US-SINGAPORE RELATIONS, 1965–1975

US-SINGAPORE RELATIONS, 1965–1975

Strategic Non-alignment in the Cold War

Daniel Wei Boon Chua

NUS PRESS
SINGAPORE

© 2017 Daniel Wei Boon Chua

Published by:

NUS Press
National University of Singapore
AS3-01-02, 3 Arts Link
Singapore 117569

Fax: (65) 6774-0652
E-mail: nusbooks@nus.edu.sg
Website: http://nuspress.nus.edu.sg

ISBN 978-981-4722-32-2 (paper)

National Library Board, Singapore Cataloguing in Publication Data

Name(s): Chua, Daniel Wei Boon
Title: US-Singapore relations, 1965–1975: strategic non-alignment in the
    Cold War / Daniel Wei Boon Chua.
Description: Singapore : NUS Press, [2017]
Identifier(s): OCN 965877527 | ISBN 978-981-4722-32-2 (paperback)
Subject(s): LLCSH: Singapore--Foreign relations--United States. | United States
    --Foreign relations--Singapore. | Cold War--Influence. | Non-alignment
    --Singapore. | Nationalism--Singapore.
Classification: DDC 327.7305957--dc23

Cover photo: President Lyndon B. Johnson meets with His Excellency Lee Kuan Yew, the late Prime Minister of the Republic of Singapore in 1967 at the Oval Office, White House, Washington, D.C. (Photo by Yoichi Okamoto, courtesy of LBJ Library, Serial # A4985-10).

Typeset by: International Typesetters Pte Ltd
Printed by: Mainland Press Pte Ltd

Contents

Acknowledgements

Several individuals contributed invaluably to the completion of this book. I thank Robert Cribb for teaching me to write and for exemplifying scholarship during my doctoral research at the Australian National University (ANU) College of Asia and the Pacific. For inspiring my interest in United States-Singapore relations, I thank Joey Long and Ang Cheng Guan. I am also grateful to Cheng Guan, as well as Rahil Ismail and Wang Zhenping, who sparked my interest in history when I studied at the National Institute of Education. Andrea Benvenuti gave me my first lesson on the use of archival sources when we met in London during my fieldwork. Former President of Singapore, Mr S.R. Nathan, along with Mr Eddie Teo, Mr Bilahari Kausikan, Mr Tan Seng Chye and Mr Mushahid Ali, generously gave of their time and allowed me to interview them for this research. I would like to register my thanks to Jennifer Sheehan from CartoGIS, ANU, for producing the maps in this book and the archivists at the National Archives of the UK, National Archives of Australia, National Archives II at College Park, Maryland, and the Presidential Libraries of Lyndon Johnson, Richard Nixon and Gerald Ford for assisting in my fieldwork. Whereas many individuals have contributed towards this book, I bear sole responsibility for the arguments made and errors that might arise.

Parts of Chapters 2 and 3 were first used in "Revisiting Lee Kuan Yew's 1965–66 Anti-Americanism", *Asian Studies Review* 38, no. 3 (Sept. 2014): 442–60. Parts of Chapters 6 and 7 have been used in "Becoming a Good Nixon Doctrine Country: Political Relations between the United States and Singapore during the Nixon Presidency", *Australian Journal of Politics and History* 60, no. 4 (2014): 534–48. I thank the editors of these two journals for allowing the use of these materials in this book.

I dedicate this book to my family: my parents for believing in me; Grace for her unstinting love and support; and Eliza, Emily and Evelyn for filling every day with joy.

Abbreviations

AAPSO	Afro-Asian Peoples' Solidarity Organisation
AMDA	Anglo-Malayan Defence Agreement; after 1963, Anglo-Malaysian Defence Agreement
ANZUK	Australia, New Zealand and United Kingdom
ANZUS	Australia, New Zealand and United States alliance
ASEAN	Association of Southeast Asian Nations
CCP	Chinese Communist Party
CIA	Central Intelligence Agency (US)
CINCPAC	Commander-in-Chief of the United States Pacific Command
CNO	US Chief of Naval Operations
COMLOG WESTPAC	Commander, Logistics Group Western Pacific
CSR	Commonwealth Strategic Reserve
CTO	Communist Terrorist Organisation
DOD	United States Department of Defense
DSA	Defense Supply Agency (US)
FCO	Foreign and Commonwealth Office (UK)
FDI	Foreign direct investments
FPDA	Five Power Defence Arrangements
GOA	The Government of Australia

GOM	The Government of Malaysia
GOS	The Government of Singapore
HMG	Her Majesty's Government (UK)
IADS	Five Power Integrated Air Defence System
ISA	International Security Agency (US)
ISC	Internal Security Council (Singapore)
ISG	Interagency Study Group (US)
KMT	Kuomintang (ROC)
LASS	Lockheed Air Services Singapore
LPM	Labour Party of Malaysia
LTBT	Limited Test Ban Treaty
MCP	Malayan Communist Party
MID	Ministry of Interior and Defence (Singapore)
MTT	Military training teams
NAM	Non-Aligned Movement
NPP	National Policy Paper (US)
OCAC	Overseas Chinese Affairs Commission (PRC)
OPD	Defence and Overseas Policy Committee (UK)
PAP	People's Action Party
PKI	Partai Komunis Indonesia; Communist Party of Indonesia
PR	Partai Rakyat (Malaysia)
PRC	People's Republic of China
PSA	Port of Singapore Authority
R&R	Rest and Recuperation Program
RELC	Regional English Language Centre (Singapore)
ROC	Republic of China on Taiwan
RSAF	Republic of Singapore Air Force
RSN	Republic of Singapore Navy
SAF	Singapore Armed Forces
SCO	Sarawak Communist Organisation

SEATO	Southeast Asia Treaty Organisation
SinSov	Singapore-Soviet Shipping Agency
SUPP	Sarawak United Peoples' Party
UMNO	United Malays National Organisation
UN	United Nations
UNGA	United Nations General Assembly
US	United States
USAF	United States Air Force
USAID	United States Agency for International Development
USDAO	US Defense Attaché Office
USG	The Government of the United States
USIA	United States Information Agency
USIS	United States Information Service
USN	United States Navy
USSR	The Union of Soviet Socialist Republics; The Soviet Union

Dramatis Personae

Singapore

Lee Kuan Yew — Prime Minister of Singapore, 1959–90

Goh Keng Swee — Minister for the Interior and Defence, 1965–67 and 1970–79

Minister for Finance, 1967–70

Lim Kim San — Minister for Finance, 1965–67

Minister for the Interior and Defence, 1967–70

S. Rajaratnam — Minister for Foreign Affairs, 1965–80

Toh Chin Chye — Deputy Prime Minister, 1965–68

Minister for Science and Technology, 1968–75

Wong Lin Ken — Singapore Ambassador to the US, 1967–68

Ernest S. Monteiro — Singapore Ambassador to the US, 1969–76

George E. Bogaars — Permanent Secretary, Ministry of the Interior and Defence, 1965–70

S.R. Nathan — Assistant Director, later Director, Labour Research Unit, 1962–66

Assistant Secretary, later Deputy Secretary, Ministry of Foreign Affairs, 1966–71

Deputy Secretary, Ministry of Home Affairs, January–August 1971

Director, Security and Intelligence Division, Ministry of Defence, August 1971–79

United States of America

1945–61

Harry S. Truman — President of the United States of America, 1945–53

Dean Acheson — US Secretary of State, 1949–53

George F. Kennan — Deputy Chief of Mission, US Embassy in the Soviet Union, 1944–46

Director, Policy Planning Staff, US Department of State, 1947–49

US Ambassador to the Soviet Union, May–September 1952

Dwight D. Eisenhower — President of the United States of America, 1953–61

John Foster Dulles — US Secretary of State, 1953–59

1961–69

John F. Kennedy — President of the United States of America, 1961–63

Lyndon B. Johnson — Vice President of the United States of America, 1961–63

President of the United States of America, 1963–69

Hubert H. Humphrey, Jr — Vice President of the United States of America, 1965–69

Dean Rusk — US Secretary of State, 1961–69

Robert S. McNamara — US Secretary of Defense, 1961–68

William P. Bundy — Assistant Secretary of State for East Asian and Pacific Affairs, US Department of State, 1964–69

Samuel D. Berger — Deputy Assistant Secretary of State for Far Eastern Affairs, US Department of State, 1965–68

Maurice D. Bean	Country Director for Malaysia and Singapore, US Department of State, 1966–70
Eugene Black	Special Assistant to the President on Southeast Asian Social and Economic Development, 1966–69
James D. Bell	US Ambassador to Malaysia, 1964–69
Richard H. Donald	Chargé d'Affaires ad interim, US Embassy in Singapore, April–December 1966
Francis J. Galbraith	US Ambassador to Singapore, 1966–69
	US Ambassador to Indonesia, 1969–74
John B. Dexter	Deputy Chief of Mission, US Embassy in Singapore, 1966–69
Marshall Green	US Ambassador to Indonesia, 1965–69
	Assistant Secretary of State for East Asian and Pacific Affairs, US Department of State, 1969–73
	US Ambassador to Australia, 1973–75

1969–78

Richard M. Nixon	Vice President of the United States of America, 1953–61
	President of the United States of America, 1969–74
Spiro T. Agnew	Vice President of the United States of America, 1969–73
William P. Rogers	US Secretary of State, 1969–73
Melvin R. Laird	US Secretary of Defense, 1969–73

Henry Kissinger	Special Assistant to the President on National Security, 1969–75
	US Secretary of State, 1973–77
Theodore J.C. Heavner	Country Director for Indonesia, Malaysia and Singapore, US Department of State, 1971–74
William H. Bruns	Chargé d'Affaires ad interim, US Embassy in Singapore, 1969
Charles T. Cross	US Ambassador to Singapore, 1969–72
John J. O'Neill, Jr	Chargé d'Affaires ad interim, US Embassy in Singapore, 1972
Edwin M. Cronk	US Ambassador to Singapore, 1972–75
William B. Grant	Deputy Chief of Mission, US Embassy in Singapore, 1972–75
Gerald R. Ford	Vice President of the United States of America, 1973–74
	President of the United States of America, 1974–77
Robert S. Ingersoll	Assistant Secretary of State for East Asian and Pacific Affairs, US Department of State, January–July 1974
	US Deputy Secretary of State, 1974–76
Arthur W. Hummel, Jr	Assistant Secretary of State for East Asian and Pacific Affairs, US Department of State, 1976–77
Edward C. Ingraham	Country Director for Indonesia, Malaysia and Singapore, US Department of State, 1974–77
John H. Holdridge	US Ambassador to Singapore, 1975–78

United Kingdom

Harold Wilson — Prime Minister of the United Kingdom, 1964–70 and 1974–78

Denis Healey — Secretary of State for Defence, 1964–70
Chancellor of the Exchequer, 1974–79

George Brown — Secretary of State for Foreign Affairs, 1966–68

George Thomson — Secretary of State for Commonwealth Affairs, 1967–68

Roy Jenkins — Chancellor of the Exchequer, 1967–70

Edward Heath — Prime Minister of the United Kingdom, 1970–74

Peter Carrington — Secretary of State for Defence, 1970–74

Australia

Harold Holt — Prime Minister of Australia, 1966–67

Paul Hasluck — Minister for Defence, 1963–64
Minister for External Affairs, 1964–69

Allen Fairhall — Minister for Defence, 1966–69

Gordon Freeth — Minister for External Affairs, February–November 1969

John G. Gorton — Prime Minister of Australia, 1968–71
Minister for Defence, March–August 1971

William McMahon — Minister for External Affairs, 1969–71
Prime Minister of Australia, 1971–72

Edward Gough Whitlam — Prime Minister of Australia, 1972–75
Minister for Foreign Affairs, 1972–73

Malcolm Fraser — Minister for Defence, 1969–71
Prime Minister of Australia, 1975–83

Thomas K. Critchley Australian High Commissioner to Malaysia, 1957–65

Alfred R. Parsons Australian Ambassador to Indonesia, 1964–67

Australian High Commissioner to Singapore, 1967–72

Australian High Commissioner to Malaysia, 1972–75

Malaysia

Tunku Abdul Rahman Prime Minister of Malaya, 1957–63

Prime Minister of Malaysia, 1963–70

Tun Abdul Razak Deputy Prime Minister of Malaya, 1957–63

Minister for Defence, 1957–70

Deputy Prime Minister of Malaysia, 1963–70

Prime Minister of Malaysia, 1970–76

Ong Yoke Lin Malayan Ambassador to the US, 1961–63

Malaysian Ambassador to the US, 1963–66

Indonesia

Sukarno President of Indonesia, 1945–67

Suharto President of Indonesia, 1967–98

New Zealand

Keith Holyoake Prime Minister of New Zealand, 1960–72

Map of Commonwealth Bases in Singapore

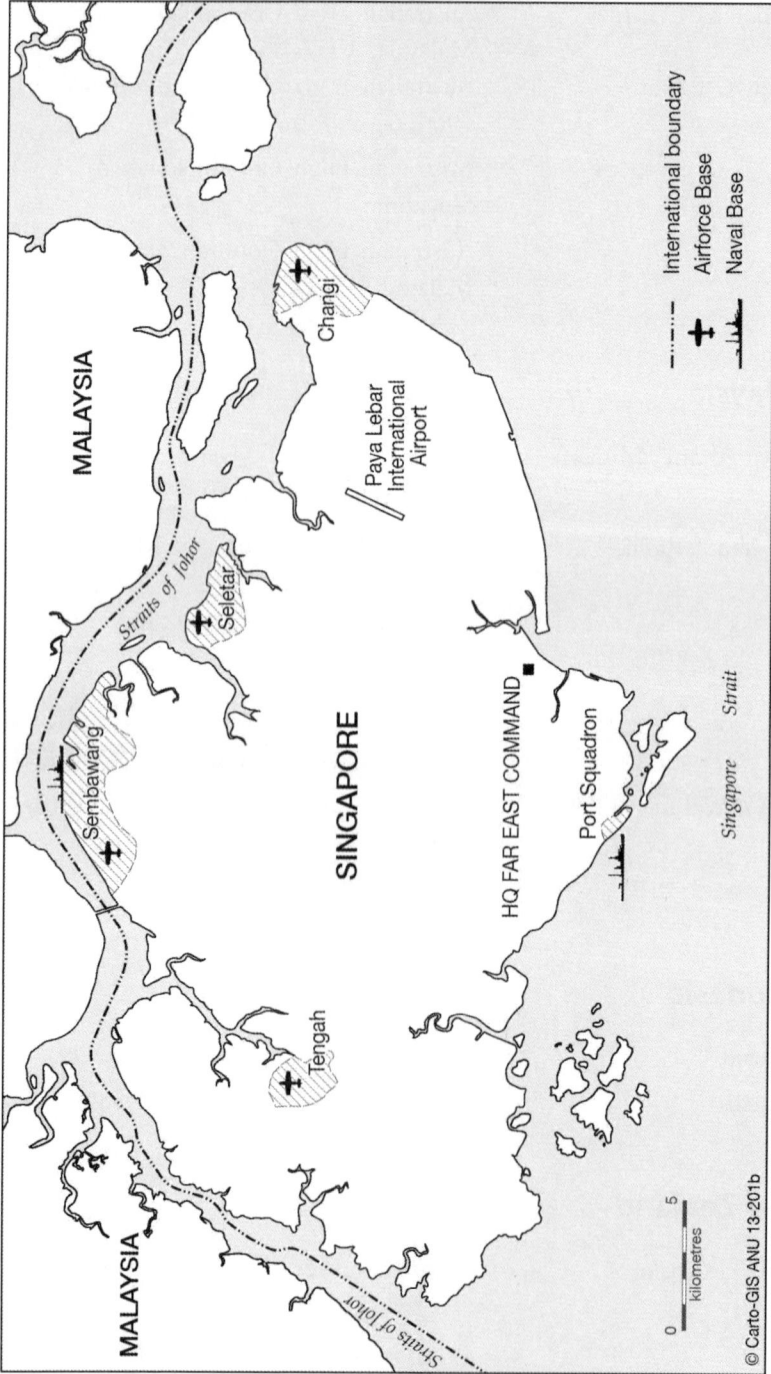

Map adapted from "The Planned British Withdrawal from Malaysia and Singapore," September 1968, British Withdrawal from Singapore and Malaysia (2 of 2), box 2, Subject Files of the Office of Indonesia, Malaysia and Singapore Affairs, 1965–74, RG 59, NACP.

Map of Commonwealth Bases in Malaysia

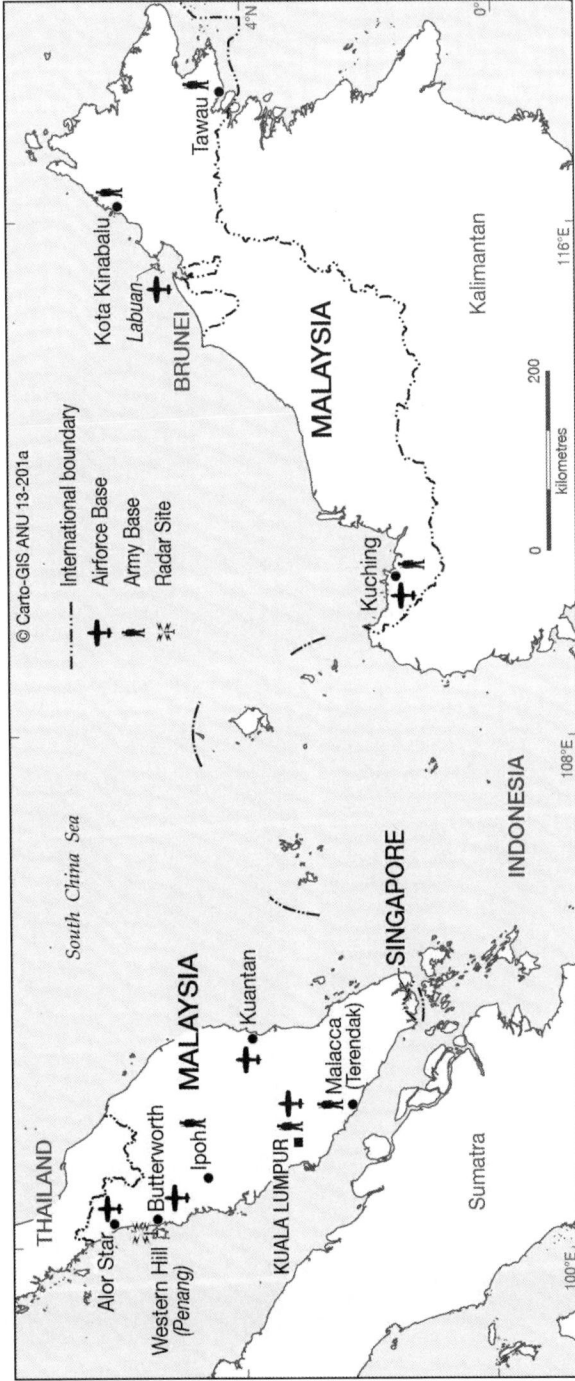

Map adapted from "The Planned British Withdrawal from Malaysia and Singapore," September 1968, British Withdrawal from Singapore and Malaysia (2 of 2), box 2, Subject Files of the Office of Indonesia, Malaysia and Singapore Affairs, 1965–74, RG 59, NACP.

Introduction

INTIMACY AT A DISTANCE

Singapore became independent on 9 August 1965 when the United States and the Soviet Union were engaged in ideological and geopolitical Cold War. During the height of the bipolar superpower conflict, while the US foreign policy in Asia was guided by a strategy to contain the spread of communism to newly decolonised Asian nations, Singapore adopted a non-aligned approach in the conduct of its external relations. Whereas the US containment strategy was fundamentally rooted in zero-sum thinking—where any Soviet gain implied a relative American loss—Singapore's non-aligned approach was premised on a positive-sum thinking of working with both sides of the bipolar conflict. Nevertheless, both the US and Singapore shared the similar objective of curbing communist influence in Southeast Asia.

In the course of a decade, from 1965 to 1975, Washington and Singapore struggled to reciprocate each other's friendly gestures. When Washington was willing to deepen US-Singapore ties during the Lyndon Johnson administration (1963–69), the Singapore government viewed US offers with suspicion. During a televised interview in August 1965, the Prime Minister of Singapore, Lee Kuan Yew, categorically dispelled any likelihood that Singapore would welcome the US military. "If the British withdraw," Lee hypothesised, "I am prepared to go on with the Australians and the New Zealanders. But, I am not prepared to go on with

Americans."[1] In 1967, after Britain announced plans to withdraw troops from east of Suez, Lee visited President Johnson and Secretary of Defense, Robert McNamara, and invited the US Seventh Fleet to utilise the naval dockyards taken over from the British military. Lee had hoped that an American military presence in Singapore would deter likely aggressors and boost investors' confidence. Washington agreed to repair US warships in Singapore but rejected further forms of US military commitment towards Singapore.

In the early 1970s, when Richard Nixon was President of the United States (1969–74), the situation was reversed. The American Ambassador to Singapore, Charles Cross, probed Lee Kuan Yew on the possibility of US Navy vessels being permanently stationed in Sembawang Naval Base in the north of Singapore.[2] But, by then, Lee was no longer worried about external threats to Singapore and hinted that an American naval presence in Singapore would benefit neither country. "Recent developments suggest that the Government of Singapore (GOS) may to some degree be in the process of changing its attitude toward U.S. military presence in Singapore and security relationships with the U.S.," wrote Theodore Heavner, Country Director of Indonesia, Malaysia and Singapore Affairs at the United States Department of State, in a memorandum in 1973. "While nothing dramatic has surfaced, the former GOS policy, i.e. holding us at arm's length and even flirting with the possibility of increased Soviet presence, now seems to be undergoing gradual change."[3] At first glance, Ted Heavner was giving a positive report on Singapore's improving attitude towards the United States. Yet, far from hitting a celebratory note,

---

[1] Lee Kuan Yew, "Transcript of an interview by foreign correspondents with the Prime Minister of Singapore Mr. Lee Kuan Yew, held at TV Singapura at 1130 hrs on 30.8.65", 30 August 1965, in Lee Kuan Yew (2 of 2), Box 2, Subject Files of the Office of Indonesia, Malaysia and Singapore Affairs, 1965–74, RG 59, NACP.

[2] Charles T. Cross, "Memorandum of Conversation: US Naval and Aircraft Repair Program in Singapore", 24 July 1971, in DEF 15 U.S. Use of Military Facilities (Singapore 1971), Box 8, Subject Files of the Office of Indonesia, Malaysia and Singapore Affairs, 1965–74, RG 59, NACP. For a map of Sembawang, see p. xviii.

[3] Theodore J.C. Heavner, "US Military Involvement with Singapore and Some Suggested Policy Guidelines", 20 February 1973, in DEF 19 Military Assistance–Army 1973, Box 11, Subject Files of the Office of Indonesia, Malaysia and Singapore Affairs, 1965–74, RG 59, NACP.

Heavner's statements were, in reality, a preamble to a warning. In his memo, he went on to caution that America should not rapidly deepen US-Singapore engagements despite signs that the Singapore government would now allow an American military presence in Singapore. The foreign policy strategy of the Richard Nixon administration had been to carry out the devolution of American military presence in Asia, while establishing détente with the Soviet Union and the People's Republic of China (PRC).[4] Heavner feared that an overly warm response to the Singapore government's overture towards the United States, though welcomed, could cause the US government to drift away from the tenets of the Nixon Doctrine, or even create such an impression among the Singapore leadership.[5]

During the Gerald Ford presidency (1974–76), US-Singapore relations became stable, having been built on solid economic and strategic cooperation. Despite the volatility of US-Singapore foreign relations during the Johnson and Nixon administrations, these formative years laid the foundation for an enduring bilateral relationship during the Cold War. During the 1960s and 1970s, the governments of both countries saw common interests between Singapore and the United States in Southeast Asia. Yet domestic conditions and external factors, such as protests in America against US involvement in the Vietnam War and the management of a Chinese majority among the Singapore population, kept both countries mostly "at arm's length".[6]

During the beginning of formal diplomatic ties between Singapore and Washington, decolonisation and Cold War dynamics dictated the relations between Singapore and the US. Both governments had not yet developed a deep understanding and empathy towards each other's interests and culture. In August 1965, Singapore emerged from close to two years of unhappy union with the Federation of Malaysia as an independent and sovereign nation. Apart from containing communist influence in domestic politics, the Singapore leadership focussed on

---

[4] Warren I. Cohen, *The Cambridge History of American Foreign Relations Volume 4: America in the Age of Soviet Power, 1945–1991* (New York: Cambridge University Press, 1993), p. 184.
[5] Heavner, "US Military Involvement with Singapore", 20 February 1973.
[6] Ibid.

developing internal social stability and economic development—the ingredients in a narrative of "survival".[7] Vietnam was high on the US government's list of priorities in Southeast Asia, although Washington's "strategic fears" proved to be "grossly exaggerated" when the eventual withdrawal from Vietnam did not severely threaten American safety.[8] The American military involvement in the Vietnam War escalated in early 1965 and ended with the signing of the Paris Peace Accord of 1973, which was soon followed by the fall of Saigon in April 1975.[9] As a result of Washington's policy of containing communist influence in Asia during the Cold War, the American military and political involvement in Southeast Asian affairs heightened between 1965 and 1975. Because of America's increasing stake in the Vietnam War, even developments in a seemingly insignificant Southeast Asian country, such as Singapore, became a concern for the US government.

---

[7] "Survival" is a recurring theme in the memoirs and biographies of Singapore's early leaders. See Lee Kuan Yew, *From Third World to First: The Singapore Story, 1965–2000* (New York: HarperCollins, 2000); Lee Kuan Yew, "The Fundamentals of Singapore's Foreign Policy: Then & Now" (paper presented at the S. Rajaratnam Lecture 2009, Shangri-La Hotel, Singapore, 9 April 2009); S.R. Nathan, "My Foreign Ministry Years", in *The Little Red Dot: Reflections by Singapore's Diplomats*, ed. Koh and Chang (Singapore: World Scientific, 2005). Scholars writing Singapore's history have also acknowledged that the theme of 'survival' is an appropriate description of Singapore's circumstances during its separation from Malaysia in August 1965. See Chan Heng Chee, "Singapore's Foreign Policy, 1965–1968", *Journal of Southeast Asian History* 10, no. 1 (1969): 2; Amitav Acharya, *Singapore's Foreign Policy: The Search for Regional Order* (Singapore: World Scientific, 2008), p. 1; Chua Beng Huat, *Communitarian Ideology and Democracy in Singapore* (London: Routledge, 1995), pp. 4–5 and 18–9; Kawin Wilarat, *Singapore's Foreign Policy: The First Decade* (Singapore: Institute of Southeast Asian Studies, 1975), pp. 29–73; Tim Huxley, *Defending the Lion City: The Armed Forces of Singapore* (New South Wales: Allen & Unwin, 2000), p. xix.

[8] Robert J. McMahon, *The Limits of Empire: The United States and Southeast Asia since World War II* (New York: Columbia University Press, 1999), p. xi.

[9] Ang Cheng Guan marks the beginning of American involvement in the Second Indochina War to be 8 March 1965 with "the landing of the first combat troops—two marine battalions consisting of 3,500 men landing on the beach of Danang". See Ang Cheng Guan, *Southeast Asia and the Vietnam War* (Oxon: Routledge, 2010), p. 24. Paul Kelemen's account of the escalation of US military involvement begins in February 1965, "marked by regular bombings of the North ... and the sending in July of 100,000 American troops to South Vietnam". See Paul Kelemen, "Soviet Strategy in Southeast Asia", *Asian Survey* 24, no. 3 (1984): 337.

As part of a new genre of Cold War history, this book places focus on Singapore as an agent influencing the course of the Cold War in Southeast Asia, and analyses the interplay between America's policy of containment in Asia and Singapore's non-aligned foreign policy. This study argues that the two governments differed in their core interests and disagreed on issues concerning America's involvement in the Vietnam War and US interference in domestic politics of newly independent Asian states. Nevertheless, economic cooperation forged a strong link between Singapore and the United States and gave the Singapore government's neutralism a strong American bias. Along with other Southeast Asian leaders, Lee prolonged the Vietnam War when he warned that a premature American withdrawal from Vietnam would result in a loss of credibility and confidence in the United States. Lee argued that the United States, by holding the line in Vietnam, was buying time for the rest of Southeast Asia to develop stable economies and governments.[10] The American military involvement in Vietnam helped in maintaining political stability of the non-communist regimes in Southeast Asia and also provided them with the years that were necessary to build their economies. It did this by offering military assistance and equipment, allowing these non-communist states to channel limited financial resources to social and economic projects. By examining the intersection of Euro-centric perspectives of the Cold War with Asian decolonisation, both the "Cold War and the local plots" interact to reveal some degree of complicity of smaller actors in the region in the protracted warfare and human suffering in Vietnam.[11]

PERCEIVING THE US-SINGAPORE RELATIONSHIP

Although Singapore was no longer a British colony in 1965, Washington still viewed the security and political stability of Singapore as a Commonwealth responsibility. Hence, as a matter of policy during the Johnson administration, the United States government avoided

---

[10] Ang, *Southeast Asia and the Vietnam War*, p. 29.
[11] Tuong Vu, "Cold War Studies and the Cultural Cold War in Asia", in *Dynamics of the Cold War in Asia*, ed. Vu and Wongsurawat (New York: Palgrave Macmillan, 2009), p. 12.

commitment to Singapore's defence. It must be noted that America was deeply entangled in the Vietnam quagmire at this time. Nevertheless, from 1965 to the middle of the 1970s, bilateral relations between the US and Singapore strengthened, reflecting an interplay between America's containment strategy in Asia and Singapore's foreign policy of neutralism.[12] Before Heavner's 1973 memorandum,[13] Singapore's policy of non-alignment with major power blocs kept the United States at a distance, not unlike Singapore's treatment of the Soviet Union and the PRC. Only Singapore's Commonwealth partners—Australia, New Zealand and the United Kingdom (ANZUK)—possessed special relations with the newly independent state.

Yet both the United States and Singapore governments, while maintaining political distance, regarded each other as significant partners in the region. Since 1966, US-Singapore relations had played a decisive role in Singapore's viability after Singapore's separation from Malaysia. After Britain's military withdrawal in 1971, the ANZUK-Singapore relations faded in importance while the US-Singapore relationship emerged as

---

[12] The terms "neutrality" and "neutralism" used in a political context during the Cold War were problematic because of the different shades in the meaning of "neutrality" in history. Peter Lyon points out that the concept of "neutralism", more often used than "neutrality" during the Cold War, branches out to "proximate equivalents" such as "non-alignment", "peaceful and active co-existence", "active formal neutralism", "positive neutralism" and "isolationism". "Neutrality", on the other hand, has an older tradition tracing back to the Roman Empire, the Middle Ages, and more recently, the French Revolutionary–Napoleonic wars, and the First and Second World Wars. More important, "neutrality" carries a narrower definition than "neutralism". Lyon argues that "neutrality means keeping aloof from shooting wars whereas neutralism means dissociation from the Cold War, while perhaps, involving efforts to remove or, at least, mitigate some of the harshness of the cold war struggle". See Peter Lyon, "Neutrality and the Emergence of the Concept of Neutralism", *Review of Politics* 22, no. 2 (April 1960): 266–7. This current study agrees with Lyon's position on the meanings of "neutrality" and "neutralism", and uses "neutralism" and "non-alignment" to mean the foreign policy stance of the Afro-Asian countries that did not align themselves with the major power blocs during the Cold War. The US Department of State documents consulted for this current study and some scholars writing on the Non-aligned Movement within the Cold War context do not make a distinction between "neutrality" and "neutralism". Hence, unless otherwise stated, sources that mention "neutral", "neutrality", or "neutralisation" will be understood to carry the broader definition of "neutralism" and "non-alignment with major power blocs".

[13] Heavner, "US Military Involvement with Singapore", 20 February 1973.

the key to Singapore's economic viability. Although the US-Singapore relationship was asymmetric, Singapore was neither a satellite nor a vassal state of the US. Because of the dynamics of international politics during the Cold War, the impact of the smaller player was significant. Tuong Vu, in his work on the Cold War in Asia, cautions that "the new Cold War scholarship should not assume that power and influence flowed only one way from the big to the small, even in highly asymmetric relationships that characterized many Cold War alliances".[14] Vu's argument, shared by Robert McMahon and Robert Litwak, is best illustrated when the US State Department found it difficult to reject the Singapore defence ministry's request for sophisticated military equipment. The US government worried that Singapore's military acquisitions would trigger an arms race but also feared that the Singapore government would turn to the Soviet Union to supply similar technology.[15]

Indeed, the importance of the United States to Singapore's viability far outweighed the importance of Singapore to the US; it was apparent that Singapore needed the US partnership more. Yet Singapore chose to be non-aligned when it gained independent statehood.[16] Both governments recognised that a formal alliance or any overt political alignment from 1965–75 would not further their respective interests; in fact, it may even be detrimental to their foreign policies and political objectives. Perceptions of Communist China and the Chinese who stayed overseas shaped the views of both American and Singaporean political leadership. Washington aimed to contain the rising influence of the PRC in Asia and associated the Chinese overseas as a communist fifth column during the 1950s. On the other hand, the Singapore government needed to build a nation from a population mostly made up of ethnic Chinese. Managing its Chinese populace was crucial for Singapore's external relations with

---

[14] Vu, "Cold War Studies and the Cultural Cold War in Asia", p. 9.

[15] Robert S. Litwak, *Detente and the Nixon Doctrine: American Foreign Policy and the Pursuit of Stability, 1969–1976* (New York: Cambridge University Press, 1984), p. 92; "Singapore: Bilateral Issues Paper", June 1972, in Briefing Papers 1972, Box 10, Subject Files of the Office of Indonesia, Malaysia and Singapore Affairs, 1965–74, RG 59, NACP; McMahon, *The Limits of Empire*, p. xi.

[16] The Singapore government's decision to be non-aligned was motivated by the fear that Singapore's membership into the United Nations would either be blocked by the Soviet Union or by members of the Non-Aligned Movement. See Chapter 2.

major powers as well as regional states. Hence, the Singapore government adopted a non-aligned approach towards the rivalry among great powers. At times, Singapore's interests were best served by drawing closer to the United States, especially when Britain first announced its intentions to withdraw troops from Malaysia and Singapore, and after the United States ceased military involvement in the Vietnam War. On other occasions, the Singapore government preferred to emphasise Singapore's foreign policy of neutralism and kept America at a distance. In other words, it was a relationship dictated by common interests.

A NEW COLD WAR HISTORY

The interplay between America's containment policy and decolonisation in Southeast Asia has gained a place of importance in the historiography of American foreign relations and Southeast Asian history during the Cold War. Since 2005, scholars of American diplomatic history during the Cold War have given much attention to the writing of "new Cold War history".[17] A "new Cold War history", as argued in Christopher Goscha and Christian Ostermann's *Connecting Histories: Decolonization and the Cold War in Southeast Asia, 1945–1962* (2009), will shift "the old debate centered on the question of who was to blame for the rise of the Cold War to rethinking some of the fundamental dynamics of the international history of the second half of the twentieth century".[18] This new genre emphasises "the role of ideas and ideology and the importance of 'smaller powers'", brings to bear findings in newly declassified documents in communist countries, and sets American foreign policy in the context of decolonisation and Asian nationalism.[19] The editors of *Connecting Histories*

---

[17] Goscha and Ostermann cite John Lewis Gaddis' 2005 publication as the forerunner of the "new Cold War History" genre. See Christopher E. Goscha and Christian F. Ostermann, eds., *Connecting Histories: Decolonization and the Cold War in Southeast Asia, 1945–1962*, Cold War International History Project series (Washington, D.C.: Woodrow Wilson Center Press, 2009), pp. 6–10; John Lewis Gaddis, *The Cold War: A New History* (New York: Penguin Books, 2005)

[18] Goscha and Ostermann, eds., *Connecting Histories: Decolonization and the Cold War in Southeast Asia, 1945–1962*, p. 7.

[19] Ibid.

note that "it is also worth recalling how the intersection of the Cold War and decolonization prolonged or hastened decolonization on the diplomatic front".[20] In the case of Singapore, Lee Kuan Yew was able to ride on America's containment strategy to promote US investments in Singapore, giving the newly decolonised country a boost in its economic development.

Tuong Vu takes the analysis further by asserting that "Asian actors—while possessing limited military and economic capabilities—were neither victims nor puppets of the superpowers as conventionally believed".[21] He outlines the importance of juxtaposing three central concepts in his assessment of Cold War historiography, "namely, 'Asia' as a geographical location, the 'Cold War' as a historical event, and 'culture' as a sphere of social activity".[22] In applying the three concepts, he argues, first of all, that the spread of the Cold War "should be reconceptualized as an intercontinental synchronization of hostilities in which Asian actors shared equal responsibilities with the superpowers in the spread of the conflict".[23] He challenges "the notion of an Asian vacuum waiting for the superpowers to fill in the late 1940s" and stresses that

> [i]t is more accurate to say that the Cold War would not have extended into Asia had some Asian actors not desired it and worked hard to get what they wanted. The Cold War did not spread to and engulf Asia as the standard narratives tell it. Asia was already engulfed in conflicts. These local conflicts in Asia intensified and lasted longer due to the Cold War. But the Cold War also intensified and lasted longer because of these local conflicts.[24]

Michael Szonyi and Hong Liu support Vu's challenge to the "standard narratives" of the Cold War in Asia by arguing that "while the history of Asia in the late twentieth century cannot simply be subsumed within a Cold War narrative, the global geo-political struggle profoundly shaped

---

[20] Ibid.
[21] Vu, "Cold War Studies and the Cultural Cold War in Asia", p. 2.
[22] Ibid.
[23] Ibid.
[24] Ibid.

the context in which regional and national change unfolded".[25] Immanuel Wallerstein challenges the "dominant historical narratives" of the US or the USSR initiating "anything important that happened" during the Cold War period, calling it "largely a fantasy".[26] The case of US-Singapore relations from 1965 to 1975 demonstrates the limited impact that superpower rivalry had on Southeast Asian decolonisation. The US, the PRC, and the USSR to a lesser extent, influenced the foreign policies and economic development of Singapore during this period, but none of them could be regarded as having dictated or solely directed key events surrounding Singapore's development of nationhood.

Second, under Vu's concept of "Cold War", he argues that "indigenous political processes in Asia (that is, nation-state building and socioeconomic development) had critical *reverse* impact on the Cold War".[27] The Asian nationalists were able to play one superpower over the other to break away from colonial rule and "to secure American or Soviet aid for their nation-building programs".[28] Szonyi and Liu assert that "the superpower perception of the conflict in bipolar, zero-sum terms implied, for the superpowers, certain logics—ways of apprehending the world and formulating policy".[29] Asian governments that understood the Cold War logic of Washington, Moscow and Beijing "could make use of those logics to force the superpowers to act in service of local interests".[30] The Singapore government occasionally took advantage of Washington's Cold War anxieties when conducting diplomacy with the United States government. At times, according to Szonyi and Liu, "tails could wag dogs".[31]

---

[25] Ibid.; Liu Hong and Michael Szonyi, "Introduction: New Approaches to the Study of the Cold War in Asia", in *The Cold War in Asia: The Battle for Hearts and Minds*, ed. Zhang, Liu and Szonyi (Leiden: Brill, 2010), p. 1.

[26] Immanuel Wallerstein, "What Cold War in Asia? An Interpretative Essay", in *The Cold War in Asia: The Battle for Hearts and Minds*, ed. Zhang, Liu and Szonyi (Leiden: Brill, 2010), pp. 7 and 17.

[27] Vu, "Cold War Studies and the Cultural Cold War in Asia", p. 3. Emphasis in original.

[28] Ibid.

[29] Liu and Szonyi, "Introduction: New Approaches to the Study of the Cold War in Asia", p. 5.

[30] Ibid.

[31] Ibid.

Finally, Vu argues that "Asian actors' visions and political loyalties during the Cold War" were not limited to the nation-state, but encompassed the nation's peoples, their ideology and their cultures.[32] In sum, Cold War scholarship must neither fall into the trap of completely ignoring the interaction between local and international histories nor disregard the influence of the superpowers during the Cold War.[33] "To use an analogy of theater," he explains, "the plays on Asian stages embedded both Cold War and local plots…. The job of Cold War analysts is to disentangle these plots."[34] This account of US-Singapore relations from 1965 to 1975 reveals the existence of differing priorities in the midst of common interests between the US and Singapore governments such as the containment of communism in Southeast Asia. The American government viewed Singapore as a partner who contributed to US interests within the larger setting of its involvement in the Vietnam War, which was a part of its containment strategy during the global Cold War. The Singapore government, on the other hand, regarded the US as a partner who helped in achieving its immediate goals of security, nation-building and socioeconomic development.

The history of US-Singapore foreign relations has attracted relatively few book-length studies. In his comprehensive study on the US-Singapore relations in the 1950s, Joey Long provides a historical background of the relationship between the two nations during the presidency of Dwight D. Eisenhower through the perspectives of the American, British and local actors.[35] According to his observation, the relations between "principal actors" from Singapore, the UK and the US went through "many twists and turns", with the Americans and British disagreeing over the "decolonization process" in the midst of conflicting local attitudes towards the western powers.[36] Long argues that the Eisenhower administration understood the People's Action Party (PAP) government to

---

[32] Vu, "Cold War Studies and the Cultural Cold War in Asia", p. 3.

[33] Ibid.

[34] Ibid.

[35] S.R. Joey Long, *Safe for Decolonization: The Eisenhower Administration, Britain, and Singapore* (Ohio: Kent State University Press, 2011).

[36] Ibid.

be "communist infiltrated" and "adverse to US and free world interests".[37] He places emphasis on Eisenhower's development of a robust Cold War strategy that deployed instruments of statecraft to make Singapore "safe for decolonization", thereby challenging the notion that Eisenhower did not exercise leadership as Commander-in-Chief, but gave his Secretary of State, John Foster Dulles, full control over foreign policy.[38] Juxtaposing the "Cold War and local plots" effectively,[39] Long's work offers an important backdrop to this study by elucidating the significance of Singapore's strategic geographical location to American administrations even before Singapore's independence.[40] In attempting to build bridges with Singapore through a myriad of strategies, the Eisenhower administration achieved mixed results but was most successful in projecting a favourable image of the United States among Singaporeans through injecting American cultural products such as popular literature and news coverage of US scientific research into the island.[41]

Shorter studies focussing on US-Singapore relations between 1965 and 1975 also provide insights into several aspects of foreign relations between the two countries. Ang Cheng Guan's study of US-Singapore relations during the Vietnam War and the Southeast Asian perspective of the Vietnam conflict examine US relations with Singapore, Malaysia, Indonesia, Thailand and the Philippines during the Vietnam War, from 1965 to 1973.[42] Ang's survey on the impact of the Vietnam War on the five Southeast Asian countries has been acclaimed for being an invaluable contribution to a deeper understanding of US-Southeast Asian relations during the Vietnam War.[43] In his other works, Ang accentuates the prominence of Lee Kuan Yew in Singapore's foreign policy planning through

---

[37] Ibid.
[38] Ibid.
[39] Vu, "Cold War Studies and the Cultural Cold War in Asia", p. 12.
[40] Long, *Safe for Decolonization*, pp. 8–19.
[41] Ibid.
[42] Ang Cheng Guan, "Singapore and the Vietnam War", *Journal of Southeast Asian Studies* 40, no. 2 (June 2009); Ang, *Southeast Asia and the Vietnam War*.
[43] Anne L. Foster, et al., "Ang Cheng Guan. Southeast Asia and the Vietnam War", *H-Diplo Roundtable Review* 11, no. 46 (2010).

an examination of Lee's strategic thoughts.[44] He asserts that Lee was "Asia's leading strategic thinker" with the ability to help other world leaders "find direction in a complicated world".[45] Drawing upon Lee's speeches and public statements, Ang argues that Lee's statements and speeches are "valuable but underrated source[s]", useful for understanding his thoughts on international politics.[46] Writing predominantly on Lee's views regarding the Vietnam War, however, Ang does allude to Lee's anti-American comments made in 1965, although he treats the anti-American thrust of Lee's statements with a light touch.[47]

Albert Lau's edited volume on the impact and legacy of the Cold War in Southeast Asia incorporates a chapter on "Decolonization and the Cold War in Singapore, 1955–9".[48] Like Joey Long, Lau's study focuses on Singapore's struggle for independence from British colonial rule, arguing that the British government had underestimated Singapore's desire to break away from colonial control during the Cold War years.[49] Lau and Long make the same observation, that London and Washington had managed relations with Singapore predominantly with a 'Cold War thinking' and had minimal appreciation for the rising nationalism in Singapore during the 1950s. As Robert McMahon cogently asserts, "nationalism, ironically, has proven at one and the same time the greatest impediment to American designs in Southeast Asia and the greatest impetus for regional order, cohesion, development, and stability".[50] This study agrees with these assertions and further argues that America's policy of containment in Asia in 1965 was slow to adjust to the conditions of Singapore's newfound independence as well. Even when the US Embassy in Singapore occasionally recommended a deeper engagement with the

---

[44] Ang Cheng Guan, "The Global and the Regional in Lee Kuan Yew's Strategic Thought: The Early Cold War Years", in *Singapore in Global History*, ed. Heng and Aljunied (Amsterdam: Amsterdam University Press, 2011); Ang Cheng Guan, *Lee Kuan Yew's Strategic Thought* (Oxon: Routledge, 2013).

[45] Ang, "The Global and the Regional in Lee Kuan Yew's Strategic Thought", p. 236.

[46] Ibid.

[47] Ibid.

[48] Albert Lau, "Decolonization and the Cold War in Singapore, 1955–9", in *Southeast Asia and the Cold War*, ed. Lau (Oxon: Routledge, 2012).

[49] Ibid.

[50] McMahon, *The Limits of Empire*, pp. xi and 221–2.

Singapore government, Washington was often slow to act. The US State Department was most successful in its relations with Singapore when its policies aligned with Singapore's need for socioeconomic development—a pillar of Singapore's nation-building project. Other forms of partnership, such as strategic and political, took a longer time to develop because of the Singapore government's decision to be non-aligned.

Although studies focussing on the United States' engagement with Singapore are relatively scant, research conducted on US relations with Southeast Asian countries often reveals insights into how Washington conducted diplomacy with non-aligned countries during the Cold War. Pamela Sodhy, in *The US-Malaysian Nexus* (1991), argues that, before 1945, the United States engaged Malaysia through a "triangular relationship", which had to involve Britain.[51] Sodhy proposes that US perception of Malaysia before its independence in 1957 was marked by three "prisms": Malaya was part of a vital area of interest, the Far East; relations with Malaya took account of British involvement; and Malaya was an "important bulwark in containing communism in Southeast Asia".[52] The US government's criticism of Britain's conduct of the Malayan Emergency (1948–60) motivated the US to become more involved in Malaya, and caused the Malayan leadership to gradually see American support as a possible alternative to the British.[53] Regional events such as the Indonesian Confrontation (*Konfrontasi*), the Vietnam War and Britain's announcement to withdraw from east of Suez resulted in the drifting apart of Malaysia and Britain, and a strengthening of US-Malaysian ties.[54] Like Malaysia, Singapore's path towards independence was characterised by the weakening of Commonwealth ties, which were replaced by closer cooperation with the US.

Indonesia's relations with the United States during the Cold War are also noteworthy to the extent that the US had different foreign policy goals related to neutralism in Singapore and Indonesia. Indonesian President

---

[51] Pamela Sodhy, *The US-Malaysian Nexus: Themes in Superpower-Small State Relations* (Kuala Lumpur: Institute of Strategic and International Studies, 1991), pp. 1–40.

[52] Ibid.

[53] Ibid.

[54] Ibid.

Sukarno was a leading voice among the Afro-Asian nations during the 1950s and 1960s. His successor, President Suharto, maintained Indonesia's non-alignment when he came to power in 1967. Richard Mason observed that "[f]or many of these newly emerged [Southeast Asian] states, neutralism in the Cold War was a domestic political imperative. At the same time, non-alignment allowed them to acquire assistance from both sides in the Cold War".[55] Using Indonesia as an example, Mason goes on to point out that "[d]espite this profession of neutralism,... the international orientation of Indonesia ... was in fact considerably closer to the Western bloc than to the Sino-Soviet bloc".[56] Mason's conclusions for Indonesia are apt when applied to Singapore between 1965 and 1975, since Singapore also "leaned discernibly toward the United States".[57] Nevertheless, the similarities between United States' objectives for Singapore and Indonesia during the early years of independent statehood end there. Whereas Washington aimed to bring Indonesia "into a full alignment with the Western powers" in 1950,[58] this study asserts that the US government was content to let Singapore remain non-aligned in the 1960s.

Sources and Approach of This Research

Grounded mainly in the analysis of declassified documents from the National Archives and Records Administration at Maryland, USA, this research provides a historical account of US-Singapore foreign relations from 1965 to 1975. Whenever necessary, records from the National Archives at Kew, London, and the National Archives of Australia at Canberra are consulted to supplement the American documents. As pointed out accurately by Ang Cheng Guan and historians writing on Singapore and Southeast Asia in general, the perspectives of Southeast Asian governments during the Cold War will remain missing as long as government documents are

---

[55] Richard Mason, "Containment and the Challenge of Non-Alignment: The Cold War and U.S. Policy toward Indonesia, 1950–1952", in *Connecting Histories: Decolonization and the Cold War in Southeast Asia, 1945–1962*, ed. Goscha and Ostermann, Cold War International History Project series (Washington, D.C.: Woodrow Wilson Center Press, 2009), p. 39.

[56] Ibid.

[57] Ibid.

[58] Ibid.

not opened for research.[59] To make up for the lack of official documents from Singapore, this study utilises speeches, memoirs and biographies of Singapore's political leaders to gain a Singaporean perspective. Interviews with former Singapore diplomats and senior officials provided critical insights into the attitudes and perspectives of the Singapore government during this period.

The interpretation of the documentary sources collected for this research benefits from the methods largely practised by scholars of diplomatic history. Beginning from the 1980s, historians John Lewis Gaddis and Melvyn Leffler have urged diplomatic historians to consider the impact of US foreign policy within an international context rather than single-mindedly criticising US diplomacy which was clearly based on how its policies and decisions would affect the American domestic environment. The focus on the global impact of US foreign relations created a generation of international historians who refrained from making America the centre of the Cold War narrative and gave a voice to other countries involved during the Cold War.[60] Often referred to as postrevisionist historians of the Cold War, Gaddis and Leffler aim to preserve two key strands of the realist school of international relations theory, which are

1. maintaining the primary focus on state-to-state interaction, and
2. avoiding synthesis of diplomatic history with other disciplines.

Leffler advocates that diplomatic history should focus on "policymaking elites, on state-to-state relations, and on national power".[61] Michael Hogan nonetheless argues that focussing on states "is essentially an analysis of perceptions, not some objective and knowable reality".[62] In response, Leffler cautions diplomatic historians against synthesising the discipline with branches of social and cultural studies, stressing that

---

[59] Ang, *Southeast Asia and the Vietnam War*, p. 1.
[60] Michael J. Hogan, "State of the Art: An Introduction", in *America in the World: The Historiography of American Foreign Relations since 1941*, ed. Hogan (New York: Cambridge University Press, 1995), p. 6.
[61] Ibid.
[62] Ibid.

[t]he pursuit of synthesis will not lead to consensus; quite the opposite. Controversy over the relative weight [that] we should assign a multiplicity of variables will open new interpretive vistas. To be persuasive we will need to be more rigorous, more complex, more creative.... But the postmodernist emphasis on culture, language, and rhetoric often diverts attention from questions of causation and agency.[63]

This research places focus on state-to-state relations between the US and Singapore, and posits a new Cold War history by examining the interaction between America's diplomacy and Singapore's decolonisation.

Situated within the field of international history, this study employs methods that are rooted in historical research, and discusses the application of international relations theory only when the need arises within the context. Gaddis posits that historians tend to keep an "open mind" in the analysis of their sources and see theory as "more often than not closing minds".[64] He explains that

theorists seek to build universally applicable generalizations about necessarily simple matters; but if these matters were any more complicated their theories wouldn't be universally applicable. From our [historians'] perspective, then, when theories are right they generally confirm the obvious. When they move beyond the obvious they're usually wrong.[65]

To be sure, Gaddis acknowledges that theory plays a role in the writing of history. When historians attempt to simulate past events, they practise what Gaddis calls "particular generalization" by embedding theory within the narrative.[66] Political scientists, on the other hand, practise "general particularization" where narrative is subordinate to the principal

---

[63] Melvyn P. Leffler, "New Approaches, Old Interpretations, and Prospective Reconfigurations", in *America in the World: The Historiography of American Foreign Relations since 1941*, ed. Hogan (New York: Cambridge University Press, 1995), p. 72.

[64] John Lewis Gaddis, "In Defense of Particular Generalization: Rewriting Cold War History, Rethinking International Relations Theory", in *Bridges and Boundaries: Historians, Political Scientists, and the Study of International Relations*, ed. Elman and Elman (Massachusetts: MIT Press, 2001), p. 302.

[65] Ibid.

[66] Ibid.

objective of testing a theoretical framework.[67] To illustrate the process of particular generalisation, Gaddis recounts that his writing of Cold War history involves the use of neorealism to explain a particular historical outcome without attempting to "encompass the entire Cold War within a neorealist framework".[68] Following Gaddis' process of particular generalisation, this research develops a historical narrative, which traces the development of US-Singapore relations and embeds concepts such as balance of power and zero-sum calculus that belong to the realist school of international relations theory.

At this juncture, it is essential to understand the points of difference and concurrence between historians and political scientists. Colin and Miriam Fendius Elman assert that "the differences between international historians and political scientists who study international relations through qualitative methods are not as stark as believed".[69] Historians and international relations theorists share the view that "the past can be studied to provide perspectives on the present and to help solve current policy problems".[70] Robert Jervis argues that the work of political scientists and diplomatic historians involve general theories and particular historical cases but they "go about the task characteristically differently".[71] A common challenge for both historians and political scientists—that Jervis points out—is the level of consistency in human behaviour.[72] Jervis observes that psychologists have found scholars putting too much emphasis on "personal dispositions" and underestimating "the power of the situation" in analysing the decision

---

[67] Ibid.

[68] Ibid.

[69] Colin Elman and Miriam Fendius Elman, "Introduction: Negotiating International History and Politics", in *Bridges and Boundaries: Historians, Political Scientists, and the Study of International Relations*, ed. Elman and Elman (Massachusetts: MIT Press, 2001), p. 6.

[70] Ibid.

[71] Robert Jervis, "International History and International Politics: Why are they Studied Differently?", in *Bridges and Boundaries: Historians, Political Scientists, and the Study of International Relations*, ed. Elman and Elman (Massachusetts: MIT Press, 2001), p. 389.

[72] Jervis, "International History and International Politics: Why are they Studied Differently?", pp. 397–8.

and the decision-maker.[73] In doing so, a tendency to assume a general consistency in human behaviour arises, which results in an inaccurate projection of the future actions of individuals. In fact, Deborah Welch Larson questions the notion of how policymakers "consciously direct their actions to achieve larger goals". She suggests that they make "snap judgments" based on the information they have and rationalise their decisions later on.[74] In this context, Larson cautions both historians and international relations theorists not to assume that decision-makers anticipated the outcomes of their actions. There is complexity involved in the analyses of archival records. Therefore, in this research, the author has made a conscious effort to avoid over-rationalising or speculating on particular situations that are wanting in sources.

Policymakers make similar observations about the limits of making generalisations about decision-making in foreign policy across different contexts. Bilahari Kausikan, a former Permanent Secretary at Singapore's Foreign Ministry, asserts that the most important factor determining foreign policy is to understand a situation accurately and respond appropriately, as he says, "something happens and you have to react!"[75] After three decades of experience in foreign policy making, Kausikan explains that

> 80 per cent of everybody's decision, as least mine, after some time when …
> I became perm[anent] sec[retary] … is intuitive…. And of course you
> have to keep adjusting the policies. Policy is always a constant series
> of adjustments. Situation change and you change, unless you are an
> idiot![76]

It is apparent, then, that both scholars and practitioners warn against generalising about rational decision making and assuming that policy makers adhere to some grand design.

---

[73] Ibid.

[74] Deborah Welch Larson, "Sources and Methods in Cold War History: The Need for a New Theory-Based Archival Approach", in *Bridges and Boundaries: Historians, Political Scientists, and the Study of International Relations*, ed. Elman and Elman (Massachusetts: MIT Press, 2001), p. 332.

[75] Author's interview with Bilahari Kausikan, Ministry of Foreign Affairs, Singapore, 8 January 2015.

[76] Ibid.

THE CHAPTERS: INTERPLAY OF CONTAINMENT AND NON-ALIGNMENT

The period covered in this book was critical to Southeast Asia's security, beginning with the entry of US ground troops into Vietnam in March 1965, and Singapore's separation from the Federation of Malaysia in August of the same year. The withdrawal of British troops from Malaysia and Singapore from 1967 to 1971 ended Britain's military influence in the sub-region. It also led to Singapore's turn towards the United States as a balancing power against the People's Republic of China. The withdrawal of the United States forces from Vietnam in 1973 was followed by the unification of Vietnam under a communist government in 1975. In that year, the Lon Nol government in Cambodia was ousted by the Khmer Rouge, setting the stage for the Vietnam-Cambodia crisis, which marked a new period of conflict. This was chosen as an apt and suitable point to end this study. The principal argument put forth in this research is that diplomatic relations between Singapore and the United States between 1965 and 1975 were determined by the interplay of the American policy of containment and Singapore's preservation of an image of non-alignment.

This book has been organised into three substantive sections that loosely reflect US-Singapore relations in different periods. Part 1 covers 1965 to 1967 and Parts 2 and 3 cover the late 1960s to 1975. The first part of this book, which contains three chapters, analyses the underlying premises of both the Singapore and American governments in their foreign policy approaches towards each other—the former declared a non-aligned posture, whereas the latter waged a global Cold War with the aim of containing the spread of communism in Asia. Although attempts were made by both governments to deepen US-Singapore relations, the relationship could best be described as 'intimacy at an arm's length'. The first chapter accounts for the nation-building imperative taken by the Singapore government when the country became independent in 1965. The need to build a nation centred on having a Singaporean identity and providing a basic standard of living to its citizens. It was this need that directed and guided the Singapore government's domestic and foreign policies. The protection of Singapore's sovereignty, economic development and the regime preservation of the PAP government formed the basis of several of Singapore's policies. Maintaining the focal point at Singapore's foreign policy, this chapter demonstrates the incompatibility of Singapore's non-aligned approach to diplomacy with the American policy of containment in Asia.

In 1965, Washington's chief objective in Singapore was to keep the island-state out of the communist orbit. The Singapore government, however, was focussed on political and economic viability more than a global containment of communism. With the objective of boosting Singapore's non-aligned credentials, Lee Kuan Yew made a series of public speeches and interviews expressing anti-American views. Chapter 2 gives an account of Lee's anti-American press campaign beginning in August 1965. US State Department documents reveal Lee's personal motivations and political objectives for making vitriolic remarks against the American administration in public. Along with Lee's anti-American speeches, steps were taken by the Singapore government to project a strong non-aligned foreign policy to gain membership into the United Nations. The souring of relations between the American and the Singapore governments caused anxiety to US officials in Washington and the Consul-General in Singapore. Governed by a zero-sum mentality, some American officials feared that Singapore's distancing of itself from the US naturally implied a close relationship with the Sino-Soviet bloc. State Department records reveal that US officials tended to overstate Singapore's propensity to align itself with the communist bloc and argued for active engagement with the newly independent Singapore, leading to the visit of senior American officials to Singapore.[77]

Part 1 of this study concludes with the US-Singapore relations moving in a positive trajectory for the first time since August 1965. William Bundy, US Assistant Secretary of State for East Asian and Pacific Affairs, met Lee Kuan Yew in March 1966. The meeting, outlined and examined in Chapter 3, was the turning point for the erstwhile difficult US-Singapore relationship. Despite the personal friendship that had developed between

---

[77] William P. Bundy, "Singapore's Economic Development and the Textile Problem (Draft Memorandum)", November 1965, in POL–Political Affairs & Rel. S-United States, Box 2, Bureau of Far Eastern Affairs. Office of the Country Director for Malaysia and Singapore. Records Relating to Malaysia and Singapore, compiled 1963–66, RG 59, NACP.

Bundy and Lee after the meeting, both governments acknowledged that a sudden change in their public positions towards each other would not serve their best interests. Recognising that economic viability would make Singapore resilient against communist ideology, Washington's containment policy in Singapore took the form of strong economic cooperation. Hence, without further ado or fanfare, US economic activities in Singapore began to increase.

Part 2 of the study, which contains two chapters, accounts for the accelerated improvement of the US-Singapore defence relationship after the British government, under the leadership of Prime Minister Harold Wilson, announced plans to withdraw British troops from Malaysia and Singapore. Chapter 4 evaluates the impact of Britain's military withdrawal, which was predicted to affect Singapore's security, as well as political and economic stability. During his visit to Washington in October 1967, Lee invited the United States Navy (USN) to maintain an American military presence in the naval bases in Singapore. The Johnson administration had already committed significant resources in Vietnam but recognised that it was in America's interest to maintain USN access to Singapore's naval dockyards after Britain's withdrawal.[78] Hence, a commercial deal was struck between the two governments to repair US ships and aircraft at Singapore's naval dockyards and air bases, respectively. Although the US government avoided direct involvement in Singapore's defence, Washington kept a close watch over the negotiations of the Five Power Defence Arrangements (FPDA), occasionally intervening behind the scenes by urging Australia to take on the leadership of the FPDA. The US government also supplied Singapore with military equipment, ranging from light weapons to heavy artillery vehicles and fighter jets. As demonstrated in Chapter 5, an increased American economic assistance to Singapore buttressed the island's defence and preserved its political stability. From 1966 onwards, there were more American private investments in Singapore, increased trade between Singapore and the US military procurement office in Vietnam, and grants for regional projects initiated by Singapore. Washington and Singapore recognised

---

[78] During the Johnson administration, US military personnel in South Vietnam increased from 16,000 personnel with no direct combat role in 1963 to 180,000 combat troops in 1965, eventually exceeding 500,000. See McMahon, *The Limits of Empire*, p. 112.

that burgeoning economic ties between Singapore and the US were compatible with containment and non-alignment.

Although economic cooperation had greatly strengthened US-Singapore relations by the early 1970s, a shifting balance-of-power caused by the Vietnam War influenced the development of bilateral ties throughout the period from 1965 to 1975. Part 3 of this study, which contains Chapters 6 and 7, analyses the practical difficulties experienced by the US and the Singapore governments in meshing containment and non-alignment. As demonstrated in Chapter 6, the United States' desire to pull out of South Vietnam motivated the Singapore government to increase engagements with the Soviet Union. After President Lyndon Johnson's announcement not to run for a second term, the Singapore government became sceptical about the American military's lasting or continued presence in South Vietnam. Fearing that a US withdrawal from South Vietnam might lead to a communist takeover in Southeast Asia, the Singapore government urged Washington to maintain American troops in Vietnam during the early months of the Richard Nixon's administration. Nevertheless, the Nixon Doctrine, aimed at minimising direct US involvement in overseas conflicts, only reinforced the perception of America's waning commitment to fight communism in Southeast Asia.

In addition to the communist threat from Vietnam, the Singapore government was also concerned that the PRC might exert its influence over the Chinese population in Singapore. The victory of the Chinese Communist Party (CCP) in 1949 after a long civil war had stirred up ethnic pride among a large section of the ethnic Chinese population in Singapore, strengthening their affiliation with China.[79] Soon after CCP assumed power, Beijing created the Overseas Chinese Affairs Commission (OCAC) to engage the overseas Chinese in Southeast Asia through Chinese organisations, schools and newspapers. During the late 1940s and 1950s, the Malayan Communist Party (MCP) established an Open United Front, which continued the communist struggle in Singapore through trade

---

[79] Constance Mary Turnbull, *A History of Modern Singapore, 1819–2005* (Singapore: NUS Press, 2009), p. 248; Liu Hong and Wong Sin-Kiong, *Singapore Chinese Society in Transition* (New York: Peter Lang, 2004), p. 125.

and student unions.[80] Trade unions such as the Singapore Federation of Trade Unions (SFTU) "made little secret of their Communist affiliation".[81] The Chinese Chamber of Commerce became openly critical of the colonial government when the Chinese language was not recognised as an official language in the Rendel commission,[82] followed by changes in the education system that disadvantaged Chinese-medium schools.[83] Resentment towards policies that affected the Chinese in Singapore sparked labour and student protests, most notably the Hock Lee Bus strike in 1955, and student protests in 1954 and 1961.[84] The Secretary General of the MCP, Chin Peng, revealed in a dialogue with scholars that there were teachers in Singapore Chinese schools who were members of the CCP.[85] The MCP had also established a Foreign Bureau in Beijing around 1954 and sought advice from the CCP.[86] After Singapore was separated from Malaysia in 1965, the Singapore government continued to regard communist subversion in Singapore as a credible threat.

Between 1968 and 1969, the Singapore government began to regard Moscow as an alternative to the US for the containment of Beijing's threat to Singapore, in case the US military would choose to withdraw from Vietnam precipitously.[87] Furthermore, Singapore's relations with Malaysia

---

[80] Lee Ting Hui, *The Open United Front: The Communist Struggle in Singapore 1954–1966* (Singapore: South Seas Society, 1996), pp. 47–54.

[81] Richard L. Clutterbuck, *Conflict and Violence in Singapore and Malaysia, 1945–1983* (Singapore: Graham Brash, 1985), pp. 51–3.

[82] Hong Lysa, "Politics of the Chinese-speaking Communities in Singapore in the 1950s: The Shaping of Mass Politics", in *The May 13 Generation: The Chinese Middle Schools Student Movement and Singapore Politics in the 1950s*, ed. Tan Jing Quee, Tan Kok Chiang and Hong Lysa (Petaling Jaya: Strategic Information and Research Development Centre, 2011), pp. 59–63.

[83] Turnbull, *A History of Modern Singapore*, p. 249; Liu and Wong, *Singapore Chinese Society in Transition*, p. 145.

[84] Lee, *The Open United Front*, pp. 79–93.

[85] C.C. Chin and Karl Hack, *Dialogues with Chin Peng: New Light on the Malayan Communist Party* (Singapore: Singapore University Press, 2004), p. 190.

[86] Ibid.

[87] "Chiefs of Mission Briefing Paper: Multi-polarity and Neutralization", 19 June 1972, in Background (Singapore 1973), Box 11, Subject Files of the Office of Indonesia, Malaysia and Singapore Affairs, 1965–74, RG 59, NACP; "Internal Political Situation", 1 February 1973, in Background (Singapore 1973), Box 11, Subject Files of the Office of Indonesia, Malaysia and Singapore Affairs, 1965–74, RG 59, NACP.

and Indonesia would be adversely affected if the Singapore government was seen to be close to the PRC.[88] Singapore established diplomatic ties with the Soviet Union in June 1968 and began allowing Soviet warships into Singapore's naval dockyards for repair. Under pressure from the ANZUK and the US, however, the Singapore government restricted access to Soviet warships even though it continued to service Soviet merchant vessels in Singapore. The Singapore government played the 'Soviet card' from 1968 to 1972 in order to keep America engaged in Southeast Asia.

Chapter 7 highlights the changes in attitude between Washington and the Singapore government after the US withdrawal from Vietnam. Although President Nixon's foreign policy strategy of superpower détente and devolution of American forces in Asia was met with suspicion by the Singapore government, America's exit from the Vietnam War in January 1973 marked a period of improved US-Singapore ties. As part of the US government's plans to withdraw from Vietnam, the US Department of Defense utilised Singapore as a staging area for its withdrawal. Bilahari Kausikan expresses the significance of US presence in Southeast Asia succinctly:

> Economies of all of us were not very strong. So the 10 years w[ere] quite valuable. It did give us a big boost at a time when our economy was down and out…. The British were going to withdraw and employment was running about 14–15% at that time. So during the Vietnam War, we were the logistics centre, we sold you [the US] things. It was quite a lifeline.[89]

The use of Singapore's ship and aircraft repair facilities by the US Army and Navy carried on after the end of the Vietnam War. During the Ford administration, the Singapore government continued to be an ardent supporter of American presence in Southeast Asia. By the end of 1975, close relations between the United States and Singapore had been firmly established.

---

[88] Huxley, *Defending the Lion City*, pp. 41–2.
[89] Interview with Bilahari Kausikan, 8 January 2015.

PART 1

Avoiding Proximity

From Conflict to Common Interests

CHAPTER 1

American Containment and Singapore Survival

Finding Common Ground

A fter Singapore gained independent statehood under the PAP government in 1965, several factors intertwined to direct the course of
US-Singapore relations.[1] Most significant among these factors were the
Singapore government's foreign policy of non-alignment with major
powers, and the US government's policy of containing Sino-Soviet
expansionism in Asia during the Cold War. The policy of containment
was the effect of America's ideological and hegemonic contest with the
Soviet Union during the Cold War. The US-Soviet competition spread
into Asia through proxy armed conflicts on the Korean Peninsula in the
1950s and in Indochina from the 1960s to 1970s. The PAP government's
foreign policy decisions were made taking Singapore's domestic conditions
into consideration, and were aimed towards achieving political, social
and economic objectives of the state. To examine the extent and impact

---

[1] Singapore became an independent state on 9 August 1965 after secession from the
Federation of Malaysia, which it had been a part of from September 1963. Government-
to-government diplomatic relations only began when Singapore became a sovereign
country, although the first United States Consul General to Singapore, Joseph Balestier,
was appointed in 1836. When Balestier was initially appointed to Riau in 1833, he
moved his residence to Singapore and lobbied Washington to change his appointment to
Singapore. See Jim Baker, *The Eagle in the Lion City: America, Americans and Singapore*
(Singapore: Landmark Books, 2005), pp. 68–9.

of the interplay between containment and non-alignment, it is essential to consider the basis of the policy approaches of both the Singapore and the United States governments. It is equally critical to evaluate the compatibility of containment and non-aligned policies between 1965 and 1975.

SINGAPORE'S FOREIGN POLICY

Foreign policy was an important instrument used by the PAP govern-ment to achieve domestic objectives of nation-building and economic development in the country after its separation from Malaysia on 9 August 1965. The Singapore government, led by Prime Minister Lee Kuan Yew, expressed the notion that Singapore's diplomatic and defence policies needed to be designed to contribute to the country's social and economic imperatives. In 1969, during the commemoration of Singapore's 150th anniversary as a British colony, Singapore's Minister for Foreign Affairs, S. Rajaratnam asserted that, "Singapore's foreign policy is … domestic policy conducted by other means."[2] Elaborating on this point in his speech, Rajaratnam made the connection between Singapore's internal and external policies by describing two "hard facts" about Singapore's role and influence in world affairs.[3] First, he stated that the equality between small and big nations was often breached by bigger powers. He then argued that a small country such as Singapore needed to possess "internal political stability, a vigorous economy and a sense of purposeful unity" if it had to "survive the storms of international life".[4] Rajaratnam's metaphor of surviving storms was a common theme in speeches made by Singapore leaders during the first few years of independence.

---

[2] S. Rajaratnam, "Speech by the Minister for Foreign Affairs & Labour, Mr. S. Rajaratnam, at the Diplomatic and Consular Corps Luncheon held at the Hollandsche Club, Camden Park, on Wednesday, 30th July, 1969", 30 July 1969, in POL 15-1 Head of State Executive Branch 1969 B, Box 3, Subject Files of the Office of Indonesia, Malaysia and Singapore Affairs, 1965–74, RG 59, NACP.

[3] Ibid.

[4] Ibid.

Since the early years of nationhood, the PAP had attributed Singapore's economic vulnerability to its geographical limitations.[5] Singapore had a land area of a mere 620 sq km, far smaller than that of its neighbours, Malaysia and Indonesia.[6] Indeed, Singapore's small size created constraints such as a lack of space and a weak domestic market as a result of a small population, and relatively inferior political position in a region with larger and more populated neighbours. The constraint of space, coupled with a lack of natural resources, also imposed limitations on the use of land for the production of commodities for trade. In the lead-up to a merger with Malaya and Britain's North Borneo territories, the PAP government posited that only a political union with the Federation of Malaysia could resolve the economic problems created by Singapore's lack of hinterland and sizeable domestic market.[7] Singapore's membership in the Malaysian federation lasted less than two years. The merger failed due to underlying tensions and mistrust between the leaders from both Singapore and Malaysia, and public spats over communal and political issues. The failed merger with Malaysia added a strong sense of crisis and urgency to the notion of vulnerability conveyed by the PAP government.

Yet Singapore's lack in size was somewhat mitigated by its geographical position. Singapore was located at the southernmost point of the Malacca Straits, where trade routes between major ports in the Far East and seaports in key Middle Eastern cities and Europe intersect. In addition, Singapore had deep harbours and was sheltered from storms by larger islands surrounding it. Therefore, since the beginning of British colonial rule in 1824, Singapore had been regarded by the British as an ideal port along the trade route to China.[8] To the region, as well as globally, Singapore's function as a trading hub had been significant.

Whereas Singapore's location at the crossroad of the Indo-Pacific Ocean trade routes made it prosperous, its strategic location also made

---

[5] Lee, "The Fundamentals of Singapore's Foreign Policy: Then & Now", pp. 5–7.

[6] Bilveer Singh, *The Vulnerability of Small States Revisited: A Study of Singapore's Post-Cold War Foreign Policy* (Yogyakarta: Gadjah Mada University Press, 1999), p. 11.

[7] William P. Maddox, "Singapore: Problem Child", *Foreign Affairs* 40, no. 3 (1962): 485; Chua, *Communitarian Ideology and Democracy in Singapore*, p. 18; Huxley, *Defending the Lion City*, p. 2.

[8] Turnbull, *A History of Modern Singapore*, pp. 28–9.

the island a target for external powers competing for a foothold in the region.[9] During the Cold War period, where the US and the Soviet Union fought each other through proxies, Singapore became a strategic target for both the free world and the communist camp.[10] Both the United States and the Sino-Soviet bloc recognised the significance of Southeast Asia because control over the region by the adversary would result in considerable strategic and political disadvantage during the conflict.[11] The United States and the Commonwealth nations calculated that a communist stronghold in Singapore would yield significant strategic advantage to the Sino-Soviet bloc in Southeast Asia.

In addition to challenges posed by its geography, the Singapore government needed to develop a national identity for Singapore. A large portion of Singapore's population was made up of ethnic Chinese— about 75 per cent of the total population. Approximately 15 per cent of Singapore's population was Malay, less than 10 per cent was Indian, and the rest of the population comprised Eurasians and other minorities. The majority of Singapore's immigrant population had come to the

---

[9] David W. Chang, "Nation-Building in Singapore", *Asian Survey* 8, no. 9 (1968): 762.

[10] Historians writing Cold War history frequently use "free world" to refer to the Anglo-American side of the Cold War conflict. The "free world" is also referred to as the "Western" countries, and such labels are used to draw attention to the difference in economic systems between the communist bloc, led by the Soviet Union and the People's Republic of China, and the capitalist countries, led by the United States. See David C. Engerman, "Ideology and the Origins of the Cold War, 1917–1962", in *The Cambridge History of the Cold War Volume 1: Origins*, ed. Leffler and Westad (New York: Cambridge University Press, 2010), pp. 31–4. The origin of the phrase "free world" used within the Cold War context could likely be traced to US President Harry Truman's speech on 12 March 1947, also known as the Truman Doctrine speech, where he juxtaposed two ways of life: "One way of life is based upon the will of the majority, and is distinguished by free institutions, representative government, free elections, guarantees of individual liberty, freedom of speech and religion, and freedom from political oppression. The second way of life is based upon the will of a minority forcibly imposed upon the majority. It relies upon terror and oppression, a controlled press and radio; fixed elections, and the suppression of personal freedoms." See Harry S. Truman, "President Harry S. Truman's Address Before a Joint Session of Congress, March 12, 1947 ['Truman Doctrine']", 12 March 1947, *The Avalon Project: Documents in Law, History and Diplomacy,* Lillian Goldman Law Library, Yale Law School. http:// avalon.law.yale.edu/20th_century/trudoc.asp. The use of "free world" in this book refers to countries that opposed the economic system of communism during the Cold War.

[11] Mason, "Containment and the Challenge of Non-Alignment", p. 42.

island in hope of better economic conditions, but remained emotionally and culturally attached to their home countries. The overseas Chinese in Singapore retained strong cultural roots with mainland China, and some continued to remit their savings to their home villages in China. Concerns over the links that ethnic Chinese in Singapore had with mainland China played a major role in bilateral relations between the Singapore and the United States governments during the Cold War and will be discussed separately in the later part of the chapter. It is sufficient to note at this point that the PAP saw an urgent need to direct the immigrant population's loyalties towards Singapore and away from their country of origin. In order to create a national identity and a common destiny for Singaporeans, the PAP government preached a shared vulnerability that put the country's survival at risk.

Apart from the problems arising from Singapore's geopolitics, violent labour and communal riots threatened its internal security and social stability during the 1950s.[12] After defeating Lim Yew Hock's Labour Front government in the 1959 elections, the PAP came to power. Intertwined in Singapore's struggle for independence was the political battle between a faction led by Lim Chin Siong and another by Lee Kuan Yew. The PAP split in 1961 when Lim and his supporters formed their own political party, the Barisan Sosialis. Lee and the PAP perceived the Barisan Sosialis to be pro-communist and asserted that Barisan could become a likely vehicle for a potential communist subversion in Singapore. One of the founding leaders of Singapore, Goh Keng Swee, asserted that Singapore merged with Malaysia in order to "break away from the Communist Party" that had controlled the PAP.[13] Months before the 1963 elections in Singapore, the government launched a raid codenamed 'Operation Coldstore' and detained individuals suspected to be communists, including Lim and prominent leaders from the Barisan Sosialis.[14] With prominent opposition politicians put under detention, the PAP won the majority of

---

[12] Stanley Spector, "Students and Politics in Singapore", *Far Eastern Survey* 25, no. 5 (1956): 65.

[13] Melanie Chew, *Leaders of Singapore* (Singapore: Resource Press, 1996), p. 146.

[14] Robert O. Tilman, "Malaysia: The Problems of Federation", *The Western Political Quarterly* 16, no. 4 (1963): 909; Chua, *Communitarian Ideology and Democracy in Singapore*, p. 16.

seats in the elections. To protest against the results of the 1963 elections, the Secretary-General of the Barisan Sosialis, Lee Siew Choh, called for a boycott of parliament by elected Members of Parliament under the Barisan Sosialis that lasted for a year.[15] From 1963 to 1965, Barisan Sosialis MPs resigned one after another and created opportunities for PAP victories in the resultant by-elections.[16] The resignation of Barisan MPs led to an enduring one-party government in Singapore with no opposition representation in parliament. The political battle came to something of a close when the PAP government achieved Singapore's full independence from the British through a merger with Malaysia and secured all seats in parliament.

Even though the Barisan Sosialis was politically impotent by the late 1960s, the PAP government continued to regard the Barisan as a threat, capable of carrying out subversive operations by inciting communal conflicts in Singapore.[17] Evoking images of the racial riots in Singapore during the 1950s and 1964, the PAP warned its citizens that Singapore would not "survive" another bout of communal riots, and should, therefore, strive to build a cohesive multi-racial society. Foreign Minister Rajaratnam's "two facts of life" speech in 1969 encapsulated the importance of building a purposefully unified society that would assure Singapore's ability to "survive the storms of international life".[18]

It is important to note that merger with Malaysia in 1963 had been deemed vital for Singapore's viability. Survival had been the overarching theme for Singapore's nation-building narrative.[19] The notion that Singapore was constantly fighting for economic survival had been built on the perception that Singapore was highly susceptible to internal shocks and

---

[15] Frances L. Starner, "Malaysia's First Year", *Asian Survey* 5, no. 2 (1965): 117.

[16] "Barisan boycott a challenge to parliamentary democracy", *Petir: Organ of the People's Action Party*, February 1966.

[17] Huxley, *Defending the Lion City*, p. 14.

[18] Rajaratnam, "Speech by Rajaratnam, 30 July 1969", 30 July 1969.

[19] See Lee, *From Third World to First*; Lee, "The Fundamentals of Singapore's Foreign Policy: Then & Now"; Nathan, "My Foreign Ministry Years"; Chan Heng Chee, *Singapore: The Politics of Survival, 1965–1967* (Singapore: Oxford University Press, 1971), p. 2; Acharya, *Singapore's Foreign Policy*, p. 1; Chua, *Communitarian Ideology and Democracy in Singapore*, pp. 4–5 and 18–9; Wilarat, *Singapore's Foreign Policy*, pp. 29–73.

external threats due the lack of natural resources. The merger had meant to provide Singapore with a hinterland after the establishment of a common market with Malaysia. But what had appeared to work in theory did not work out in reality. After the Malaysian federal government and the PAP government struggled for almost two years to find a viable political arrangement between Singapore and Malaysia, the Deputy Prime Minister of Singapore, Goh Keng Swee, met Malaysian Deputy Prime Minister Tun Razak and Foreign Minister Tun Ismail on 20 July 1965 and "persuaded [them] that the only way out was for Singapore to secede, completely".[20] In fact, both Malaysian leaders had already "come to the conclusion that Singapore must get out", and what was left to discuss was how separation could be accomplished without British awareness.[21]

The political separation from Malaysia left Singapore without a hinterland. After the separation in 1965, the PAP government focussed on the immediate need for an economic model that had to work without dependence on a common market with Malaysia.[22] Another problem that added to Singapore's struggle at that time was a lack of significant manufacturing and agricultural industries. In other words, Singapore did not produce enough goods that could be exported. Hence, reducing Singapore's economic dependence on Malaysia became an urgent task for the PAP government. Singapore's economic condition had already worsened when Indonesia cut its trade with Singapore in 1963 after Sukarno's protestation against the Malaysian Federation.

One of the main aims of Singapore's foreign policy had been to emphasise its sovereignty and adopt a non-aligned position with regard to the major powers. In Rajaratnam's 1969 speech, credit was attributed to Britain for setting in motion the making of "modern Singapore" 150 years ago.[23] Yet 1969 marked the fourth year of Singapore's independence, a result of a protracted anti-colonial struggle against British rule after the end of the Second World War. Rajaratnam noted that his audience "might find baffling that the people of Singapore should at one and

---

[20] Chew, *Leaders of Singapore*, p. 146.
[21] Ibid.; Lee Kuan Yew, *The Singapore Story: Memoirs of Lee Kuan Yew* (Singapore: Times Edition, 1998), pp. 628–31.
[22] Chua, *Communitarian Ideology and Democracy in Singapore*, pp. 4–5.
[23] Rajaratnam, "Speech by Rajaratnam, 30 July 1969", 30 July 1969.

the same time be celebrating the founding of a colonial outpost and its final liquidation".[24] The foreign minister used the occasion and the speech to illustrate that Singapore's long association with the British had become history. He also stressed that an independent Singapore must not align itself with the major powers if it hoped to achieve economic and social stability during the Cold War. Rajaratnam called attention to similar matters when Singapore was admitted into the United Nations General Assembly in September 1965. To the UN General Assembly, Rajaratnam said

> Singapore has chosen the path of non-alignment. It simply means that we do not wish to be drawn into alliances dedicated to imposing our own way of life on other countries. Friendship between two countries should not be conditional on the acceptance of common ideologies, common friends and common foes.[25]

Although Rajaratnam's statements reflected the Singapore government's resolve to be non-aligned, British military bases still remained on the island until 1971, and the Singapore government publicly supported US involvement in the Vietnam War from 1968 to 1973. It is important to observe that if Singapore had taken its neutralism to an extreme, it would have alienated the United States, which was a key supporter of non-communist regimes in Southeast Asia.

UNITED STATES' POLICY OF CONTAINMENT

Underpinning Washington's approach towards Singapore was the containment of Sino-Soviet influence in Southeast Asia. The foundation of America's containment policy was set soon after the Second World War ended. George Kennan, a US diplomat stationed in Moscow, wrote a long telegram to US Secretary of State James Byrnes in 1946, outlining the ideological differences between the Union of Soviet Socialist Republics (USSR) and the capitalist world led by the United States of America

---

[24] Ibid.
[25] Speech by S. Rajaratnam quoted in S.R. Nathan, *An Unexpected Journey: Path to the Presidency* (Singapore: Editions Didier Millet, 2011), p. 292.

and Britain.[26] Kennan's telegram, known as the 'Long Telegram', was followed by an article, which called for the containment of the Soviet Union.[27] John Foster Dulles, Secretary of State during the Eisenhower administration, advocated a more aggressive strategy of rolling back Soviet influence.[28] Although the US and the USSR possessed equal animosity towards each other, notions about the nature of the Cold War conflict were not completely similar in Washington and the Kremlin; the United States government defined the Cold War as a conflict between a free world and a totalitarian world, whereas the Soviet Union described the Cold War conflict as a struggle between a capitalist world and a socialist world.[29] Although Washington and Moscow were fighting for somewhat dissimilar objectives during the early period of the conflict, both posited that "there was an irreconcilable ideological gulf between the two camps, and that it was incumbent on everyone to choose sides".[30] To the West, a rejection of the containment of the USSR amounted to an endorsement of totalitarianism. Hence, "neutralism was immoral", as Dulles was reported to have said.[31]

In Asia, the United States government aimed to contain the influence of communist China after Beijing and Moscow reached a "strategic 'division of labor' agreement" in 1949 that placed the Soviet Union chiefly responsible for promoting communist revolutions in the West, whereas the Chinese Communist Party (CCP) would stir up revolutions in the East.[32] Chen Jian notes that during the 1950s, CCP leaders vigorously promoted the PRC's successful revolution as a model

---

[26] George Kennan, "Telegram, George Kennan to James Byrnes ['Long Telegram']", 22 February 1946, Harry S. Truman Administration, Elsey papers. http://www.trumanlibrary.org.

[27] George Kennan, "The Sources of Soviet Conduct", *Foreign Affairs* 25 (1947): 566–82; Wallerstein, "What Cold War in Asia?", p. 16.

[28] Wallerstein, "What Cold War in Asia?", p. 16.

[29] Ibid.

[30] Ibid.

[31] Ibid.; Sodhy, *The US-Malaysian Nexus*, p. 143.

[32] Chen Jian, "Bridging Revolution and Decolonization: The 'Bandung Discourse' in China's Early Cold War Experience", in *Connecting Histories: Decolonization and the Cold War in Southeast Asia, 1945–1962*, ed. Goscha and Ostermann, Cold War International History Project series (Washington, D.C.: Woodrow Wilson Center Press, 2009), pp. 144–5.

for achieving "national independence and people's democracy" in Asia.[33] Beijing gained some level of acceptance among leaders of independence movements through its participation in the 1954 Geneva Conference and the Bandung Conference in 1955.[34] Prior to the Bandung Conference, in June 1954, Chinese Premier Zhou Enlai, together with Indian Prime Minister Jawaharlal Nehru and Burmese Prime Minister U Nu, introduced the "Five Principles of Peaceful Coexistence", which included:

> 1. mutual respect for sovereignty and territorial integrity, 2. non-aggression, 3. noninterference in other countries' internal affairs, 4. equal and mutual benefit, and 5. peaceful coexistence.[35]

Led by Premier Zhou, the PRC delegation to the 1955 Bandung Conference projected a reconciliatory image of Beijing and expressed willingness to work with the United States to reduce "tensions in the Far East".[36] Chen, in his analysis of the PRC's foreign policy during the early Cold War period, argues that "the emergence of the Bandung discourse" was Beijing's attempt to establish "China's centrality in international affairs and expand China's influence in the non-Western world".[37] Washington's opposition to the Non-aligned Movement was a response to Beijing's successful engagement with non-aligned countries during the Bandung Conference. State Department officials during the Eisenhower administration "uncritically assumed" that ethnic Chinese communities in Southeast Asia, especially Singapore, which had a majority Chinese population, were particularly responsive to Beijing's overtures.[38]

Beijing's engagement with the Afro-Asian countries was premised on exploiting anti-imperial and nationalist sentiments that were prominent in states that were decolonising during the Cold War period. Beijing's attempt to connect "decolonization and revolution" in Asia was demonstrated by the PRC's support of the revolutions in Korea and Indochina, where Beijing backed the communist regimes of Kim Il-Sung in Pyongyang,

---

[33] Ibid.
[34] Ibid.
[35] Ibid. Also see No. 4 of Chen's notes.
[36] Ibid.
[37] Ibid.
[38] Long, *Safe for Decolonization*, p. 16.

and Ho Chi Minh in Hanoi.[39] Although Beijing's participation in the Korean War led to a high number of casualties within the People's Liberation Army, the war experience in Korea and Indochina bolstered the CCP's ability to mobilise Chinese domestic masses through nationwide campaigns, which promoted revolutionary nationalism.[40] Beijing's rhetoric during the Bandung Conference, however, was not matched by deeds. Despite the Chinese leadership's advocacy of peaceful coexistence in the Five Principles, the aggressive actions of the PRC in Korea, Indochina and the Taiwan Strait contradicted the tenets of non-aggression and non-interference. By shelling the Nationalist-controlled Jinmen islands in 1958, Beijing abandoned a foreign policy of moderation and embraced an overtly aggressive approach in resolving international disputes.[41] In his evaluation of Mao Zedong's speeches in the 1950s, Chen argues that Beijing had all along held "a deep and consistent belief ... that revolution would never emerge in peaceful settings".[42] Beijing's ostensible espousal of the Five Principles was a strategy to turn countries in Asia and Africa "into allies in anti-imperialism and anti-colonialism struggles, and that 'in the end the United States will certainly be isolated'".[43] As much as Beijing attempted to isolate the US from the East, Washington strived just as hard to contain the PRC's influence in Asia.

The American strategy of containment was delineated in a joint State-Defense long-range China study conducted by the US Defense and State Departments in late 1965. The document outlined five possible strategies that the US government could take against the growing influence of the PRC in Asia. Washington could seek an "early showdown" with the PRC, adopt "close-in containment and forward defense" by maintaining US military presence in Northeast and Southeast Asia, develop an off-shore island chain of US bases or allies to contain the PRC, develop "remote containment and mid-Pacific defense behind buffer zones",

---

[39] Chen, "Bridging Revolution and Decolonization", pp. 144–7.
[40] Ibid.
[41] Ibid.
[42] Ibid.
[43] Ibid. Chen quotes part of Mao's speech during a meeting with Harry Pollitt, chair of the British Communist Party. Also see No. 62 of Chen's notes.

and disengage with the region but maintain "mid-Pacific defense".[44] The most extreme strategies—showdown and disengagement—were excluded after preliminary consideration because they were deemed less advantageous than the other strategies. Hence, containment manifested in three forms— close-in, remote, or from an island chain—became the basis for US deployment of political, military, economic and psychological instruments of diplomacy.[45]

Until the early 1960s, the United States had adopted a strategy of close containment and forward defence in Northeast and Southeast Asia. The Defense and State Departments considered the strategy to be costly, strategically inflexible and one that "unavoidably" led to "frictions with the host governments and peoples".[46] US government planners, therefore, preferred the offshore island chain containment strategy in the interim period of 1965 to 1975, and aimed to move towards remote containment from a buffer zone in the mid-Pacific region as a long-term policy.[47] But neither strategies was practicable under the current circumstances in Northeast and Southeast Asia because, as stated by the joint Defense and State Department China study, abandonment of close containment was "out of the question" while the US was "locked in a struggle to preserve the freedom of South Vietnam and to demonstrate our [US] will and ability to repel indirect, as well as direct, Communist aggression".[48] "Swift, complete withdrawal," the study concluded, "might be misinterpreted by both our friends and our enemies and undermine our continuing efforts to deter renewed Communist insurgency and bolster the internal stability of South Vietnam...."[49] America should not be seen to be abandoning its allies in Asia. Hence, the US government maintained a close-in containment strategy despite its high cost.

---

[44] Ibid.; US Department of State, "Chapter V: U.S. Strategy Over the Next Decade", December 1965, in State, Department of Policy Planning, Vol. 6 [1 of 2], Box 52, National Security File. Agency File, LBJL.

[45] Ibid.

[46] Ibid.

[47] Ibid.

[48] Ibid.

[49] Ibid.

The State Department designed different forms of close-in containment strategy in Northeast and Southeast Asia that could be implemented to handle three types of regimes in Asia.[50] Towards established communist regimes in Asia, the United States government would deter or defeat overt attacks and counter "communist subversion, psychological warfare and disruptive diplomacy".[51] With respect to non-communist states, the US government would strengthen their economic, political and social stability and assist in their aspirations for modernisation. Furthermore, Washington would induce Asian communist leaders to "moderate, and eventually abandon, their expansionist policies".[52] In the face of greater recognition of Beijing in the UN and the PRC's growing nuclear capabilities, the study concluded that "[s]trengthening the free nations around Communist China is in fact essential to the success of a strategy of remote containment in South Asia and to any hope of moving back from close-in containment in East and Southeast Asia".[53] In order to strengthen non-communist countries in Southeast Asia, the study recommended a slew of diplomatic instruments ranging from economic and military aid, providing support for education, offering a nuclear deterrence, and promoting regional cooperation. Significantly, the US government, according to the study, needed to strengthen ties with non-communist Southeast Asian nations by acquiring a better understanding of the systems and people of these countries. Nevertheless, Beijing's overtures towards the non-aligned countries during the 1950s had coloured the American perception of the NAM. Singapore, which declared its affiliation with the non-aligned camp after gaining independence, was also perceived to be pro-Beijing by the US. Governed by a bipolar Cold War logic, London and Washington concluded that Beijing could—if it wanted—potentially mobilise Singapore's Chinese population to promote communist revolution in Southeast Asia.

---

[50] Ibid.
[51] Ibid.
[52] Ibid.
[53] Ibid.

SINGAPORE'S CHINESE MAJORITY

During the early Cold War period, the US Department of State identified the overseas Chinese in Asia as an avenue along which Beijing could exert economic and political influence. In 1946, the Truman administration held the view that "[i]f these [overseas] Chinese were turned into a fifth column to advocate local communist revolutions, or convinced to use their economic power to support the communist machine, then the entire region would fall, endangering US security and foreign policy interests, not to mention weakening US allies in the region like the ROC [Republic of China on Taiwan], Japan and South Korea."[54] After the declaration of the PRC in October 1949, the US government paid specific attention towards overseas Chinese and formulated "an overseas Chinese policy, which sought to deny the overseas Chinese to the Chinese communists; encourage the diaspora to identify their interests with those of their countries of residence; and ensure that they look to the ROC on Taiwan for leadership and sources of cultural or ethnic pride".[55]

During the 1950s, Washington regarded Singapore's majority Chinese population as "especially vulnerable to communist subversion",[56] a perception that informed the way Washington conducted its diplomacy towards Singapore during the Eisenhower administration. The PRC encouraged overseas Chinese to send their children for education in China and helping to rebuilding the motherland. In reaction to Beijing's overtures, the colonial authorities in Singapore prohibited the Chinese from returning to Singapore after visiting China.[57] The Chinese Chamber of Commerce in Singapore resented the harsh treatment of the British authorities against what the Chinese regarded as acts of patriotism towards their homeland. The Chamber became openly critical of the colonial government when the Chinese language was not recognised as an official language in

---

[54] Ibid.; Meredith Oyen, "Communism, Containment and the Chinese Overseas", in *The Cold War in Asia: The Battle for Hearts and Minds*, ed. Zhang, Liu and Szonyi (Leiden: Brill, 2010), p. 64.

[55] Ibid.

[56] Long, *Safe for Decolonization*, p. 16. Clutterbuck argues that Chinese schools were "particularly vulnerable to Communist propaganda". See Clutterbuck, *Conflict and Violence in Singapore and Malaysia, 1945–1983*, p. 75.

[57] Turnbull, *A History of Modern Singapore*, p. 248.

Singapore by the Rendel commission.[58] In addition to this, the funding for English-medium schools was disproportionally higher than it was towards Chinese-medium schools. This disparity drew students away from poorly staffed and inadequately funded Chinese schools, and widened the rift between the Chinese community and the colonial government.[59] Chinese schools thus became "particularly vulnerable to Communist propaganda".[60] The National Service Ordinance announced in 1954 sparked violent clashes between students of Chinese middle schools and the police, although reports vary on whether the Malayan Communist Party instigated the protests.[61] In 1961, Chinese middle school students boycotted examinations to protest against changes in the education system, this time with allegations by Prime Minister Lee Kuan Yew that left-wing opposition political parties had fuelled the protests.[62] It was more likely that most of the Chinese students protested because of dissatisfaction about policies rather than with the intention of subverting the government. Nevertheless, the communists took advantage of the student movements to create unrest and gather supporters.[63] Many young Chinese students were drawn to the communist party and developed an admiration for Marxism, and soon, Beijing became a source of inspiration to them.[64]

In fact, the loyalty of Singapore's Chinese towards mainland China was more a matter of "ethnic pride" than an ideological alignment.[65] Lim Chin Siong also claimed in a conversation with Douglas Hyde, who interviewed Lim in the mid-1960s, that his supporters were "pro-Chinese rather than pro-Communist".[66] Looking back at the 1950s and 1960s, Kausikan observes that there was "certain sentimentality towards

---

[58] Hong, "Politics of the Chinese-speaking Communities in Singapore in the 1950s", pp. 59–63.

[59] Turnbull, *A History of Modern Singapore*, p. 249; Liu and Wong, *Singapore Chinese Society in Transition*, p. 145.

[60] Clutterbuck, *Conflict and Violence in Singapore and Malaysia, 1945–1983*, p. 75.

[61] Liu and Wong, *Singapore Chinese Society in Transition*, pp. 142–3; Clutterbuck, *Conflict and Violence in Singapore and Malaysia, 1945–1983*, pp. 84–6.

[62] Liu and Wong, *Singapore Chinese Society in Transition*, pp. 153–5.

[63] Ibid.

[64] Clutterbuck, *Conflict and Violence in Singapore and Malaysia, 1945–1983*, pp. 63–5.

[65] Long, *Safe for Decolonization*, p. 16.

[66] Clutterbuck, *Conflict and Violence in Singapore and Malaysia, 1945–1983*, p. 137.

the distant, once upon a time, ancestral homeland" and that the Chinese population in Singapore "may be proud of China" without being communist.[67] Regardless of the motivation behind overseas Chinese affiliation towards the PRC, however, a competition for the loyalty of the overseas Chinese ensued during the early 1950s. At least three parties vied for the support of the overseas Chinese: the PRC, the Republic of China on Taiwan, and the United States to a lesser extent. A fourth group competing for the loyalties of the Chinese immigrants was the host country that the overseas Chinese resided in. During the Cold War, the host governments that were not aligned with major power blocs frequently "added their voices in opposition to both communist and containment themes".[68] The PAP government in Singapore was no different and was determined to gain the allegiance of the Chinese population towards Singapore.

The Chinese Communist Party government's ultimate goal was to limit the political and economic support from the overseas Chinese towards Nationalist China. Beijing's policy towards overseas Chinese was articulated in five points by the OCAC. Meredith Oyen translates and summarises the five points as follows:

> unifying the patriotic overseas Chinese; exposing attacks on the overseas Chinese by Chiang Kai-shek's government; protecting the rights of the Chinese living abroad (including their ability to send remittances, but also protecting them against local discriminations and violence and opening immigration opportunities); promoting cultural and language education abroad; and improving relations between the overseas Chinese and the local societies in which they lived.[69]

Although the OCAC seemed to prioritise improvement of relations between the overseas Chinese and the local societies that they lived in, the Commission's major policy objectives pointed towards the chief aim of unifying the overseas Chinese behind Beijing's leadership and maintaining cultural and language links between overseas Chinese and the PRC.

---

[67] Interview with Bilahari Kausikan, 8 January 2015.
[68] Oyen, "Communism, Containment and the Chinese Overseas", pp. 60–1.
[69] Ibid.

In the psychological and information battle among the US, the PRC and the ROC, Beijing enjoyed the greatest success in Singapore during the 1950s because of its more palatable propaganda messages. Pro-communist Hong Kong newspapers, such as *Ta Kung Pao* and *Wen Wei Po*, focussed on shared love for the Chinese mainland and tactfully avoided reports about internal campaigns so that the Chinese in Singapore would not form negative perceptions of mainland China after reading about political developments in the PRC.[70] Since many overseas Chinese were engaged in private enterprise in Singapore, the PRC newspapers avoided negative commentary that criticised capitalist thought. Beijing's priority was not to "get the entire diaspora behind every domestic policy" but rather to promote general opposition to the ROC and support for the PRC.[71] The United States Information Service (USIS) counteracted PRC propaganda by providing articles that were sympathetic to free world ideologies for Southeast Asian Chinese newspapers, which were often in need of well-written Chinese articles. But the success of USIS was heavily dependent on indigenous circumstances.[72] Whereas the USIS managed to distribute 90 per cent of its articles through Hong Kong newspapers, its articles were not as well-circulated through Singapore's Chinese newspapers because the press in Singapore was able to produce its own material rather than use "pieces offered by USIS".[73] Although both the USIS and the PRC propaganda machinery had limited influence over Singapore's newspapers, the PRC had an edge because it produced Chinese textbooks used in Singapore schools.

In tandem with its relatively successful propaganda campaign towards overseas Chinese, the PRC modified its citizenship policy towards overseas Chinese in the mid-1950s. Beijing's willingness to compromise on its "dual nationality" stance improved China's relations with African and Asian governments that had emerged from decolonisation and independence movements as the policy would allow overseas Chinese to assimilate into their host countries. During the Qing dynasty, ethnic Chinese born in China or abroad were recognised as Chinese nationals or citizens though

---

[70] Ibid.
[71] Ibid.
[72] Ibid.
[73] Ibid.

they could also be recognised as citizens of another state.[74] After the end of the Qing dynasty, when the Kuomintang (KMT) government came to power, it retained the dual nationality policy in its attempt to make overseas Chinese "culturally loyal to China".[75] With the establishment of the PRC in 1949, the loyalty of overseas Chinese in Southeast Asia towards mainland China became a source of problems for Beijing's relations with newly independent governments in the region.[76] Overseas Chinese residing in Southeast Asia were perceived to be more loyal to mainland China than to their host country, and were seen as an extension of Beijing's influence in the region. During the Bandung Conference of 1955, the PRC delegation led by Zhou Enlai indicated that Beijing was willing to abandon its policy of dual nationality.[77] Once the dual nationality policy was abolished, the Chinese residing overseas could either choose to remain as Chinese citizens and give up political rights in their host countries, or give up Chinese citizenship to assimilate better into their host societies.[78]

The PRC's decision was largely welcomed by Southeast Asian governments at that time, improving Beijing's goodwill among the non-aligned countries during the conference in Bandung.[79] The British accused the PRC of allowing the Chinese in Malaysia and Singapore "to naturalize so that they could better promote communism from within the country as citizens, rather than as aliens".[80] Washington, too, was doubtful about whether Beijing would be any less influential to the overseas Chinese after

---

[74] Leo Suryadinata, *Understanding the Ethnic Chinese in Southeast Asia* (Singapore: Institute of Southeast Asian Studies, 2007), pp. 90–3.

[75] Ibid.; Wang Gungwu, *China and the Chinese Overseas* (Singapore: Times Academic Press, 1991), p. 176.

[76] Suryadinata, *Understanding the Ethnic Chinese in Southeast Asia*, p. 105.

[77] In 1955, Beijing offered to enter into a "dual nationality" treaty with Southeast Asian countries and Indonesia was the only country that signed the treaty with Beijing. The treaty allowed local-born Chinese to choose local citizenship and their children to do the same when they would reach 18 years of age. Nevertheless, in the wake of the 1965 coup in Jakarta, the Indonesian government repudiated the treaty unilaterally to prevent "undesirable" Chinese children from gaining Indonesian citizenship. In 1980, Beijing declared its nationality law to recognise only single citizenship; all Chinese overseas with local citizenships automatically lost their Chinese citizenship. Ibid.

[78] Oyen, "Communism, Containment and the Chinese Overseas", p. 88.

[79] Chen, "Bridging Revolution and Decolonization", pp. 158–9.

[80] See Note No. 74 of Oyen, "Communism, Containment and the Chinese Overseas", p. 89. Oyen cites US archival records under US Foreign Service Posts, Record Group 84.

the elimination of dual nationality. The Anglo-American fear was not entirely unfounded. When China was invaded during the Second World War, the overseas Chinese living in Southeast Asia exhibited patriotic sentiments towards China, demonstrated through efforts to invest their wealth and skills towards the Sino-Japanese war in mainland China.[81] After the war ended, the Chinese residing overseas, regardless of their birthplace, developed strong anti-colonial and anti-western values, and participated in the nationalist movements against European powers.[82] These patriotic feelings became so strong that "all the colonial powers as well as native rulers began to develop genuine … deep-seated fears, about the ambitions of China and its Overseas Chinese".[83] Regardless of Beijing's motivation for changing its citizenship policy, what was clear was that the manoeuvre was calibrated to gain friends among the Afro-Asian nations. By precipitating the assimilation of the overseas Chinese into their local societies, Beijing had put into motion the erosion of support for the KMT government in the ROC, which had depended on support from the overseas Chinese as a counterweight against the PRC. Beijing's policy eventually forced the KMT's hand and persuaded it to follow the PRC lead by conceding that it was better for the overseas Chinese to become citizens of their host countries.[84]

In addition to the PRC's diplomatic triumph over the ROC, Beijing also picked up some gains when Southeast Asian governments hosting the overseas Chinese implemented "abrupt and drastic" policies to hasten the assimilation of these new citizens from China.[85] These policies resulted in stiffened resistance against integration and pent-up resentments, which Beijing could exploit.[86] According to a CIA report on overseas Chinese in Southeast Asia, governments such as Indonesia, Thailand, South Vietnam, and the Philippines imposed economic restrictions on their own Chinese citizens and simultaneously forced the Chinese to assimilate faster by

---

[81] Wang, *China and the Chinese Overseas*, p. 177.

[82] Ibid.

[83] Ibid.

[84] Central Intelligence Agency Office of Research and Reports, "Overseas Chinese in Southeast Asia", 22 January 1960, *CIA-RDP79-01006A000100160001-9*, CIA Records Search Tool (CREST).

[85] Oyen, "Communism, Containment and the Chinese Overseas", p. 90.

[86] Ibid.

assuming greater responsibility towards the host government.[87] The CIA report concluded that in "all the host countries [in Southeast Asia] the Chinese have resisted assimilation".[88] Assimilation of the Chinese population was even more difficult in Singapore than in other Southeast Asian nations because the majority of Singapore's population was Chinese, many of whom were immigrants. Under Britain's colonial administration, the Chinese population in Singapore resisted assimilation into a British colonial identity and was responsible for much of the social unrest on the island during the 1950s.

During the period of self-governance in Singapore, the Labour Front government in Singapore was openly hostile towards communist slogans in Singapore and displayed intolerance towards communist-incited activities by quelling riots and protests involving Chinese workers and high school students during the mid-1950s. The Singapore government showed toughness in containing leftist influence in Singapore but the US government, though acknowledging the resolve of the Labour Front government to be non-communist, foresaw that if Singapore became independent from British rule, it could quickly get drawn into Beijing's orbit. "Given the earnest concern about stemming the communist tide," argues Joey Long, "a consensus on the Eisenhower administration's Singapore policy had emerged within top policymaking circles in Washington: whether in concert with the British or unilaterally, the United States would have to intervene more forcefully to preserve American interests."[89] Putting together a repertoire of diplomatic, cultural and covert tactics, the Eisenhower administration cajoled local politicians, disseminated USIS material in local libraries established with US resources, and deployed CIA agents to gather intelligence by bribing Singapore Special Branch officers.[90]

By the late 1950s and well into the 1960s, the PRC seemed to have reduced its emphasis towards the overseas Chinese when the CCP

---

[87] Office of Research and Reports, "Overseas Chinese", 22 January 1960.

[88] Ibid.

[89] Long, *Safe for Decolonization*, p. 38.

[90] For an account of successful and unsuccessful operations carried by the Eisenhower administration to keep Singapore "safe for decolonization", refer to Long, *Safe for Decolonization*.

disbanded the Overseas Chinese Affairs Commission.[91] Washington began to change its position towards the overseas Chinese as well. The United States government became more active in integrating Chinese Americans into American society, and revised its foreign policy to reflect the lesser threat it now attributed to the overseas Chinese. In particular, the US State Department moved Washington's overseas Chinese policy "out of the realm of China policy and into the realm of US-Southeast Asian relations".[92] Overseas Chinese affairs became regarded as part of the domestic affairs of host governments, and fundamentally detached from developments in the PRC. Unlike during the 1950s, Washington eventually began to recognise that a significant number of overseas Chinese in Southeast Asia were in fact "more pro-China than pro-Communist".[93]

In 1965, driven to some extent by the fear that Singapore could still fall under Beijing's political influence, the US government directed policies to build "reasonably good relations" with Singapore.[94] Assistant Secretary of State for East Asian and Pacific Affairs William Bundy's views on Singapore in late 1965 were that

> [a] hostile Singapore could develop into a difficult strategic problem for us in Southeast Asia, particularly if the UK goes ahead with certain military phase-downs in the area which it has intimated strongly on several recent occasions. The temptation to a hostile government of an overwhelmingly Chinese state to act in concert with Peking's objectives, even if it maintained its anti-communist personality, would be substantial. While we may not be able to prevent this eventuality, I believe we have a definite obligation to take constructive actions to lessen its attractiveness to those in and out of the Singapore government who are willing to consider constructing reasonable good relations with us as a desirable policy option.[95]

"For the sake of our future relations with this small, but key country," argued Bundy, "I believe we must demonstrate in a concrete way our genuine desire to do what is politically possible to ensure its continued

---

[91] Oyen, "Communism, Containment and the Chinese Overseas", p. 92.
[92] Ibid.
[93] Office of Research and Reports, "Overseas Chinese", 22 January 1960.
[94] Bundy, "Singapore's Economic Development", November 1965.
[95] Ibid.

economic viability."[96] Clearly, the US government had become more willing to engage favourably with Singapore by the mid-1960s.

Months before his first official visit to Washington in 1967, Lee Kuan Yew stated that he wanted to change Washington's perception that Singapore was pro-Beijing. In an interview conducted by the Chinese media in Singapore, before his October trip, a question was raised: "We know the Americans generally have some misconceptions about the overseas Chinese, and believe that they have strong ties with China and are acting as agents for China....Why should the Americans hold such an attitude towards the overseas Chinese?" Without challenging the premise that Washington, indeed, held misconceptions about the overseas Chinese, Lee told his questioner that there might be several factors in play and that he wished to "take the opportunity of [his] coming visit to clarify this matter".[97] To the US administration, Lee wanted to clarify that Singapore was not a malleable instrument at the disposal of the PRC. In October 1967, Lee visited Washington and met with President Johnson, Secretary of State Dean Rusk, Secretary of Defense Robert McNamara and other senior US officials. The press statements Lee gave during his visit were supportive of American involvement in the Vietnam War and contrasted with the anti-American speeches he had made in the latter half of 1965.[98] Lee's meeting with the Johnson administration was fruitful in two ways: Lee had somewhat convinced the American President and senior officials in Washington that the Singapore government was more pro-American than pro-Beijing, and had also become convinced that the US government no longer held the view that Singapore was pro-communist. The US Department of State realised in the 1970s that

---

[96] Ibid.

[97] Francis J. Galbraith, "Lee Visit", September 1967, in V-46A Visit of Prime Minister Lee Kuan Yew of Singapore—October 17–18, 1967. Admin. Misc and sub misc, Box 34, Executive Secretariat. Visit Files, 1966–70, RG 59, NACP.

[98] Francis J. Galbraith, "Singapore Prime Minister Lee Kuan Yew's Visit to the United States", November 1967, in V-46A Visit of Prime Minister Lee Kuan Yew of Singapore—October 17–18, 1967. Admin. Misc and sub misc, Box 34, Executive Secretariat. Visit Files, 1966–70, RG 59, NACP; Lee Kuan Yew, "PM Lee Interview on 30.8.65", 30 August 1965; James D. Bell, "Telegram to US Department of State", 17 September 1965, in Lee Kuan Yew (2 of 2), Box 2, Subject Files of the Office of Indonesia, Malaysia and Singapore Affairs, 1965–74, RG 59, NACP.

Singapore was far more fearful of intimacy with Beijing than Washington had initially perceived.

After the Nixon administration's rapprochement with Beijing in 1972, the Singapore government, unlike other Southeast Asian governments, was reluctant to follow America's lead in engaging the PRC. The US State Department reported in 1973 that Lee and his government were confident that the Chinese people of Singapore would "eventually break their emotional ties with the mainland and develop a Singaporean identity" but the process had not been completed.[99] Formal diplomatic ties between the Singapore government and Beijing during the early 1970s might lead to close affiliation between Singapore's Chinese population and the PRC, and could weaken the nascent sense of a Singaporean identity that the PAP had been promoting among Chinese Singaporeans. Hence, according to US observers, the Singapore government would have liked "another generation of isolation from the mainland".[100] At this time, Lee also feared that other countries in the region, particularly Malaysia, would develop close ties with Beijing "too quickly".[101] Malaysia was the first member of the Association of Southeast Asian Nations (ASEAN) to establish formal ties with the PRC.[102] The Singapore government calculated that Kuala Lumpur was engaging the PRC so that Beijing would reduce support for the Communist Party of Malaya, which was still active in the Thai-Malaysia border.[103] It is not clear whether the Malaysian government benefitted from formal ties with Beijing but there was a risk that recognition of the Chinese Communist Party regime in Beijing could re-energise the leftist political factions that had been on the fringes of Malaysia and Singapore politics. The Singapore government was perhaps more cautious than the Malaysian government about the prospects of a rejuvenated left-wing in Singapore politics. Hence, Lee expressed concern that official diplomatic

---

[99] "Singapore-China", 2 February 1973, in Background (Singapore 1973), Box 11, Subject Files of the Office of Indonesia, Malaysia and Singapore Affairs, 1965–74, RG 59, NACP.

[100] Ibid.

[101] Ibid.

[102] Sodhy, *The US-Malaysian Nexus*, p. 328.

[103] Robert Chin, "Some GOS Perceptions of Malaysia", 12 June 1972, in Background (Singapore 1973), Box 11, Subject Files of the Office of Indonesia, Malaysia and Singapore Affairs, 1965–74, RG 59, NACP.

presence of the PRC in Kuala Lumpur "would put great pressure" on the Singapore government, too, to establish diplomatic ties with Beijing.[104]

In 1974, Deputy Chief of Mission at the American Embassy in Singapore, William B. Grant, reported to the State Department regarding the concerns related to Singapore's recognition of the PRC after a conversation with his British counterpart, Deputy High Commissioner John Watts. According to Watts, the British High Commissioner, Peter Tripp, had met with Lee earlier to discuss possible ramifications if Singapore were to decide to recognise the PRC.[105] "Lee told High Commissioner Tripp," reported Grant, "that he could only count on about 10% of the population of Singapore being totally loyal to Singapore and its government. Another 15% were out and out Chinese chauvinists who looked to Peking for inspiration and direction."[106] Lee described the remaining 75 per cent as "rather pathetic and could be easily swayed one way or another by events and personalities".[107] Lee seemed to be telling the British High Commissioner that more Chinese in Singapore were loyal towards the PRC than towards Singapore, which ironically was a perspective Lee had wanted to change in American circles when he had visited Washington in October 1967.

The perception that closer relations with Beijing could disrupt the progress of Singapore's nation-building project was echoed by the Soviet Counsellor to Singapore, Valentin Pasentchuk. The Soviet diplomat, who was stationed in Beijing during the Cultural Revolution, noted that "the school books used by Chinese children clearly showed parts of Southeast Asia including Malaysia and Singapore as belonging to 'Greater China'".[108] Whether Beijing had territorial interests in Singapore or not,

---

[104] "Singapore-China", 2 February 1973.

[105] William B. Grant, "Memorandum of Conversation: Consequences of GOS recognition of PRC", 1 August 1974, in POL People's Republic of China, Box 12, Subject Files of the Office of Indonesia, Malaysia and Singapore Affairs, 1965–74, RG 59, NACP.

[106] Ibid.

[107] Ibid.

[108] William B. Grant, "Memorandum of Conversation between Mr. Valentin M. Pasentchuk, Counsellor, Embassy of the Union of Soviet Socialist Republics, and Mr. William B. Grant, Deputy Chief of Mission, American Embassy Singapore", 18 April 1974, in POL USSR 1974, Box 12, Subject Files of the Office of Indonesia, Malaysia and Singapore Affairs, 1965–74, RG 59, NACP.

the Soviet diplomat would have seen some benefit in sharing this view with the Singapore leaders. If Pasentchuk's report was reliable, and the PRC did view Singapore as a part of its territory, then the Singapore government would, indeed, want to maintain a distance from Beijing for as long as possible. Furthermore, an entente between Beijing and the Singapore government would jeopardise Singapore's relations with its close neighbour, Indonesia, who had suspended diplomatic relations with the PRC.[109] Pasentchuk mentioned to William Grant in a conversation that "Singapore had made it clear it would be the last ASEAN Government to establish relations with the PRC".[110] Indeed, preoccupation with the risks arising from communist China was a common thread that bound the US and Singapore governments closely.

SINGAPORE AND NON-ALIGNMENT

Another factor that determined US-Singapore relations during the Cold War was the way Washington viewed Singapore's non-aligned foreign policy. Along with the change of American attitude towards the Chinese in Singapore during the early 1960s, America's foreign policy towards non-aligned countries also shifted decisively. The Secretary of State, Dean Rusk, who served under Presidents John F. Kennedy and Lyndon B. Johnson, publicly stated that Washington no longer held a hostile position towards the NAM. In 1962, Rusk indicated the shift of the Kennedy administration's approach towards the NAM. During a press conference, Rusk explained that the Kennedy administration did not "regard neutrals as enemies, or allies as satellites",[111] a departure from the views of the Eisenhower administration which regarded non-aligned

---

[109] Michael Leifer, *Singapore's Foreign Policy: Coping with Vulnerability* (Oxon: Routledge, 2000), p. 78.

[110] Grant, "Memcon: Pasentchuk and Grant", 18 April 1974.

[111] James L. Greenfield, "Telegram: Greenfield to Manning", 1 May 1962, in 19.1 ANZUS Council Mtg–May 8–9, 1962 Canberra, Australia (Administrative Arrangements–OIC) 1962–AUST/NZ Desk Files, Box 6, Bureau of East Asian & Pacific Affairs. Country Director for Australia, New Zealand, and Pacific Islands. Subject Files, RG 59, NACP.

states as being closer to the communist bloc than the US. In fact, Rusk "deplore[d] the earlier American misunderstanding of the Neutrals".[112]

Although the Department of State had adopted a new approach towards non-aligned countries, some sections of American officials and politicians remained unfriendly and suspicious towards the NAM. That the United States was a popular target for anti-imperialist propaganda by some non-aligned countries contributed to the remnants of mutual distrust between the NAM and the US. In 1963, the United States Information Agency (USIA) reported that the Indonesian government was using the Afro-Asian Journalists' Conference held in Jakarta as a platform to garner support from non-aligned countries against the proposed Federation of Malaysia. The Conference launched "poorly camouflaged anti-Western, anti-American denunciations", accusing the US of "imperialist intervention in Cuba, Laos, Korea and South Viet-Nam".[113] The Acting Director of USIA, Donald M. Wilson, called for retaliatory measures, which included lodging formal protests to the Indonesian Department of Foreign Affairs, launching propaganda campaigns through American press and radio, and circulating "materials refuting specific charges levied against the U.S. and its allies and exposing Chinese communist tactics in their attempts to capture the Afro-Asian movement".[114] The US State Department did not see benefits in taking such a confrontational approach and instructed the USIA to focus its propaganda campaign on specific issues of contention "without bringing Indonesia into the picture in any denigrating fashion".[115]

Discussions among State Department officials revealed that the US administration had begun to interpret the internal affairs and external relations of non-aligned countries based on local perspectives rather than

---

[112] Ibid.

[113] Donald M. Wilson, "Plan to Counter Afro-Asian Anti-American Propaganda", 17 May 1963, in POL 3 Organizations & Alignments Afro-Asian (POL–Political Affairs & Rel. Gen. '63), Box 15, Bureau of Far Eastern Affairs. Office of Regional Affairs. Office of the Regional Planning Adviser. Subject Files, 1955–64, RG 59, NACP.

[114] Ibid.

[115] Edward E. Rice, "Plan to Counter Afro-Asian Anti-American Propaganda", 24 June 1963, in POL 3 Organizations & Alignments Afro-Asian (POL–Political Affairs & Rel. Gen. '63), Box 15, Bureau of Far Eastern Affairs. Office of Regional Affairs. Office of the Regional Planning Adviser. Subject Files, 1955–64, RG 59, NACP.

through bifurcated Cold War logic. State Department official, Robert L. Kinney, advised that the United States

> must assume for the present that the Indonesians, whatever their peculiarly Javanese motives, are going to be playing the communist and particularly the Chicom [the People's Republic of China] game: the cards in Djakarta are simply stacked that way (Sukarno's pet propaganda lines, weak Cabinet Ministers and a rampant internal network of communist fronts allied with the Chicoms).[116]

The US State Department might have advocated putting up with anti-American propaganda from Jakarta. But what really troubled the US government was Indonesia's dependence on the Soviet Union for military equipment. Even after power shifted from Sukarno to Suharto, the Indonesian Air Force and Navy continued to be 70–80 per cent equipped with Soviet weaponry in 1968, and relied on the USSR for spare parts.[117] Washington was concerned that a communist Indonesia would "outflank the struggling noncommunist states of mainland Southeast Asia ... isolate Australia and New Zealand, deny to the West Indonesia's tremendous oil, tin, and rubber resources, and challenge the U.S. base complex in the Philippines".[118] Therefore, the US government was prepared to offer generous military assistance and grants for Indonesia to acquire US defence equipment in order to reduce Jakarta's military reliance on Moscow.

To be sure, Washington did not view Singapore's non-aligned position as a hindrance to having close US-Singapore relations in the 1960s.[119] The Singapore government had, on several occasions, proclaimed that

---

[116] Robert L. Kinney, "Letter of Ambassador Jones to Assistant Secretary Hilsman (5-16-63) Re U.S. Posture Toward Indonesian Afro-Asian Conference Efforts", 3 June 1963, in POL 3 Organizations & Alignments Afro-Asian (Political Affairs & Rel. Labor Conf '63), Box 15, Bureau of Far Eastern Affairs. Office of Regional Affairs. Office of the Regional Planning Adviser. Subject Files, 1955–64, RG 59, NACP.

[117] US Department of State, "National Policy Paper: Indonesia, Malaysia and Singapore Subregion", 6 February 1968, in Department of State. Policy Planning, filed by LBJ Library [1 of 2], Box 55, National Security File. Agency File, LBJL.

[118] McMahon, *The Limits of Empire*, p. 120.

[119] Francis J. Galbraith, "Letter to William P. Bundy, Assistant Secretary, Bureau of East Asian and Pacific Affairs", 24 June 1968, in POL 15-1 Amb. Galbraith's Off.-Inf. Lets. 1968, Box 4, Subject Files of the Office of Indonesia, Malaysia and Singapore Affairs, 1965–74, RG 59, NACP.

Singapore's non-alignment did not preclude its preference towards the US.[120] Furthermore, officials from the US government had developed personal relations with Singapore's political leaders and government officials even before Singapore was separated from Malaysia, contributing to an emerging sense of empathy for the attitudes in both governments. Lee Kuan Yew was a firm believer in the domino theory,[121] which suggested that the communist influence would eventually spread to other countries in Southeast Asia if Vietnam became unified under a communist regime. During the Kennedy and Johnson administrations, the domino theory influenced decisions in Washington as much as it did in Singapore and Malaysia.[122] The Malaysian Prime Minister, Tunku Abdul Rahman, warned his parliament in January 1967 that "the intention of the Communists is not just to take over South Vietnam…. Once South Vietnam is taken over by the Communists, it will only be a matter of time before Malaysia goes under".[123] There was genuine anxiety among Southeast Asian leaders against a communist takeover. Hence, throughout the early years of independence, the Singapore government kept to a foreign policy position that retained a public image of non-alignment with major power blocs, while leaning towards the free world.[124] During the Nixon administration, the US foreign policy in Asia was undergirded by a dual strategy of superpower détente and devolution of direct American military involvement in the region. The most significant foreign policy pronouncement of the Nixon

---

[120] Ibid.

[121] Ang, "Singapore and the Vietnam War", p. 360; Ang, *Lee Kuan Yew's Strategic Thought*, p. 31.

[122] McMahon, *The Limits of Empire*, p. 113. In summing up US intervention in Southeast Asia, McMahon further argues that "the domino theory appears never to have been based on anything other than illusory, worst-case projections. Moreover, the persistent worry about the disastrous political repercussions sure to follow retreat or defeat in Southeast Asia appear as equally fanciful now as they should have seemed at the time". See McMahon, *The Limits of Empire*, p. 221.

[123] "The kinds of Reds I hate – by Tengku", *The Straits Times*, 21 January 1967, p. 7.

[124] Author's interview with Mushahid Ali, S. Rajaratnam School of International Studies, Singapore, 27 November 2014. Former Singapore diplomat Mushahid Ali explains that because the threats came from "communist parties supported by communist countries like China and the Soviet Union", the Singapore government chose to be closer to the west.

administration was the Nixon Doctrine, also known as Guam Doctrine, outlined by President Richard Nixon on 25 July 1969 at the US military base in Guam.

Speaking to reporters during a visit to US bases in Guam, President Nixon declared his administration's foreign policy approach thus:

> One, that we [the US government] will keep our treaty commitments…; two, that as far as the problems of internal security are concerned, as far as problems of military defense, except for the threat of a major power involving nuclear weapons, that the United States is going to encourage and has a right to expect that this problem will be increasingly handled by, and the responsibility for it taken by, the Asian nations themselves.[125]

In November 1969, President Nixon reiterated the Guam Doctrine in a speech to the 'silent majority' to plead for support. He outlined the key principles of his administration's foreign policy doctrine, this time adding a third point:

> [I]n cases involving other types of aggression [i.e., not involving nuclear weapons], we [the US government] shall furnish military and economic assistance….[126]

Initially suspicious of the intentions of the Nixon Doctrine, the Singapore government came to realise that the approach was complementary to Singapore's non-aligned foreign policy.

According to the Nixon administration, "[n]eutralization in principal [*sic*] meshes with the Nixon Doctrine concepts, and in the long run could provide a framework for stability in SEA requiring a minimum of U.S. security resource inputs".[127] The US State Department described

---

[125] Richard M. Nixon, "Informal Remarks in Guam with Newsmen", 25 July 1969, *The American Presidency Project,* Online by Gerhard Peters and John T. Woolley. http://www.presidency.ucsb.edu/ws/?pid=2140 [accessed 24 May 2013].

[126] Richard M. Nixon, "Remarks of the President on Vietnam delivered to national television and radio audiences from the White House at 9:32 p.m. EST", 3 November 1969, in Nixon Doctrine, 1969–71 (1), Box A82, Melvin R. Laird Papers, GRFL. This pronouncement of the Nixon Doctrine is more commonly cited by scholars because it was given in a formal setting.

[127] "PARA - Malaysia", 1973, in POL 2/3 PARA (Malaysia 1973), Box 11, Subject Files of the Office of Indonesia, Malaysia and Singapore Affairs, 1965–74, RG 59, NACP.

Singapore as "a good Nixon Doctrine country", praising Singapore for its contribution towards Southeast Asian stability, and for being a supporter of American involvement in the Vietnam War.[128] In 1972, the US State Department commented on Singapore's balance of power approach in Southeast Asia:

> GOS theory (Rajaratnam and Lee) is that multi-polarity is an established and on balance favorable situation. The belief is that the great powers have agreed on no direct confrontation, and that small countries must at all costs avoid becoming too closely dependent on one great power or they run the danger of becoming the field for indirect big power competition.... It would be more accurate... to say that what the GOS really desperately wants is for someone to counter the potential threat of Communist China.... They [GOS] do not really consider the US as a threat to their security, however, and they do so consider both the PRC and the USSR. Thus, they would much prefer that the US remain as the principal counter to China and would like the USSR to play this role only if we will not.... Neutralization in the GOS view is a non-starter.... [T]hey do not even really believe that.[129]

The State Department, in 1973, described Singapore's non-aligned foreign policy as "non-alignment with a Western bias".[130] Despite the "distinctly Western bias", Washington acknowledged that the Singapore government guarded its "public posture of non-alignment" and would "avoid actions or statements which would appear to line [Singapore] up politically on the side of any major power or bloc".[131]

---

[128] "Singapore PARA - FY 1974", 15 December 1972, in POL 2/3 PARA (Singapore 1973), Box 11, Subject Files of the Office of Indonesia, Malaysia and Singapore Affairs, 1965–74, RG 59, NACP. For a more detailed analysis on the effects of the Nixon Doctrine on US-Singapore relations, see Chapter 7.

[129] "Chiefs of Mission Briefing Paper: Multi-polarity and Neutralization", 19 June 1972.

[130] "Policy of Non-Alignment", 3 February 1973, in Background (Singapore 1973), Box 11, Subject Files of the Office of Indonesia, Malaysia and Singapore Affairs, 1965–74, RG 59, NACP.

[131] Ibid. See also Huxley, *Defending the Lion City*, p. 34.

CONCLUSION

The United States-Singapore bilateral relations from 1965 to 1975 were established under Cold War circumstances where the US government aimed to keep Singapore out of the communist bloc. The Singapore government, on the other hand, was less caught up with the Cold War and more preoccupied with maintaining Singapore's social, political and economic stability through adopting a non-aligned approach towards great power rivalries. Although Washington and Singapore shared a common objective of limiting the PRC's influence in Singapore and Southeast Asia, the Lee Kuan Yew government regarded the Soviet Union as a possible partner who could contain Beijing's influence in the region if the US were to leave the region. Not surprisingly, Singapore's diplomatic ties with the Soviet Union became a source of friction in US-Singapore relations. Whereas Washington valued cordial bilateral ties with Singapore, Malaysia and Indonesia, the US-Singapore relationship was considered the least critical to American interests among the three Southeast Asian countries.[132] Since Washington would not risk alienating the Malaysians and Indonesians by appearing overly sympathetic towards Singapore, the US government preferred to keep Singapore at arm's length.

Similarly, the Singapore government preferred to maintain a distance, at least politically, between Washington and Singapore. Although the Singapore government sought American economic assistance, close political alignment with the United States would draw criticism from Singapore's Chinese media and potentially damage the credibility of the PAP government. To balance out the notion that Singapore was relying too much on American economic engagement, the Singapore government established some economic cooperation with the Soviet Union and the PRC. Nevertheless, Singapore's economic nexus with the US far outweighed Singapore's trade and economic ties with Moscow and Beijing. To Lee and the PAP government, if Singapore was seen as an American stooge, dissent among the Chinese population might,

---

[132] Theodore J.C. Heavner, "Memorandum: Theodore J.C. Heavner to Cmdr. Robert A. Shaid: Comments on JCS Questions and Proposed Answers", 17 August 1971, in DEF 15 U.S. Use of Military Facilities (Singapore 1971), Box 8, Subject Files of the Office of Indonesia, Malaysia and Singapore Affairs, 1965–74, RG 59, NACP.

in the most extreme circumstances, result in a political comeback of the Barisan Sosialis, which had had strong support from Chinese voters in Singapore before the mid-1960s. This desire to manage the opinions of Singapore's Chinese population explains why US-Singapore relations had a somewhat acrimonious beginning in August 1965.

CHAPTER 2

"Never the Americans"

Behind Lee Kuan Yew's Anti-American Press Campaign

Shortly after Singapore's separation from Malaysia in August 1965, Lee Kuan Yew made strong anti-American statements during media interviews over the next several months. 1965 marked the beginning of American military escalation in the Vietnam War with the deployment of the first US combat troops, consisting of 3,500 men in Danang.[1] It was also a year that saw a waning of British military superiority in Southeast Asia. It would not have been surprising for the Singapore government, which claimed to be economically and socially vulnerable, to seek the protection of a major power such as the United States. Yet, barely one month after the signing of the Separation Agreement between Malaysia and Singapore, Lee launched a public relations campaign that was highly critical of the United States government. Lee Kuan Yew's 1965 anti-American press campaign reflected both political calculation and an underlying hostile attitude towards the Americans. This chapter asserts that Lee's fundamental distrust towards the American administration was the most important factor that drove his negative press campaign towards the US.

---

[1] Ang, *Southeast Asia and the Vietnam War*, p. 24; McMahon, *The Limits of Empire*, p. 118.

LEE'S ROLE IN US-SINGAPORE RELATIONS

Lee Kuan Yew's leadership had a profound impact on the development of Singapore. Some academics and world leaders, therefore, describe Lee as the "official mascot" of Singapore.[2] In 1969, the US Secretary of State, William P. Rogers, went as far as to remark that "Lee is Singapore".[3] Even Lee seemed to perceive Singapore as an extension of his political persona when he entitled his personal memoir as *The Singapore Story: Memoirs of Lee Kuan Yew*. The Singapore government was oligarchic in its decision-making process and in its rudimentary foreign affairs ministry in 1965. This meant that key foreign policy decisions were often made by the Prime Minister and senior members of the Singapore cabinet. When Singapore became independent, the Ministry of Foreign Affairs was not a "sophisticated bureaucratic apparatus", but more of an inexperienced outfit of novice diplomats.[4] As explained by S.R. Nathan, a senior official in Singapore's Ministry of Foreign Affairs during the 1960s and 1970s, Prime Minister Lee Kuan Yew, with advice from Foreign Minister Rajaratnam, set the foreign policy direction for Singapore.[5] Lee was the main decision-maker in Singapore's foreign relations, especially during the first few years of Singapore's independence. "I soon realised," recounts Nathan, "that the Foreign Minister did not make 'foreign policy'. It was the Prime Minister who made it with inputs from the Foreign Minister and his other Cabinet colleagues."[6] Even when the Singapore Foreign Ministry had evolved into a professional foreign service in the early 1970s, Lee remained "an articulate spokesman of Singapore's international concerns and policies".[7]

In a study on Lee Kuan Yew's strategic thoughts, Ang Cheng Guan argues that "Lee is generally acknowledged as Asia's leading strategic thinker, one who does not flatter but 'who is known, from time to time, to

---

[2] Acharya, *Singapore's Foreign Policy*, p. 19.
[3] William P. Rogers, "Memorandum for the President: Your Meeting with Prime Minister Lee Kuan Yew of Singapore, May 13", 2 May 1969, in POL 7 Prime Minister Lee's Visit 1969, Box 3, Subject Files of the Office of Indonesia, Malaysia and Singapore Affairs, 1965–74, RG 59, NACP.
[4] Acharya, *Singapore's Foreign Policy*, pp. 18–9.
[5] Nathan, "My Foreign Ministry Years", p. 13.
[6] Ibid.
[7] Acharya, *Singapore's Foreign Policy*, p. 19.

speak bluntly', and someone who helps 'us find direction in a complicated world'".[8] In fact, Lee's speeches and public statements can be regarded as "valuable but underrated source[s]" useful for understanding his thoughts on international politics.[9] In a study written during the first years of Singapore's independence, Chan Heng Chee mentions Lee's "seemingly senseless outburst" towards the Americans during the 30 August 1965 interview.[10] With sources from newspapers and speeches of Lee and other contemporary observers, Chan argues that the factors leading to Lee's anti-American press campaign from August 1965 to early 1966 were twofold: to bolster Singapore's non-aligned credentials, and to prevent a precipitous withdrawal of the British forces from Singapore that would leave the island without a credible defence force.[11] This chapter amplifies Chan's analysis and adds a new dimension to understanding Lee's anti-American press campaign by uncovering his motives behind the harsh statements made during the first months of Singapore's independence.

Lee's Anti-Americanism

Lee Kuan Yew's verbal attacks on the American administration in August 1965 caught Washington by surprise because Lee had not been known in United States' policy-making circles to be anti-American prior to August 1965. In fact, a memorandum of conversation, dated 19 January 1965, between Lee, US Ambassador to Malaysia, James Bell, and US Consul General to Singapore, John Lacey, revealed their close and cordial ties with Lee.[12] Furthermore, the US Department of State briefly considered inviting Lee to Washington in July 1965 but eventually held back the invitation for fear that the US would become projected into Malaysia's

---

[8] Ang, "The Global and the Regional in Lee Kuan Yew's Strategic Thought", p. 236.
[9] Ibid.
[10] Chan, *Singapore: The Politics of Survival*, p. 43.
[11] Ibid.
[12] John A. Lacey, "Malaysian Politics and U.S. Military Credit Offer (Memorandum of Conversation between Ambassador James D. Bell and Prime Minister Lee Kuan Yew)", 19 January 1965, in POL 18 Provincial, Municipal & State Government (Singapore 1965), Box 1, Subject Files of the Office of Indonesia, Malaysia and Singapore Affairs, 1965–74, RG 59, NACP.

political controversy between the Alliance government in Kuala Lumpur and the People's Action Party government in Singapore.[13] For Lee to display such a hostile attitude towards the American administration was, therefore, puzzling to the Americans. But for Lee and the PAP government, being openly critical of American policies in Southeast Asia accentuated Singapore's non-aligned foreign policy and bolstered Singapore's image of independence from western powers. Lee's vitriol against the US administration was later explained by the Singapore government as Lee's attempt to gain the acceptance into the group of the non-aligned Afro-Asian nations. It had another motive: to serve notice to listeners in Whitehall that the US would not be an acceptable alternative to Britain should the British government decide to withdraw from Singapore bases.

In a televised interview conducted on 30 August 1965, Lee began to articulate anti-American sentiments for the first time since Singapore's separation from the Federation of Malaysia on 9 August 1965. The interview began with discussions on Singapore's internal security and the British military bases in Singapore, and culminated in Lee's criticism of the American administration. Lee said: "[I]f the British withdraw I am prepared to go on with the Australians and the New Zealanders. But, I am not prepared to go on with Americans."[14] Lee supported his low opinion of the American government by recounting three incidents that had led him to conclude that the US government lacked "depth and judgment or wisdom which comes out of an accumulation of knowledge".[15] The first incident Lee cited was an attempt by the US Central Intelligence Agency officers to suborn a Singapore Special Branch officer in 1961. The second involved Lee and Goh Keng Swee missing a flight from Hawaii to Washington. The third incident involved Lee's unsuccessful attempt to bring an American doctor to treat his wife's illness in Singapore. Since Lee expounded more on the first and third incidents, this chapter will

---

[13] William P. Bundy, "Action Memorandum: Mr. Gordon Walker's Proposal That Singapore Prime Minister Be Invited to Visit the United States", 13 July 1965, in POL 18 (from July 1, 1965/Dec. 31/ '65) POL–Political Affairs & Rel. Singapore, Box 1, Subject Files of the Office of Indonesia, Malaysia and Singapore Affairs, 1965–74, RG 59, NACP.

[14] Lee, "PM Lee Interview on 30.8.65", 30 August 1965.

[15] Ibid.

focus on the incidents involving the CIA covert operations in Singapore and Lee's attempt to enlist the help of the US government to bring in a doctor to treat his wife's illness. The two incidents are significant also because Lee continued to refer to the two incidents during media interviews through late 1965.[16]

The CIA Incident

During the TV interview mentioned above, Lee described the American government as inferior to the British. He further claimed that the US administration's inferiority was "crucial to the whole of [his] thinking" towards the Americans.[17] Lee narrated a 1961 incident involving the CIA to demonstrate American inferiority to the British in carrying out crucial intelligence operations:

> [W]e caught an American C.I.A. agent trying to subvert our Intelligence Special Branch Officer, bribe him, so that the Special Branch Officer will feed the C.I.A. because the C.I.A. wants to know what is happening. Subverting a Singapore officer! ... I am proud the officer, offered a large sum of money and continuing sums of money ... refused and reported the matter to his chief who reported it to me.... I told my officers, "Lay a trap: microphones, everything.["] The man was caught, [and] arrested, [with] enough evidence to send him to gaol for anything up to twelve years. We had him by the throat. The American Consul General, shaking at his knees, knew nothing about it.... Do you get confidence in an outfit like that?[18]

When the CIA incident occurred in 1961, Lee asked the American government for $100 million economic assistance in exchange for a quiet release of the two arrested CIA agents.[19] The American government turned down Lee's request and counter-offered Lee and his political party $10 million instead. Lee felt that the US offer was "an unbelievable insult" and rejected it.[20] Eventually, at the repeated urgings of the British High Commissioner, Lord Selkirk, the Singapore government released the CIA

---

[16] Bell, "Telegram to US Department of State", 17 September 1965.
[17] Lee, "PM Lee Interview on 30.8.65", 30 August 1965.
[18] Ibid.
[19] Ibid.; Lee, *From Third World to First*, pp. 449–51.
[20] Lee, *From Third World to First*, p. 450.

agents a month later.[21] After Lee revealed the incident during the 30 August 1965 interview, the US State Department denied Lee's allegations in a routine press conference. The next day, Lee backed his claim by releasing a letter from US Secretary of State Dean Rusk written in 1961. In the letter, Rusk expressed regret that the incident had occurred and assured the Singapore Prime Minister that the Kennedy administration would carry out disciplinary action against the concerned officers. The letter did not mention the attempted bribe.[22] Embarrassed, the US State Department was later compelled to acknowledge the authenticity of Lee's claims that the Secretary of State had written the letter to the Singapore government but refused to confirm that any bribe had been offered for the release of the CIA agents.[23] US Ambassador to Malaysia James Bell, who was Director of the Office for Southwest Pacific Affairs when the CIA incident happened, also denied Lee's allegation that Washington offered Lee a bribe to cover up the failed CIA operation.[24] Joey Long's detailed account of the 1961 CIA incident affirms the authenticity of Lee's claims regarding the bribes, and blames the debacle on the lack of consultation between the CIA and the US Consulate General in Singapore.[25] By exposing the incident on national television, Lee was attacking American prestige by highlighting the covert intelligence-gathering operations undertaken by the US in Singapore and how they had failed miserably.

The Doctor Incident

To further support his argument that the United States government was inferior to the British, Lee revealed another encounter he had had with the US government. During the interview, Lee told his interviewer that "somebody very dear" to him "was in need of specialist treatment" and their doctor in Singapore had recommended an American specialist who was

---

[21] Ibid.

[22] Peter Boyce, *Malaysia and Singapore in International Diplomacy: Documents and Commentaries* (Sydney: Sydney University Press, 1968), pp. 167–8.

[23] Lee, *From Third World to First*, p. 450.

[24] Robert J. McCloskey, "Memorandum for the files", 2 September 1965, in Lee Kuan Yew (2 of 2), Box 2, Subject Files of the Office of Indonesia, Malaysia and Singapore Affairs, 1965–74, RG 59, NACP.

[25] Long, *Safe for Decolonization*, pp. 172–8.

described as the best person to treat the illness.[26] Later, in September 1965, Lee disclosed that his wife, Kwa Geok Choo, was that person, and she had been suspected of having a terminal illness after her doctor, Benjamin Sheares, had conducted a preliminary diagnosis. Dr Sheares had recommended an American specialist, Dr Howard Taylor of Columbia University, as the "best man on Mrs. Lee's problem".[27] Lee had then sought the help of Ambassador Bell and Consul General Richard Donald to invite the American doctor to see Mrs Lee in Singapore. Samuel Berger, Deputy Assistant Secretary for the Far East at the US State Department, approached Dr Taylor with Lee's request, stressing that "the State Department regarded this [request] as a matter of national importance" and urged Taylor to fly to Singapore.[28] Lee told his interviewer in 30 August 1965:

> Do you know what was the answer [from the American doctor]? The Professor was busy. He recommends Professor XYZ, but he does not know whether Professor XYZ will come or not.... And if the patient was prepared to fly to Geneva, the Professor would look at him or her.... You know, the impudence and the impertinence of it![29]

It turned out that Dr Taylor had scheduled a professional trip to Geneva for commitments "which he could not break" and had refused to go to Singapore.[30] When Donald asked Lee Kuan Yew if Mrs Lee could go to the US for treatment instead, Lee

> [r]epeatedly and forcefully said he would not permit his wife to go to US irregardless [*sic*] of consequences to her: It would 'blow my [Lee's] chances' with Afro-Asian group.... [Lee] believes two or three weeks, possibly a month, margin [was] available [for treatment]. 'Unless it is cancer, where every day counts'.... [Lee] said he [was] under intolerable pressure from his wife who is quarreling with him (I [Donald] assume [she was] wanting to fly to US).[31]

---

[26] Lee, "PM Lee Interview on 30.8.65", 30 August 1965.

[27] Samuel D. Berger, "Memorandum for files - Subject: LEE KUAN YEW: The Incident of the Doctor", September 1965, in Lee Kuan Yew (2 of 2), Box 2, Subject Files of the Office of Indonesia, Malaysia and Singapore Affairs, 1965–74, RG 59, NACP.

[28] Ibid.

[29] Lee, "PM Lee Interview on 30.8.65", 30 August 1965.

[30] Berger, "Lee: Incident of the Doctor", September 1965.

[31] Ibid.

After the US State Department officials' repeated pleas with Dr Taylor, the doctor finally agreed to fly to Singapore to treat Mrs Lee's illness. Nevertheless, several days had passed and Lee finally told Donald that Mrs Lee was "no longer interested in seeing [a] doctor who had no interest in seeing [his] patient.... She would seek out a British doctor."[32] In his memoir, Lee recalled that the failure of the United States government to arrange for Dr Taylor to treat his wife's ailment in Singapore drove him to "[fire] a broadside at the Americans" during the August 1965 interview.[33] Lee commented that he was "angry and under stress" due to his wife's critical condition,[34] and was "venting [his] anger on the Americans for being unhelpful".[35]

The events that transpired after the August interview led Lee to conclude that the Americans had not acted in good faith from the start. Dr Taylor was worried that Lee's mention of the case in his August interview would tarnish his professional reputation and created the impression that the US State Department had conveyed Lee's request to him inaccurately. In a letter to Dr Sheares explaining his initial refusal to go to Singapore, Dr Taylor claimed inaccurately that US State officials had not told him the identity of the patient and the nature of the sickness when they had first approached him.[36] On 15 September 1965, in an interview with *New York Times* correspondent Jerry King, Lee

> produced [a] letter from Dr Taylor ... in which Taylor said that State Dept had not informed him who [the] patient was or [the] nature of [the] problem and that if he [Taylor] had known his initial response to Dept[']s request might have been different.[37]

Lee apparently bought into Taylor's side of the story and accused Washington of insidiously forcing him to send his wife to the US for treatment.

---

[32] Ibid.
[33] Lee, *From Third World to First*, p. 449.
[34] Ibid.
[35] Ibid.
[36] Berger, "Lee: Incident of the Doctor", September 1965.
[37] Bell, "Telegram to US Department of State", 17 September 1965.

Lee said this proved his point that USG [United States Government] wanted to get Mrs Lee into US while he, Lee, was struggling to develop a neutralist policy in Singapore. [Jerry] King tried to argue with Lee that this was nonsense but got nowhere.... Lee was highly emotional on [the] subject.[38]

Lee Kuan Yew's Criticisms of America's Vietnam Policy

Lee Kuan Yew's verbal attack on the US administration then shifted from his personal encounters with American officials to Washington's conduct of foreign policy in Southeast Asia. During the interview on 30 August 1965, Lee mocked the US government's unsuccessful, and unpopular, intervention in Vietnam:

But, the Americans, they lack depth. And, they don't understand the overseas Chinese. They don't understand the Vietnamese. That is why it is such a mess—they (the Americans) would have had somebody more brutal than Lim Yew Hock (ex PM of Singapore), like Ngo Dinh Diem. And, when finally they decided that their own creation was an embarrassment. They closed their eyes, looked the other way, and he [Diem] got bumped off. I thought, well, they must have a plan, you know. Ngo Dinh Diem, bumped off. "A" takes over. Then Plan Alpha moves into operation. But, my god, they had no plans. There have been no less than 15 to 20 governments since Ngo Dinh Diem.[39]

To be sure, Lee was not the first Southeast Asian leader to criticise the US for its unpopular war in Vietnam. His comments, however, reflected his attempt to echo the views of non-aligned African and Asian governments, who were often critical of America's foreign interventions.

---

[38] Ibid.

[39] Lee, "PM Lee Interview on 30.8.65", 30 August 1965. The US State Department document mistakenly identified Lim Yew Hock as the "ex PM of Singapore". Lim's title was, in fact, "Chief Minister", before his Labour Front Party lost the Singapore elections to the PAP in 1959.

Lee's Fading Anti-American Sentiments

Lee's anti-American press campaign continued into September 1965. In an interview with the Chinese press in Singapore, Lee told reporters on 13 September 1965 that

> America has a comparatively short history [compared with Britain] of only a few hundred years.... They may never understand us, that we would rather die than be politically bludgeoned in this way.... They are used to all sorts of preposterous transactions. For example, they buy and sell political leaders in South Korea and South Vietnam.... They think that Singapore is a small country and that her people can be bought and sold.[40]

On 11 December 1965, Lee spoke with a group of foreign correspondents at the studios of Television Singapore, distinguishing his personal sentiments against the Americans from the policy of the Singapore government towards the US. A reporter from the *Daily Mail* of London, Arthur Cook, referred to the 30 August 1965 interview with Lee, when Lee displayed "great personal bitterness towards the Americans".[41] Lee interrupted Cook in mid-sentence, asserting that:

> My personal bitterness is irrelevant in matters of national policy.... One does not conduct national affairs on the basis of personal likes and dislikes. If you do that, then you perish.[42]

In his account of the mood at that time, former Singapore diplomat, Mushahid Ali, explains that the incident "coloured his approach" towards the Americans and took some time to fade.[43] During the same interview, Lee was less strident against the US, saying that he now felt "the Americans are intelligent people and when they find they have got to buy goods instead of buying people, as they do in some other parts of Asia, it may be cheaper in the long run for them".[44] Perhaps one good point to mark

---

[40] Lee, *The Papers of Lee Kuan Yew: Speeches, Interviews and Dialogues, Vol. 3: 1965–1966* (Singapore: Gale Asia, 2012), pp. 98–9.
[41] Ibid.
[42] Ibid.
[43] Interview with Mushahid Ali, 27 November 2014.
[44] Lee, *The Papers of Lee Kuan Yew: Speeches, Interviews and Dialogues, Vol. 3: 1965–1966*, pp. 98–9.

the end of Lee's anti-American speech would be in the middle of 1966. On 15 June 1966, Lee delivered a speech titled "Big and Small Fishes in Asian Waters".[45] In response to questions after the speech, Lee gave a sympathetic analysis on US involvement in Vietnam:

> You know, American presidents have the unfortunate disability of having to face election every four years. In 1968, there will be any number of Robert Kennedys around to put all kinds of highly attractive formulae for resolving all the discomfort of by then probably three-quarters of a million Americans [affected by the Vietnam War].... Hundreds of Vietnamese are dying every day, for what? For Vietnam? No! To decide that Vietnam shall not be repeated.... But whilst we buy time, if we just sit down and believe people are going to buy time forever after for us, then we deserve to perish.[46]

At an address given at the Political Study Centre on 13 July 1966, Lee no longer attributed the lack of leadership in South Vietnam to poor US foresight and planning, but portrayed the developments in Vietnam as unpredictable:

> Nobody really knows because so many factors are involved [in] just what this [presumably the course of the Vietnam War] is going to lead to. Not even the Russians, not even the best of the whiz bids in Washington—they really do not know. If you ask them, 'Look, what is going to happen in Vietnam? You tell me now, spell out step by step where you think this will end,' and I do not think they can really spell it out to you and say, 'Well, in the year X which is three years or five years from now, we shall have accomplished this and so many years from thence, we will have accomplished that'.... They are playing on the basis that certain factors are in a process of flux and change. Whatever happens, they cannot withdraw.[47]

In both instances, Lee aimed to encourage US involvement in the Vietnam War, and that non-communist states in Southeast Asia had to make good use of the time that America was buying.

---

[45] Ibid.
[46] Ibid.
[47] Ibid.

US PROPOSAL FOR AN EMBASSY

Whether Lee's criticisms of the United States was for publicity or a reflection of official doctrine towards the US, the Singapore government did try to use Singapore's non-aligned and anti-American position to gain some leverage over the United States. An example is the US government's request to upgrade the American Consulate General to an embassy in late 1965. By November 1965, the Johnson administration felt some urgency to raise the Consulate General to an embassy because "if we [the US government] wait too long Lee may accuse us of lack of confidence or other shortcoming in our relations with him".[48] Upon receiving the request, Rajaratnam, Singapore's foreign minister, used the opportunity to request for a more open American market for Singapore textiles and other forms of economic assistance from the US.[49] When Washington refused to tie the US Embassy issue to American economic assistance, Washington's proposal to establish an embassy in Singapore was shelved for months.[50]

Lee's August 1965 interview and Rajaratnam's refusal to elevate the US Consulate General to an American Embassy suggested that the Singapore government intended to keep the Americans at a distance. Yet, in both instances, there were hints that the PAP government actually desired for greater US economic assistance—most clearly in the CIA bribe incident and Rajaratnam's conditions for the establishment of an American Embassy in Singapore. After Singapore's independence was recognised and it had become a member of the United Nations on 21 September 1965, Lee's criticism of the US began to fade from his public statements.

---

[48] George Ball, "Outgoing Telegram: Department of State to Amconsul Singapore", 17 November 1965, in Cables – Singapore (Vol. 1) 8/65–7/67, Box 281, National Security File. Country File. Asia and the Pacific, LBJL.

[49] Robert J. Morris and Albert D. Moscotti, "Briefing Paper: Singapore", 17 February 1966, in POL 1 Gen. Policy Background (Singapore 1966), Box 1, Subject Files of the Office of Indonesia, Malaysia and Singapore Affairs, 1965–74, RG 59, NACP.

[50] Samuel D. Berger, "Letter of Credence for Chargé in Singapore", 11 April 1966, in POL 17 Diplomatic and Consular Repr. (Singapore 1966), Box 1, Subject Files of the Office of Indonesia, Malaysia and Singapore Affairs, 1965–74, RG 59, NACP.

REASONS FOR LEE KUAN YEW'S ANTI-AMERICANISM

Singapore's Non-aligned Foreign Policy

It seemed apparent that the chief aim of Lee's anti-American speeches was to gain recognition from the non-aligned Afro-Asian countries for Singapore's sovereignty after its separation from Malaysia in 1965. Since the establishment of the Non-aligned Movement in 1961, the group had almost doubled, from the 25 founding members to 47 full members in 1964. Based on a 1965 estimate by the Director of the League of Arab States Information Center for the Southwestern United States, Khalid I. Babaa, out of the 112 member nations in the United Nations, 54 claimed to belong to the NAM, "although the shades and degrees of belonging to that group vary".[51] One notable characteristic of the NAM states was that they did not distinctly vote as a bloc, largely due to the principle of non-alignment with major power blocs and their ideologies.[52] The UN voting records nonetheless showed that non-aligned members in the UN consistently voted along anti-colonial and anti-imperialist lines.[53] To gain the recognition of the NAM, Singapore needed to be distinctly anti-colonial and anti-imperialist. Furthermore, extra effort had to be made to emphasise its non-aligned stance because its ties with Commonwealth defence partners had inadvertently placed Singapore within the pro-West camp.

The Singapore delegation to the United Nations in September 1965 also feared that "the Soviet Union might veto [Singapore's] membership of the UN".[54] In September 1964, a draft resolution submitted by the Norwegian delegate called for peaceful negotiations to end the Indonesia-Malaysia *Konfrontasi,* which was a low-level conflict or confrontation initiated by Indonesia in opposition to the federation of former British colonies into a new political entity.[55] A Soviet veto

---

[51] Khalid I. Babaa, "The 'Third Force' and the United Nations", *Annals of the American Academy of Political and Social Science* 362 (November 1965): 88.

[52] Ibid.; Richard L. Jackson, *The Non-aligned, the UN, and the Superpowers* (New York: Praeger, 1983); Leon Gordenker, "The United Nations and Its Members: Changing Perceptions", *International Journal* 39, no. 2 (1984).

[53] Jackson, *The Non-aligned, the UN, and the Superpowers.*

[54] Nathan, *An Unexpected Journey*, p. 292.

[55] S/5973, United Nations Security Council, "Norway: draft resolution", 15 September 1964, New York (United Nations Security Council Official Records).

had successfully blocked the Norwegian resolution. The Russian delegate, P.D. Morozov, explained the Soviet veto in anti-colonial and, essentially, anti-British terms. Morozov's speech highlighted that the Soviet Union disagreed with the resolution because it did not mention the root of the problem, which it felt was the British presence in Southeast Asia:

> We [the USSR] consider it necessary to stress once again that the situation in South-East Asia is essentially a struggle against the remnants of the rotten colonial system to which the colonialists are still obstinately trying to cling.... It is in fact the aim of the United Kingdom and the other colonial Powers to preserve their colonial domination and to continue to suppress the national liberation movement of the peoples of South-East Asia.... The colonialists must finally leave their former colonies in peace.[56]

Because the British military presence in Malaysia and Singapore had not yet been removed, it was a cause of anxiety within the Singapore government. Singapore felt that the USSR would veto Singapore's application for the UN membership. In fact, Malaysia's well-intended sponsorship of Singapore's entry into the UN in September 1965 might have actually increased the likelihood of a Russian veto. Furthermore, the Singapore government could not take UN admission to be automatic because territories such as Southern Rhodesia, Angola, Mozambique, Portuguese Guinea, South West Africa and British Guiana had been denied independence and recognition by the UN.[57] Hence, Singapore actively sought the support of powerful non-aligned countries such as India and Egypt to "mobilise support" for Singapore's recognition by the UN.[58] Chan Heng Chee, observing the developments during the Lee Kuan Yew's anti-American press campaign, argued that Lee's "seemingly senseless outburst" against the American government was prompted by the "slow response" from African governments to recognise Singapore's

---

[56] S/PV.1152, United Nations Security Council, "1152nd Meeting Held in New York, on Thursday, 17 September 1964, at 10.30 a.m.", 17 September 1964, New York (United Nations Security Council Official Records), p. 10.

[57] A/PV.1332, United Nations Security Council, "United Nations General Assembly Twentieth Session, 1332nd Plenary Meeting, Tuesday, 21 September 1965, at 3 p.m.", 21 September 1965, New York (United Nations General Assembly Official Records).

[58] Nathan, *An Unexpected Journey*, p. 292.

independence. Almost a month after Singapore's independence, most of the Afro-Asian nations had not officially recognised Singapore.[59] "Thus on the eve of Singapore's application for membership in the UN," Chan concludes, "Lee probably felt expedient to assert strongly his country's genuine non-alignment."[60] Eventually, Singapore was admitted into the UN with unanimous accord by the Security Council without the need to call for a vote.[61] But Singapore's entry into the United Nations did not immediately reduce the frequency of Lee's anti-American comments. The US State Department reported that Lee "repeatedly returned in public and on background basis to correspondents to [the] themes in his August 30 diatribe against U.S.".[62]

Senior cabinet ministers tried to play down Lee's anti-Americanism during media conferences. During an interview before attending the UN General Assembly in September 1965, Foreign Minister Rajaratnam was asked if Lee's anti-Americanism was intended to gain support from non-aligned countries. Rajaratnam alluded to the possibility that some Afro-Asian nations might interpret Lee's anti-American comments as "a badge of acceptance" by the Afro-Asian group, but defended Lee's anti-American statements as criticisms that focussed on US policies that the Singapore government disagreed with.[63]

In September 1965, US State Department officials observed that Lee wanted Singapore-US relations to be "correct but distant", offering two likely intentions behind Lee's acrid remarks about America and its people:

> Prime Minister Lee has been attacking the U.S. publicly in an effort to (a) establish his neutralist credentials with the Afro-Asians and gain admission to the Algiers Conference, and (b) serve notice on the Malaysians and UK that the U.S. cannot be regarded as an alternative

---

[59] Chan, "Singapore's Foreign Policy, 1965–1968", p. 182.

[60] Ibid.

[61] A/PV.1332, United Nations Security Council, "UNGA 1332nd Plenary Meeting", 21 September 1965.

[62] Berger, "Lee: Incident of the Doctor", September 1965.

[63] S. Rajaratnam, "Press conference given by Mr. S. Rajaratnam, Minister for Foreign Affairs at Paya Lebar Airport before his departure for United Nations on 16th September, 1965", 16 September 1965, in POL 3 United Nations Malaysia. 1965, Box 2, Bureau of Far Eastern Affairs. Office of the Country Director for Malaysia and Singapore. Records Relating to Malaysia and Singapore, compiled 1963–66, RG 59, NACP.

to the British and Commonwealth as the primary guarantors of Malaysian-Singapore security.[64]

Lee's desire to court the Afro-Asian nations was not new. Even before Singapore was separated from Malaysia, Lee had posited that Singapore and Malaysia needed to win the friendship of the non-aligned group of countries. In 1964, Lee warned the Malaysian parliament that

> [i]solation from the growing body of Afro-Asian opinion and identification with imperialist and colonialist nations must in the end mean death. For us life must mean a growing identification with the hopes and aspirations of the political attitudes of Asian countries.[65]

Despite Lee's admonitions, the Malaysian government was unenthusiastic about engaging the Afro-Asian nations in the Algiers Conference.

In 1964, Lee sought the domestic advantage that non-alignment would give to the PAP. The Algiers Conference, or the Afro-Asian Peoples' Solidarity Organisation Conference (AAPSO), was well attended by political parties, labour unions and other organisations that represented "radical elements and liberation movements in Asia and Africa".[66] Entry to the Algiers Conference was vital to the PAP's political position in Singapore because Singapore's strongest opposition party, the Barisan Sosialis, had earlier gained support from the Partai Komunis Indonesia (PKI) and the PRC in 1964. S.R. Nathan explained the importance of Singapore's membership in the AAPSO in his memoir:

> Victory [in the form of international recognition] at the AAPSO would have given them [the Barisan Sosialis] a wider range of international supporters. Such a development threatened to undermine the NTUC's [National Trade Union Congress in Singapore] and potentially PAP's efforts to win wider domestic support in the ongoing struggle

---

[64] Robert J. Morris, "Twentieth General Assembly, New York–September 1965: Talking Paper (Singapore)", September 1965, in POL 3 United Nations Malaysia, 1965, Box 2, Bureau of Far Eastern Affairs. Office of the Country Director for Malaysia and Singapore. Records Relating to Malaysia and Singapore, compiled 1963–66, RG 59, NACP.

[65] Chan, *Singapore: The Politics of Survival*, p. 41.

[66] Nathan, *An Unexpected Journey*, p. 266.

against pro-communist elements in Singapore. Acceptance by this movement of the NTUC-led Singapore committee, rather than the Barisan Sosialis, was considered critical for the NTUC and indirectly for the PAP.[67]

Acceptance by non-aligned Afro-Asian countries had been critical to the PAP's political survival in Singapore before independence, and being recognised by the Afro-Asian countries became even more crucial for Singapore after its separation from Malaysia. Chan argues that Lee's tart remarks against the US from the August 1965 interview were instrumental in increasing Afro-Asian votes for Singapore's entry into the UN.[68]

In spite of the intensity of Lee's anti-American statements, the Singapore government, and even Lee himself, had no intention to alienate the US completely. In a daily staff report to President Johnson, White House staff members, Chester Cooper and McGeorge Bundy, informed Johnson that Lee was keeping to his anti-American press campaign.[69] Nevertheless, the staff report added that Consul General Donald had received "private statements from Lee confirming that his intent in all this [anti-American press campaign] is to discourage the UK from serious consideration of a military withdrawal".[70] Concurring with the White House staff report, State Department also observed that the Singapore government

[c]ontinued normal close and friendly relations between ConGen [Consulate General] and GOS and PAP officials, (with one middle grade PAP official [on] Sept 16 explicitly seeking out ConGen officer and telling him that no instructions had been passed by Prime Minister [Lee] to be cool to Americans).... [The] September 16 assurances to ConGen officers ... by permanent Secretary [of] Ministry [of] Defense that 'all that (Lee's anti-American statements) [were] for public consumption only.'[71]

[67] Ibid.
[68] Chan, *Singapore: The Politics of Survival*, pp. 43–6.
[69] Chester L. Cooper and McGeorge Bundy, "The Week's Developments in Asia", 23 September 1965, in Daily Regional Staff Report to the President, Box 19, Files of McGeorge Bundy, LBJL.
[70] Ibid.
[71] Berger, "Lee: Incident of the Doctor", September 1965.

Keeping British Bases in Singapore

The US State Department seemed to accept that Lee's anti-American remarks made during the 30 August 1965 interview were his attempts to ensure the continued military presence of the Commonwealth powers in Singapore.[72] When Singapore was a British colony, it had been under the protection of the Commonwealth Strategic Reserve based in the subregion. Hence, even after Singapore obtained self-governance and independence, Australia, New Zealand and the United Kingdom (ANZUK) continued to underwrite Singapore's security. Furthermore, Commonwealth military bases on the island benefited Singapore's economy through employment and consumption of goods, and boosted investor confidence. A reduction of Commonwealth military presence could, in such a scenario, trigger security and economic problems in Singapore.

By publicly dismissing the possibility that Singapore could turn to the US for its security, Lee had intended to convince the Commonwealth military forces to remain committed to, and in, Singapore.[73] Lee argued for British superiority over the Americans, when he gave the example of the botched CIA operation to illustrate American incompetence. In addition, he insinuated that the US Department of State had acted in bad faith when he had sought their assistance to bring the American specialist to Singapore to treat his wife's illness. Nevertheless, Lee's diatribe against the US, a close ally of the British, was a questionable strategy for forestalling a British withdrawal. In fact, it now appears that rushing to acquire some form of assurance from the US government to take over Singapore's defence would have been a more viable strategy, had the Singapore government indeed sensed that a British withdrawal was imminent.

Like the Singapore government, the US government also wanted the ANZUK powers to remain committed to Singapore's defence for as long as possible. The US Department of State outlined America's position on Singapore's strategic importance and Washington's desire to keep the British committed to its bases in Singapore in 1965 thus:

---

[72] Maurice D. Bean, "Visit of Prime Minister Lee Kuan Yew of Singapore, October 17–18, 1967: Scope Paper", 10 October 1967, in V-46A Visit of Prime Minister Lee Kuan Yew of Singapore—October 17–18, 1967. Briefing Book (1 of 2), Box 34, Executive Secretariat. Visit Files, 1966–70, RG 59, NACP.

[73] Lee, *From Third World to First*, p. 451.

We [the US government] regard continued maintenance of the UK military presence, and specifically the Singapore base, as vital to the Western position in Southeast Asia. Alternative base sites in Australia or elsewhere would not meet either strategic or political requirements.[74]

Since both the US and Singapore governments shared a common aim of keeping the British in Singapore bases, it seemed counterintuitive that Lee should publicly criticise the American administration instead of working in tandem with the US government to persuade the British to maintain military deployment in Singapore.

Indeed, with Indonesia's *Konfrontasi* against the Malaysian Federation still unresolved, the British government did not harbour any intention of announcing a reduction of forces in Singapore and Malaysia, even though the Harold Wilson government was planning for a reduction of Britain's defence commitments overseas. In light of Singapore's separation from Malaysia, the Defence and Overseas Policy Committee reported on the impact of Singapore's secession on Britain's long-term interests in August 1965. The Committee stressed that Britain must "ensure that this important area [Singapore-Malaysia subregion] does not fall under Chinese Communist domination".[75] In this respect, Washington, London and Singapore shared a common goal—that of containing the influence of the People's Republic of China. Additionally, the Committee advised the Cabinet that British forces needed to remain in the Singapore bases to maintain "some influence on United States policies in the Far East".[76] Hence, due to these vital strategic and political considerations, it was unlikely that Whitehall would hastily announce a military withdrawal from Singapore in 1965. It was also doubtful whether Lee's criticism of the US administration in August 1965 would change any decision made in Whitehall about reducing Britain's military commitments to Singapore. It appeared, therefore, more probable that Lee was trying to repair the damage done to the US-Singapore relationship when he told Donald that

---

[74] Morris, "Twentieth General Assembly, New York", September 1965.
[75] CAB 148/22, Defence and Overseas Policy Committee, "Repercussions on British Policy in South East Asia of the Secession of Singapore from Malaya", 25 August 1965, The National Archives of the UK (TNA).
[76] Ibid.

his anti-American speeches were intended for public consumption and especially for the Labour Party government in Whitehall.

Perceiving a US-Malaysian 'Alliance'

Gaining acceptance by the Afro-Asian nations and keeping the British forces in Singapore bases were perceptible objectives behind Lee Kuan Yew's anti-American comments made in late 1965 and early 1966. American archival sources, however, point to more fundamental causes driving Lee's decision to project an anti-American image. Lee's decision to disparage the American government was greatly motivated by his perception of the American position towards Singapore, based on the Malaysian government's engagement with the United States during *Konfrontasi*.

Lee had keenly observed the dismal consequences that Kuala Lumpur's bungled attempt of attaining military aid and credit from Washington during *Konfrontasi* had had. When the United States government had offered to sell Malaysia military equipment amounting to US$7 million on credit, at interest of less than 5 per cent over five years, the Malaysian government and news media had responded angrily at the offer.[77] Malaysian Prime Minister Tunku Abdul Rahman (also known as 'the Tunku'), at that time, had felt that Malaysia deserved far more favourable credit terms, since the Americans had previously given Indonesia outright grants. The Malaysian reactions surprised Ambassador Bell and State officials as they thought that "[m]ilitary credits would increase Malaysia's confidence in the U.S. and should strengthen relations between the two countries".[78] In fact, the State Department felt that the military credit sales offer was already given at the "best

---

[77] James D. Bell, "Discussions with British Regarding Military Sales to Malaysia", 15 October 1963, in DEF 19 Military Assistance (Defense Affairs Malaysia '63), Box 1, Bureau of Far Eastern Affairs. Office of the Country Director for Malaysia and Singapore. Records Relating to Malaysia and Singapore, compiled 1963–66, RG 59, NACP.

[78] David Cuthell, "Sales of Military Equipment to Malaysia", 1964, in DEF 19 Military Assistance (Defense Affairs Malaysia '63), Box 1, Bureau of Far Eastern Affairs. Office of the Country Director for Malaysia and Singapore. Records Relating to Malaysia and Singapore, compiled 1963–66, RG 59, NACP.

credit terms available" at that time.[79] Still, the US administration's offer to Malaysia backfired. Robert Barnett, Deputy Assistant Secretary of State for Far Eastern Economic Affairs, spoke with the Malaysian Ambassador to the US, Ong Yoke Lin, to mitigate the diplomatic fallout. No progress was made, however, as the US was not willing to offer more favourable terms unless the Malaysian government moved swiftly to quell "over-excited public opinion" in Malaysia.[80] The Malaysian government finally turned down the military credit sales offer from the US but received financial aid from Canada. As it turned out, Canada had given Malaysia the grant after consultations with London and Washington.[81] Praises for Malaysia's "courageous Canadian brothers" of the Commonwealth were sung, while at the same time disparaging caricatures were levelled at the Americans.[82] By the time the storm involving military credit sales blew over, State Department officials had learnt a lesson about the sensitivities of Malaysia's government and its people.

Lee Kuan Yew, too, had gained a lesson at Malaysia's expense by witnessing US reluctance to provide Commonwealth countries such as Malaysia and Singapore with any substantial aid. But since Singapore's separation had not occurred until the later part of 1965, Lee's attention was mainly towards US-Malaysian relations. When asked for his opinion on the military sales credit fiasco, Lee lamented to Ambassador Bell in January 1965 that "this kind of ultra-nationalism only serves to

---

[79] Ibid.

[80] Robert W. Barnett, "Memo of Telephone Conversation: Robert W. Barnett and Ambassador Ong Yoke Lin", 30 December 1964, in DEF 19 DOD Team Visit November 1964 (DEF Defense Affairs Malaysia), Box 1, Bureau of Far Eastern Affairs. Office of the Country Director for Malaysia and Singapore. Records Relating to Malaysia and Singapore, compiled 1963–66, RG 59, NACP.

[81] Jerrold I. Berke, "Malaysia: Meeting with Canadian Representatives, 9/17/64", 21 September 1964, in 1 General Policy. Plans. Coordination. (AID), Box 1, Bureau of Far Eastern Affairs. Office of the Country Director for Malaysia and Singapore. Records Relating to Malaysia and Singapore, compiled 1963–66, RG 59, NACP.

[82] "Press Statement by Enche' Hassan bin Hj. Mohd., Member of the Presidium of the National Afro-Asian Solidarity Committee of Malaysia", 26 January 1965, in POL–Political Aff. & Rel. United States, 1965, Box 2, Bureau of Far Eastern Affairs. Office of the Country Director for Malaysia and Singapore. Records Relating to Malaysia and Singapore, compiled 1963–66, RG 59, NACP.

weaken the fabric of the country".[83] Lee commented that the Malaysian government had high hopes that the US would be willing to help Malaysia because of "the GOM's feeling of frustration with respect to the British, Australian and New Zealanders who are constantly telling the GOM what not to do".[84] Even before 1965, the Tunku had shown apparent "annoyance at unsolicited advice" from the British.[85] The Malaysian government was annoyed that the British had advised the Tunku to negotiate for a settlement with Jakarta.[86] Also, the Malaysian government complained that the British were not enforcing the ceasefire agreements strictly enough and were unwilling to pursue the Indonesian guerrilla forces into Indonesian borders.[87] Malaysia's disappointment in the US would not have been so deep, had their annoyance with Britain not been so great.

That the Malaysian government was leaning closer to the Americans was already well-known to the American ambassador. Ambassador Bell explained that the Malaysian government disapproved of the manner in which the British military forces had fought during *Konfrontasi* against Indonesia. In his letter to the Assistant Secretary of State for Far Eastern Affairs, Roger Hilsman, Ambassador Bell wrote that

> [h]aving moved away from political ties with the U.K. and having developed a reluctance to accept British political advice, the Malaysians may, over the next few months, seek a closer relationship with the United States. In this connection, the Tunku mentioned to the Attorney General [Robert Kennedy] his desire to have Malaysian military officers trained by the United States.[88]

---

[83] Lacey, "Memcon: Bell and Lee", 19 January 1965.

[84] Ibid.

[85] James D. Bell, "Letter from Ambassador Bell to Roger Hilsman, Assistant Secretary of State for Far Eastern Affairs", 28 January 1964, in 1, Box DEF 19 Military Assistance (Defense Affairs Malaysia '63), Bureau of Far Eastern Affairs. Office of the Country Director for Malaysia and Singapore. Records Relating to Malaysia and Singapore, compiled 1963–66, RG 59, NACP.

[86] CAB 130/239, Working Party on Singapore, "The Repercussions on British Policy in South East Asia of the Secession of Singapore from Malaysia", 12 August 1965, TNA.

[87] Bell, "Bell to Hilsman", 28 January 1964.

[88] Ibid.

At the onset of *Konfrontasi*, however, US enthusiasm for deeper engagement with Kuala Lumpur had fizzled out for fear of being drawn into a conflict with Indonesia. Lee understood, then, that Washington ranked Malaysia below Indonesia among important Southeast Asian countries because of Malaysia's relatively insignificant geopolitical impact on the region's security; and Singapore surely ranked even lower.

More crucially, Lee told Ambassador Bell that the Tunku and his lieutenants "had been allowed to believe that the United States, in support of anti-communism, always stood ready to help other free nations, if requested to do so…. [T]hese men came to think that they could call on the Seventh Fleet and on the United States material aid so that … they could bequeath a fortune to their children."[89] According to Lee, the Eisenhower administration ought to have borne some responsibility for having encouraged the Malaysian government to shift its reliance from the United Kingdom to the United States in the 1950s. When Malaya became independent in 1957, the Tunku was confident that the anti-communist position of the US would compel the American government to aid Malaysia, should communist-inspired Chinese in the Malay Peninsula attempt to take over Kuala Lumpur. In fact, the Tunku believed that the US also underwrote Malay dominance as the political elites after federation in 1963. When the Tunku admonished Lee to give up the idea that Chinese Malaysians in Singapore could attain a greater political influence within the Federation of Malaysia in July 1964, Lee found reason to believe that the Tunku had full confidence in America's support.[90] Bell heard Lee's views with great interest in January 1965. It was, however, difficult to determine whether Lee's second-hand account of Tunku's attitude was Lee's attempt to mislead the American ambassador, or the Tunku's attempt to mislead Lee. More than a year later, Lee met with the US Assistant Secretary of State for East Asian Affairs, William Bundy, and reiterated his views on US-Malaysian relations.

---

[89] Lacey, "Memcon: Bell and Lee", 19 January 1965.

[90] "Memorandum of Conversation: Prime Minister Lee Kuan Yew, Assistant Secretary William Bundy, Sim Kee Boon and Richard H. Donald", 8 March 1966, in POL 7–1 Visits, Meetings (Singapore 1966), Box 1, Subject Files of the Office of Indonesia, Malaysia and Singapore Affairs, 1965–74, RG 59, NACP.

CONCLUSION

Lee Kuan Yew promulgated a non-aligned foreign policy and amplified Singapore's non-alignment by making harsh anti-American comments in the media from late 1965 to early 1966. Lee's vitriol against the US administration was interpreted as an attempt to gain the acceptance of the non-aligned Afro-Asian camp and also calibrated to cause Whitehall to think twice before planning a military withdrawal from British bases in Singapore. But beyond these two apparent reasons, Lee's understanding or misunderstanding from Tunku Abdul Rahman—that US President Lyndon Johnson had pledged to support Malays against the Chinese in an event of a communal conflict in Malaysia and Singapore—had driven Lee to project a hostile attitude towards the US in August 1965. The US-Singapore relations did not remain strained for long, however, as the political elites in Singapore maintained a fairly pliable foreign policy and gradually drifted from their erstwhile image of staunch non-alignment to a deeper engagement with the United States. A few events precipitated the shift; and the event that led to intimate US-Singapore relations was the meeting of Lee Kuan Yew with William Bundy in March 1966.

CHAPTER 3

United States-Singapore Entente

Removing Doubts and Building Trust

Singapore's relations with the United States ameliorated in March 1966 after more than six months of strain caused by a series of anti-American statements made by Prime Minister Lee Kuan Yew. With his anti-American press campaign, the Singapore leader had aimed to bolster his country's non-aligned credentials and also warn the British government that the Americans would not be welcomed in Singapore if Whitehall intended to reduce British forces in Singapore in the near future. Lee also signalled his willingness to allow the Soviet Union's Pacific Fleet to have some presence in Singapore's naval dockyards.[1] But Lee's anti-American comments were also a result of his distrust of the US government, which had grown out of his political experience when Singapore had been a member state of the Federation of Malaysia. When Singapore was still a part of Malaysia in 1964, Lee had formed a perception of the Americans based on his cognizance of an unverified US-Malaysian pact. Lee had been under the impression that US President Lyndon Baines Johnson had promised Malaysian Prime Minister Tunku Abdul Rahman that Washington would assist the Tunku in suppressing the Chinese if communal riots in Malaysia got out of hand. Lee interpreted Johnson's promise to the Tunku as a sign that Washington would preserve Malay political dominance in Malaysia in order to contain communist Chinese influence in Southeast Asia.

---

[1] Seth S. King, "Singapore's Prime Minister Would Consider Offering Base to Russians if Malaysia Brings in G.I.'s", *The New York Times*, 16 September 1965.

Nevertheless, Lee's perception of the Johnson administration's position towards Malaysia and Singapore had been erroneous. This misperception was discovered after he had a meeting with US officials in March 1966. United States' ties with Singapore greatly improved after that meeting; and Lee's first official visit to Washington in October 1967 further enhanced US-Singapore relations.

MEETING WITH WILLIAM BUNDY

In March 1966, William Bundy met Lee Kuan Yew in Lee's office and discussed what had transpired between US President Johnson and the Malaysian Prime Minister during the Tunku's visit to Washington in July 1964. Both Bundy and Lee had some knowledge of what had been discussed during the Tunku's visit to Washington but had different impressions about the outcome of the Johnson-Tunku meetings. When Bundy, together with US Consul General Richard Donald, called on Lee on 8 March 1966, Lee spent a large part of the meeting probing Bundy on US policy towards overseas Chinese, especially the Chinese living in Singapore and Malaysia. He wanted to know if the Americans "believed that every Chinese was a potential communist and therefore the best way to handle the problem was by 'containing' Malaysia and Singapore".[2] Bundy claimed to have "never heard of 'containment' of Singapore and Malaysia" and pointed out that Washington had maintained its support and friendship towards Malaysia.[3] Lee then described the problems between the Malay and Chinese communities in Malaysia and asserted that American interference in Malaysia's racial problems had eliminated "the possibility of an accommodation" between the Malays and the Chinese in Malaysia.[4]

In his rejoinder to Lee's accusations of American interference, Bundy alluded to the Tunku's visit to Washington in 1964 when President Johnson "expressed 'U.S. support for a free and independent Malaysia'".[5]

---

[2] "Memcon: PM Lee and Bundy", 8 March 1966.
[3] Ibid.
[4] Ibid.
[5] Ibid.

Bundy had been "very close to the scene" during that visit and "could categorically tell Mr. Lee that nothing else had been added".[6] He promptly assured Lee that equal support would be given to Singapore by the American President. Lee expressed relief upon hearing Bundy's assurance of US support, but pressed further by asking whether "the United States would support Singapore if it were attacked by the Malays".[7] Seeing that his American visitors appeared puzzled by the question, Lee explained that he had an "obsession" over America's policy towards the Malay-Chinese conflict in Malaysia and Singapore.[8] According to records of the meeting,

> [Lee] stated that in 1964 soon after the Tunku's return from Washington he had joined the Tunku in the mountains where the Tunku was trying to decide whether to accept Lee into the Alliance Party [the ruling party of Malaysia]. At that time, the Tunku had brushed aside Lee's suggestions for ways of dealing with the Chinese problem and had said that the way to handle any Chinese who presented a problem was to shoot them. Lee had objected that this was not a practical matter, and if by so doing the Tunku drove more and more of the Chinese into opposition where would the Tunku get the strength to shoot so many Chinese? The Tunku had replied with calm confidence that he would do so from the United States.[9]

There was no record of Lee's elaboration on what could have led to the Tunku's confidence wherein the Tunku felt that help for the Malays would come from the United States. But one thing was certain: the Tunku had become confident of American support after visiting Washington in July 1964. The Tunku's confidence that the Malays, with American help, would prevail against the Chinese had eliminated any prospects of a compromise between Malay-Chinese differences during Singapore's membership in the Federation of Malaysia. As part of the Chinese 'problem' in Malaysia during 1964, Lee and Singapore would have been the targets of a joint Malaysian-American action should the US have intervened in a clash

---

[6] Ibid.
[7] Ibid.
[8] Ibid.
[9] Ibid.

between the Malays in Malaya and the Chinese in Singapore. Lee was afraid that the Johnson administration's containment policy would mark Singapore as a potential Chinese communist fifth column after Singapore's failed merger with Malaysia in August 1965. As long as the American government distrusted Singapore's Chinese majority and regarded Singapore as a potential threat, Lee was hesitant about having close relations with the US. American efforts to engage Singapore, Lee feared, might be a ploy to 'contain' Singapore; hence, it was safer for Singapore to keep the US at an arm's length. But since Bundy had insisted that President Johnson had not promised America's support for the Malays in a Malay-Chinese clash, Lee could now be less wary of the motives behind US policies towards Singapore. Lee concluded his meeting with Bundy by urging the US government to correct Kuala Lumpur's misperception, stating that

> [t]he Malays have a very simple mind…and if they have any grounds for believing that the United States will move in and pick up the pieces, the possibility of an accommodation between the Malay and Chinese communities in Malaysia is gone.[10]

All in all, Lee was satisfied with the outcome of his meeting with Bundy, having found an answer to his "obsession".[11] He now began to gradually shift away from his erstwhile anti-American rhetoric. Bundy and Donald observed that Lee began to "mellow" after the latter's public display of anti-Americanism.[12] Despite signs that Lee was no longer critical of the American administration, the US State Department cautioned that it was "vitally important to him [Lee], however, that there be no abrupt change in his public posture".[13] There was, nonetheless, clear indication that Bundy's meeting with Lee had revised the State Department's portrayal of Lee. In October 1967, State Secretary Dean Rusk wrote to President Johnson stating that

---

[10] Ibid.
[11] Ibid.
[12] William P. Bundy, "From Lee Kuan Yew to Chiang Kai-shek: Far East–March 1966", 14 March 1966, LBJ Library online database.
[13] "Memcon: PM Lee and Bundy", 8 March 1966.

at one time, he [Lee] <u>had the suspicion</u> that <u>Americans were convinced</u> that the <u>overseas Chinese were a Chinese Communist fifth column</u>. If he gets on this topic, you should <u>leave him in no doubt we have no such belief today</u>, and that we fully share his basic view.[14]

The Bundy-Lee meeting removed obstacles hindering more intimate US-Singapore bilateral ties. Yet centred in their discussion were the meetings between President Johnson and the Tunku in July 1964. The fact that Lee's account of the Johnson-Tunku meetings was so different from Bundy's understanding of what he had witnessed in July 1964 creates some puzzling uncertainties. There could at least be a few possibilities; either the Tunku had been trying to intimidate Lee by misleading him in 1964, or Lee had been trying to mislead Bundy in 1966. Both scenarios beg a crucial question: what actually transpired between Johnson and the Tunku in 1964? Reports related to the Tunku's visit to Washington have now been declassified and held by the US archives and the Lyndon B. Johnson Presidential Library. There is, however, no evidence that Johnson had promised America's support against the Chinese in Malaysia. Johnson's intention for inviting the Tunku was really to assure the latter of the United States' support for Malaysia against Indonesia when *Konfrontasi* had been ongoing.

TUNKU'S JULY 1964 VISIT TO WASHINGTON

On 19 May 1964, President Johnson invited the Tunku to Washington for an official visit. The Tunku accepted the invitation within a week and the dates of the visit were set to be 22–23 July 1964.[15] The Tunku's visit to Washington was part of his two-week visit to the US and Canada, on his way back from the Commonwealth Prime Ministers' Conference held in

---

[14] Dean Rusk, "Your Meeting with Prime Minister Lee Kuan Yew of Singapore, October 17: Memorandum for the President", 13 October 1967, in V-46A Visit of Prime Minister Lee Kuan Yew of Singapore—October 17–18, 1967. Briefing Book (1 of 2), Box 34, Executive Secretariat. Visit Files, 1966–70, RG 59, NACP. Emphasis in original.

[15] Benjamin H. Read, "Read to Bundy: Proposed White House Press Release: Official Visit of Prime Minister of Malaysia, Tunku Abdul Rahman (Washington July 22, 23)", 26 May 1964, in Malaysia Tunku Visit 1964, Box 276, National Security File. Country File, LBJL.

London in early July. In preparation for the Tunku's visit, Robert Komer from the National Security Council advised that President Johnson should raise the following talking points in his first meeting with the Tunku:

> No one who's looked at US policy for the last 15 years can doubt our [US] will to protect free nations in [the] Far East.
>
> This is why we're in Vietnam now. <u>We regard this effort as directly protecting Malaysia too</u>....
>
> You [Johnson] could also describe your deep admiration for Tunku's leadership since Malaya's independence in 1957. Its prosperity, democratic institutions, and staunch anti-communism are much appreciated here.[16]

When Komer had stressed to the President that the US regarded its efforts in Vietnam "as directly protecting Malaysia too", there was certainly a risk that President Johnson could have over-emphasised the protection of Malaysia, or the Tunku may have misunderstood the American President's assurance. But it is hard to be sure and probably not worth speculating here. With respect to the Malaysia-Indonesia conflict, Komer also added that Johnson should assure the Tunku that the Americans fully supported Malaysia in *Konfrontasi*, but must strongly urge the Tunku not to over-stress America's support when talking to the media in order for "the US not to burn all its bridges to Sukarno"; Johnson's invitation for Tunku's visit was sufficient proof of US-Malaysian "solidarity".[17]

Komer's worries came true after the first Johnson-Tunku meeting. In a press conference after meeting President Johnson, the Tunku announced that he had accepted Johnson's "offer" to train "a sizeable number of Malaysian troops in [the] US".[18] According to the Tunku, President Johnson had "instructed [US] DefSec McNamara to 'confer immediately'

---

[16] Robert W. Komer, "Talking Points for Tunku Meeting", 22 July 1964, in Malaysia Tunku Visit 1964, Box 276, National Security File. Country File, LBJL. Emphasis in original.

[17] Ibid.

[18] Donald B. McCue, "Telegram: US Embassy in Kuala Lumpur to US Department of State", 23 July 1964, in Malaysia Tunku Visit 1964, Box 276, National Security File. Country File, LBJL.

with [Malaysian] MinDefSec Kadir on details of training program".[19] The Tunku also disclosed that Johnson had sanctioned the sale of sophisticated military equipment such as jet aircraft, large helicopters and landing craft to Malaysia, ostensibly designed to counter the Indonesians during *Konfrontasi*. The Tunku, in his eagerness to accentuate America's support of Malaysia during the conflict, inflated the extent of US military assistance to the press. Much of Komer's briefing notes to President Johnson for his second meeting with the Tunku focussed on getting the American President to qualify some of the assurances given to the Tunku during their first meeting. Komer reported that the Tunku was "pleased at the overt signs of [US] support, which strengthens him at home and vis-à-vis Sukarno (however, he's gone a little far in using Washington as a platform for tough anti-Indo talk, and in baldly telling the press about everything you [Johnson] told him)".[20] "The problem now," according to Komer, "is to make sure that he doesn't get too cocky towards Sukarno because he thinks he's got us in his hip pocket."[21] With respect to US military credit sales to Malaysia, Komer cautioned that "we don't want Tunku to think he has a blank check".[22] Johnson might have attempted to calibrate his support for the Tunku in their second meeting, but events occurring after the visit seemed to show that the President had not been very effective. Not only did the Tunku leave Washington thinking that he had received a blank check, but he also misled the Malaysian government to conclude that the US government was willing to give them unqualified aid and military assistance. Malaysia's soaring expectations of the Johnson administration inadvertently led to a diplomatic imbroglio between Malaysia and the US, which involved US military sales to Malaysia.

Clearly, the Johnson-Tunku meetings in July 1964 were focussed mainly on the Malaysia-Indonesian *Konfrontasi*. Singapore was hardly mentioned during the Tunku's call on President Johnson, except for once during their second meeting, and then only because the riots in Singapore

---

[19] Ibid.

[20] Robert W. Komer, "Memorandum for the President", 23 July 1964, in Malaysia Tunku Visit 1964, Box 276, National Security File. Country File, LBJL.

[21] Ibid.

[22] Ibid. Emphasis in original.

had reached a death toll of fourteen.[23] The memorandum of conversation for that meeting recorded that

> [t]he President asked the Tunku about the riots in Singapore, saying that we had our own problems in New York. He hoped the Tunku was more successful than he had been in stopping this sort of trouble. The Prime Minister replied that the situation in Singapore was still tense. There had been three more deaths but the situation seemed to be quieting down.[24]

Based on US records, the Tunku did not seem to have asked the American President for assistance to deal with the communal problems in Malaysia. He, too, was more concerned about *Konfrontasi*. Perhaps a possible occasion on which the Tunku and Johnson could have discussed Singapore was during a private meeting on 22 July, where no notes were recorded.[25] Insofar as the American documents show, it was unlikely that President Johnson had given the Tunku any assurance that in case of a clash between the Malays and Chinese in Malaysia, the Johnson administration would "shoot" the Chinese.[26] It is difficult to speculate whether the Tunku regarded Johnson's rhetoric on US-Malaysian solidarity to include American assistance against internal and external threats to Malaysia, or whether he had assumed that Johnson would not refuse him if he approached Washington for help against the Chinese in Malaysia.

What seems clear, and most significant within the context of Lee's conversation with William Bundy, is that Lee distrusted the Johnson administration's motives in engaging with Singapore between 1964 and 1966. Regardless of what transpired between President Johnson and the Tunku in 1964, it is sufficient, within the purpose of understanding Lee's anti-American press campaign, to note that Lee was willing to go

---

[23] William B. Kelly, "Telegram: Amconsul Singapore to Secstate WashDC", 23 July 1964, in Malaysia Cables Vol. II 4/64–7/64 [2 of 2], Box 275, National Security File. Country File, LBJL.

[24] Robert W. Komer, "Memorandum of Conversation: President's Second Meeting with the Prime Minister of Malaysia", 23 July 1964, in Malaysia Memos Vol. III 7/64–11/64, Box 275, National Security File. Country File, LBJL.

[25] Albert D. Moscotti, "Memorandum of Conversation: The Prime Minister of Malaysia and the President", 22 July 1964, in Malaysia Memos Vol. II 4/64–7/64, Box 275, National Security File. Country File, LBJL.

[26] "Memcon: PM Lee and Bundy", 8 March 1966.

along with William Bundy's account of the Johnson-Tunku meetings, and began to gradually change his anti-American position in the months after meeting with Bundy. At least that much was apparent in the official American documents.

US EMBASSY

After the Lee-Bundy meeting, Lee began to improve ties with Washington, and closer US-Singapore relations ensued without much publicity. In fact, Lee's hostile public demeanour towards the US took almost a year to change. The Singapore government finally acceded to the US proposal to elevate the status of the American Consulate General to an embassy in April 1966.[27] Richard Donald became the Chargé d'Affaires ad interim pending the appointment of an American ambassador to Singapore. A few months later, Francis J. Galbraith was appointed the first ambassador to the newly established American Embassy in Singapore and presented his credentials to Singapore's Yang di-Pertuan Negara, Yusof Ishak, in December 1966.

The elevation of the American Consulate General to an embassy illustrated how Lee took sure steps to develop bilateral ties with the US. But, outwardly, he maintained a cold response towards American officials. At the initial stage, Ambassador Galbraith received a rather cool treatment from the Prime Minister's Office. When the Head of the political section of the US Embassy, Roger Sullivan, contacted Lee's office to arrange for a meeting between Galbraith and the Prime Minister, he was snubbed by Lee's personal assistant, Lim Tiong Ann.[28] Based on Galbraith's account, Lim told Sullivan that

> Lee does not see Ambassadors and only sees them if they are from countries important to Singapore. Roger made the obvious point that [Galbraith] came from such a country and also that [his] visit would not be purely a courtesy call, but would be for the purpose of discussing [his] mission.[29]

---

[27] Berger, "Chargé in Singapore", 11 April 1966.
[28] Francis J. Galbraith, "Letter from Francis Galbraith to Maurice D. Bean", 9 December 1966, in POL 17 Diplomatic and Consular Repr. (Singapore 1966), Box 1, Subject Files of the Office of Indonesia, Malaysia and Singapore Affairs, 1965–74, RG 59, NACP.
[29] Ibid.

Lim firmly stood by his initial response and refused Galbraith a meeting with Lee. Galbraith would not speculate whether that reflected "Lee Kuan Yew's own attitude toward [him] or whether it [wa]s the automatic result of a general instruction".[30] Eventually, Galbraith managed to meet with Toh Chin Chye, the Deputy Prime Minister. The meeting went well and Galbraith used the opportunity to assure Toh that the two countries shared common interests in promoting US investments in Singapore and regional stability. Francis Galbraith also reported to the Country Director for Malaysia and Singapore, Maurice D. Bean, the positive results from American investments in Singapore's Jurong Industrial Park. American investors in Singapore praised the Singapore government's "ability to conceptualize, plan, and execute", and "the productivity of [Singapore's] labor".[31] Overall, Ambassador Galbraith's first memo back to Washington was one of cautious optimism.

Galbraith's optimism was eventually rewarded and his relationship with Lee improved with time. "My own relationship with Lee has progressed," reported Galbraith, "from icy reception of our first encounter to an easy relationship which enables me to see him or to get others in to see him if it is necessary and desirable to do so."[32] In fact, Galbraith later developed great sympathies for the Singapore government during his tenure as US ambassador to Singapore. Correspondence between Galbraith and the State Department in Washington reflected his frustrations with Washington's "meanness" and "lack of response" more than complaints of difficulties with Lee or the Singapore government.[33] By 1966, the United States administration and the Singapore government were taking the first steps along a path of closer and deeper engagement. William Bundy's meeting with Lee Kuan Yew was a turning point for the US-Singapore relationship. The next significant event that set US-Singapore bilateral ties in a positive trajectory was Lee's visit to Washington in October 1967.

---

[30] Ibid.

[31] Ibid.

[32] Francis J. Galbraith, "Official-Informal Letter to William P. Bundy, Assistant Secretary, Bureau of East Asian and Pacific Affairs", 7 July 1967, in POL 15–1 Ambassador Galbraith's Official-Informals, Box 5, Subject Files of the Office of Indonesia, Malaysia and Singapore Affairs, 1965–74, RG 59, NACP.

[33] Galbraith, "Letter to Bundy", 24 June 1968.

LEE KUAN YEW'S OCTOBER 1967 VISIT TO WASHINGTON

US Intentions for Inviting Lee

In July 1967, William Bundy wrote to Lee, inviting him on an official visit to Washington. The American invitation came in the same month that Britain announced the intention to withdraw its forces from Singapore and Malaysia. Despite being advised that the timing of the visit would create an impression that Singapore was nervous about the British withdrawal, Lee accepted the invitation, surmising that "Bill Bundy must have had a reason for wanting me to go to Washington that year".[34] The Johnson administration's goals for inviting Lee Kuan Yew for an official visit to Washington were twofold: to use Lee as a spokesperson for US policies in Southeast Asia, and to develop personal ties between American officials and the Prime Minister of Singapore.

The US Embassy in Singapore hinted that Lee Kuan Yew could be a credible advocate for American strategy in Southeast Asia since he had become more affable to the US. American Embassy officials noted that the Singapore government projected a degree of impartiality since it frequently pointed out that the Americans "spend too much time justifying [American] objectives in terms Asians do not understand".[35] Lee could, therefore, take on the role of a 'neutral' commentator who could explain US actions in Vietnam in terms more acceptable to an Asian audience. Apart from being credible to the Afro-Asian audience, State Department officials also recognised that Lee was a strong orator. In June 1967, when Lee was in London to meet Prime Minister Harold Wilson and members of the British Cabinet, US Ambassador to the UK, David Bruce, sent reports to Washington that described

---

[34] Lee, *From Third World to First*, p. 454; Maurice D. Bean, "EXDIS Ref: Singapore 2079", 5 July 1967, in V-46A Visit of Prime Minister Lee Kuan Yew of Singapore—October 17–18, 1967. Admin. Misc and sub misc, Box 34, Executive Secretariat. Visit Files, 1966–70, RG 59, NACP.

[35] Donald W. Ropa, "Memorandum for Mr. Rostow: Your meeting today with Singapore Defense Minister Dr. Goh Keng Swee", 19 September 1966, in Memos - Singapore (Vol. 1) 8/65–7/67, Box 281, National Security File. Country File. Asia and the Pacific, RG 59, NACP.

Lee's endorsement of the US as "most effective".[36] Bruce's panegyric of Lee lauded that

> Lee's vivid English, shrewd sophisticated political sense, and professed pragmatic socialism won him attention at all levels [of] HMG [Her Majesty's Government] and with Labor MP's.... [S]ome of Lee's remarks on situations in Asia are worth recording as examples of most effective arguments for use with left-wing and other British critics of U.S. policies in Asia.[37]

Bruce's telegram also stressed that Lee's views on America's role in Southeast Asia were very much in line with Washington's position.

> [Lee] could see no substitute for American military presence in Asia for many years to come, although he was uncertain about the form that [the American] presence should take. If American power were withdrawn, there could only be a Communist Chinese solution to Asia's problems.... [The] important thing was that North Viet-Nam could not be allowed to win. Therefore, 'holding operation' for an indefinite period—ten to twenty years—might do the trick ... for non-communist Asian states by then would be stronger. He said in effect he was [a] believer in domino theory and he personally had no doubt if [the] US were defeated in Viet-Nam that Thailand and Malaysia would quickly carry their symbolic tribute to Peking.[38]

Impressed with the impact of Lee's arguments in front of a British audience, William Bundy, therefore, wrote to Lee in July 1967 congratulating him for having "made a real dent in the inadequate grasp" that British Labour Party politicians had on the "facts of life in Southeast Asia", calling Lee "the ideal mentor" to British Parliamentarians.[39] To reciprocate Lee's support of US efforts in Vietnam, Bundy concluded his letter assuring Lee that, in return, the US "shall continue to be in the front row of the pavilion ... on

---

[36] David K.E. Bruce, "Visit of Singapore Prime Minister Lee Kuan Yew", 28 June 1967, in V-46A Visit of Prime Minister Lee Kuan Yew of Singapore—October 17–18, 1967. Admin. Misc and sub misc, Box 34, Executive Secretariat. Visit Files, 1966–70, RG 59, NACP.

[37] Ibid.

[38] Ibid.

[39] William P. Bundy, "Letter to Lee Kuan Yew", 12 July 1967, in UK East of Suez (July–December), Box 1, Subject Files of the Office of Indonesia, Malaysia and Singapore Affairs, 1965–74, RG 59, NACP.

the East of Suez matter".[40] Formerly a fierce critic of the United States, Lee was now sought after by Washington to be a spokesperson for Vietnam.[41]

Nevertheless, Lee Kuan Yew's statements supporting the United States in Southeast Asia would only be effective if quoted sparingly. Ambassador Francis Galbraith cautioned the State Department

> about our [US] making too much use of his [Lee's] frequent statements supporting our position in this part of the world [Southeast Asia]. One of his great values to us is, of course, his credibility before Afro-Asian and other audiences that are unsympathetic to our position in Southeast Asia. The more we exploit his words, the more danger we run of eroding that credibility.[42]

Lee once told Galbraith: "I will be of more use to you if I don't seem too involved with you."[43] The last thing Washington—and Singapore—wanted was for Lee to be labelled an "Anglo-American stooge".[44]

Lee's Own Intentions for the Visit

Lee Kuan Yew had his own agenda for visiting Washington in 1967. Observing his speeches a month before his trip, Ambassador Galbraith concluded that

> [f]rom Lee's general description of objectives he hopes to achieve with this visit to [the] U.S., I [Galbraith] conclude that he is somewhat torn between a direct appeal for assurances of future support and a feeling that to start down this road would compromise Singapore's non-alignment and his own political position unacceptably.[45]

---

[40] Ibid. By "East of Suez", Bundy was referring to the announcement by the British government that British forces based east of the Suez Canal would be reduced and completely withdrawn by the mid-1970s. The British military withdrawal included bases in Singapore and Malaysia.

[41] McMahon, *The Limits of Empire*, p. 142.

[42] Francis J. Galbraith, "Official-Informal Letter to Maurice D. Bean, Country Director of Malaysia/Singapore", 26 July 1967, in POL 15-1 Ambassador Galbraith's Official-Informals, Box 5, Subject Files of the Office of Indonesia, Malaysia and Singapore Affairs, 1965–74, RG 59, NACP.

[43] Galbraith, "Letter to Bundy", 7 July 1967.

[44] Galbraith, "Letter to Bean", 26 July 1967.

[45] Galbraith, "Lee Visit", September 1967.

Galbraith thought that Lee sincerely hoped to enhance his understanding of America and its people before deepening US engagements with Singapore. Galbraith reported that

> [Lee] is also uncertain about us and about our probable response.... I suspect that he is still in the exploratory stage of determining [the] best course to insure Singapore's survival in the 1970's and that he wants to study [the] U.S. and probe [the] thinking [of] our leaders as part of his explorations. Lee unquestionably regards [his] forthcoming visit as [a] truly major step of crucial importance [to] Singapore and his own career.... [O]ne basic objective Lee clearly has in mind is to improve his knowledge and understanding of the U.S. He wants to see what the American 'establishment' is like, how it works, and to determine whether it is possible for him to deal with it in [a] way satisfactory to him.[46]

Finally, and perhaps most importantly, Lee Kuan Yew wanted to find out how the US government could mitigate the security and economic repercussions of the impending British military withdrawal. Lee told Galbraith that he was "reconciled to the British withdrawal" but thought that there was a risk that the British would pull out even more rapidly if the British pound sterling continued to weaken.[47] Lee concluded that the United States would remain the only "countervailing power to communism" after the British withdrawal and wanted to know what the United States would do to maintain security in the area.[48] Having categorically rejected the possibility of an American military presence in Singapore in the past, it would be embarrassing for Lee to be asking for US protection now. Hence, Lee told the American ambassador that he was merely suggesting ways in which the US "might be able to help" in the region's security.[49] Lee made clear in his discussion with Galbraith and his deputy, John B. Dexter, that he did not want US troops to replace

---

[46] Ibid.
[47] John B. Dexter, "Memorandum of Conversation between Lee Kuan Yew, S. Rajaratnam, Wong Lin Ken, Francis Galbraith and John B. Dexter: Lee's Visit to the U.S.", 5 September 1967, in POL 7 Visits. Prime Minister Lee Kuan Yew Background Material, Box 4, Subject Files of the Office of Indonesia, Malaysia and Singapore Affairs, 1965–74, RG 59, NACP.
[48] Ibid.
[49] Ibid.

British troops "on the ground" in Singapore.[50] After consulting with Lee, Rajaratnam and Singapore's Ambassador to the US Wong Lin Ken, Ambassador Galbraith reported three areas that Lee was interested in working closely with the United States.

> One is economic. He [Lee] would obviously like to use the [bases] as a continuing source of employment and minimize the [effects] of the [British withdrawal]. In addition, he probably [wants] America's use of Singapore's facilities as a means of drawing U.S. deterrent power into this area. [Finally], there is probably a political [function] that [Lee] hopes to see the U.S. perform and which may be the most [important] of all in his mind, namely, protection from Indonesian and/or Malaysian dictates.[51]

Galbraith also detected Lee's concern that the American press might revive "questions relating to [Lee's] outbursts against the United States" in late 1965 during this visit.[52] He concluded that Lee was "anxious" not to be "goaded into" saying something that would "spoil his image in the United States, Australia or Singapore".[53] Lee indicated to Galbraith that he would require "qualified" US Embassy staff to accompany him when he would meet the press during his visit to Washington.[54] It was possible that he wanted to use the Washington trip to repair his image in America, without sending a wrong message to his Commonwealth observers. If the Australians saw that Singapore was cleaving to the US, Lee feared that the Australians might decide to withdraw together with the British.

Sensing that he might have moved too far from a neutralist position by accepting President Johnson's invitation, Lee indicated that he would have accepted an invitation from the PRC as well if he had received one from Beijing.[55] Galbraith noted that Lee was clearly making efforts to

---

[50] Ibid.

[51] Galbraith, "Lee Visit", September 1967.

[52] Francis J. Galbraith, "Memorandum of Conversation between Lee Kuan Yew, Goh Keng Swee and Francis J. Galbraith: Lee's Visit to the United States", 8 September 1967, in POL 7 Visits. Prime Minister Lee Kuan Yew Background Material, Box 4, Subject Files of the Office of Indonesia, Malaysia and Singapore Affairs, 1965–74, RG 59, NACP.

[53] Ibid.

[54] Ibid.

[55] Galbraith, "Lee Visit", September 1967.

"protect his 'left flank' exposed to Chinese chauvinists" by stressing that his trip to the US did not imply that Singapore was "moving into American camp".[56] As the date of his visit drew nearer, Lee expressed that he deemed a replacement of the British by US forces "as unprofitable 'either from their [the US] point of view or mine [Lee's]'", and that he would welcome the US Seventh Fleet and Soviet vessels to use the dockyard facilities in Singapore.[57] Lee was also cautious about Singapore's domestic response to his US visit. While planning for his visit to Washington in October 1967, Lee was "dubious about stopping in Honolulu".[58] Apparently, Lee's in-laws resided in Hawaii. He feared that Singapore's Chinese media might get the impression that he had plans to make the Chinese in Honolulu "models" for the Chinese in Singapore.[59] As far-fetched as such a prospect might be, Lee was concerned that "speculation about political significance of his Hawaiian connections" would be "politically damaging" to him.[60] Hence, he wanted Galbraith to ensure that his stopover at Hawaii was brief and low key.

The British Foreign and Commonwealth Office (FCO) also took considerable interest in Lee's October 1967 visit to Washington. In an FCO brief submitted to the Permanent Under-Secretary, British officials gathered from Lee's speeches that Lee was "not seeking an American presence in Singapore but may be hoping to secure ship-repairing business from the U.S. Navy".[61] The FCO brief hinted that Lee now saw America as "the power that will secure Singapore's long-term future independence".[62] In this regard, Lee's visit to Washington had clearly been an important step towards an enduring US-Singapore relationship. In fact, it was so important that Lee requested for his British hosts to conduct a briefing

---

[56] Ibid.
[57] Ibid.
[58] Galbraith, "Lee's Visit to the United States", 8 September 1967.
[59] Ibid.
[60] Ibid.
[61] FCO 7/875, C.E. Diggines, "The Prime Minister of Singapore", 10 October 1967, TNA.
[62] Ibid.

for him about senior US foreign policymakers before he left London for the US in October 1967.[63] Since it was in the interest of the United Kingdom that Singapore and the US develop closer ties, the FCO obliged and scheduled a briefing session for Lee on the evening of 11 October 1967 to explain the workings of the US administration, including the vital role of the Senate Foreign Relations Committee, as well as the rivalry between its influential chairman, Senator William Fulbright, and President Johnson.[64] By the time his London visit ended, Lee had gone through considerable British tutelage to handle his first official visit to Washington.

The Visit

When Lee arrived in Washington in October 1967, the State Department and White House staff gave him a generous reception. Lee recalled in his memoir that he was "embarrassed by the extravagant praise" that President Johnson lavished on him and Singapore when he arrived,[65] and considered it "most un-British".[66] Nevertheless, Lee reciprocated the kindness of his host by endorsing the Johnson administration's policies in Southeast Asia and commended Washington's perseverance in Asia. Lee thought that it was vital for Singapore that the US remained committed in Vietnam, so he avoided criticising the bombing of Vietnam. Most of Lee's statements during his US trip were aimed at projecting a positive image of himself to his American hosts. As Lee noted in his memoir, he "was not prepared to do what was against Singapore's interest" by criticising Johnson during the visit.[67] According to Galbraith's report of the visit,

---

[63] FCO 7/875, J.O. Moreton, "Visit by the Prime Minister of Singapore to the United States", 5 October 1967, TNA.

[64] FCO 7/875, Diggines, "PM of Singapore", 10 October 1967.

[65] Lyndon B. Johnson and Lee Kuan Yew, "Exchange of remarks between President Lyndon Baines Johnson and Prime Minister Lee Kuan Yew of Singapore on the latter's arrival at the White House", 17 October 1967, in V-46A Visit of Prime Minister Lee Kuan Yew of Singapore—October 17–18, 1967. Admin. Misc and sub misc, Box 34, Executive Secretariat. Visit Files, 1966–70, RG 59, NACP; Lee, *From Third World to First*, p. 455.

[66] Lee, *From Third World to First*, p. 455.

[67] Ibid.

> Lee asked me [Galbraith] several times if anything he had said would
> make it more difficult for the President, and the impression was
> reinforced through to the end of the visit that Lee was trying to be
> helpful to the President on Viet-Nam.... Lee went even further than
> this in defense and praise of the President on two or three occasions....
> [H]is implied and often explicit praise of the President and the
> Secretaries of State and Defense seemed to spring from conviction as
> a result of his talks with them.[68]

Although able to create a positive impression at most times, Lee's anxiety
about British announcement of withdrawal from Singapore led to "one
of his poorest performances" of the trip when meeting Secretary of
State Dean Rusk.[69] Lee spoke critically of America's tendency to favour
relations with Europe over Asia, and attributed America's bias against
Asians to the former's racist attitude. Dean firmly rejected Lee's insinuation
of America's racism and urged him to assess America's determination and
commitment by recounting US actions in Asia since World War II rather
than seek verbal assurance from the US government.[70] Galbraith observed
that, during the meeting,

> Lee's expressions were overdrawn and he sounded less reasonable
> and attractive than he was on most other occasions. He seemed to
> be trying to draw the Secretary into a statement of commitment,
> or of willingness to consider commitment, to Singapore as a *quid
> pro quo* for more explicit Singapore support for the United States on
> Viet-Nam. In the face of the Secretary's non-committal responses, Lee's
> argumentation took on an urgent, almost desperate note.[71]

Lee told Rusk that "he didn't know when or whether he would be
able to come to the United States again" and urged Rusk to give him

---

[68] Galbraith, "Lee's Visit to US", November 1967.

[69] Ibid.

[70] Francis J. Galbraith, "Singapore Prime Minister Lee Kuan Yew's Meeting with the
Secretary", 17 October 1967, in V-46A Visit of Prime Minister Lee Kuan Yew of
Singapore—October 17–18, 1967. Admin. Misc and sub misc, Box 34, Executive
Secretariat. Visit Files, 1966–70, RG 59, NACP.

[71] Galbraith, "Lee's Visit to US", November 1967.

an assurance that the US would commit to Singapore's security.[72] Galbraith later opined that Lee could have been nervous about meeting the President later on, or was just under strain from a long day of meetings. In any case, Lee's intention was clear: he wanted the US defence commitment in exchange for Singapore's support of the Vietnam War. In this regard, Lee's request was similar to what Tunku Abdul Rahman had tried to achieve in 1964 when he had offered President Johnson a staunch non-communist partner in Malaysia in exchange for American protection.[73]

In other meetings related to Singapore's security, Lee was more successful in achieving what he wanted. He convinced Defense Secretary Robert McNamara to send a mission to assess the feasibility of American use of the Singapore naval dockyards and military airfields for maintenance and repairs on a commercial basis.[74] Lee also spoke with William Bundy "of his [Lee's] desire to arm Singapore sufficiently to 'give anyone a bloody nose who is going to rob the house and take my jade pieces'".[75] Bundy assured Lee that the United States could supply Singapore with the "rifles already ordered ... and perhaps permit the supply of other light weaponry".[76] Again, Lee tried to press the US to offer protection over Singapore so that Malaysia and Indonesia would not be a threat to the island's sovereignty. To that effect,

---

[72] Galbraith, "Lee's Meeting with Rusk", 17 October 1967.

[73] King, "Singapore's Prime Minister Would Consider Offering Base to Russians if Malaysia Brings in G.I.'s", 16 September 1965; "Memcon: PM Lee and Bundy", 8 March 1966.

[74] Galbraith, "Lee's Visit to US", November 1967; William P. Bundy, "Memorandum: Discussions with Australia of Future Defense Arrangements in Singapore and Malaysia–Action Memorandum", 1968, in Malaysia/Singapore [Lot File 71D3], 1967, Box 21, Bureau of East Asian and Pacific Affairs. Office of the Country Director for Australia, New Zealand, and Pacific Islands, 1969–74, RG 59, NACP.

[75] Galbraith, "Lee's Visit to US", November 1967.

[76] Ibid. Prior to Lee's visit, Singapore had placed an order for US-made AR-15 rifles. After much debate in the US Congress about fears of Singapore re-exporting the rifles to communist countries, the decision was made for the sale to proceed after America's own orders for the weapon had been filled. It is understood that Bundy was going to convey Congress's decision eventually and the fact that Lee had brought it up merely gave Bundy an opportunity to do so.

Lee asked whether the Seventh Fleet couldn't 'drop a word' that would give Singapore assurance that it would be safe against Malaysian/Indonesian incursions. Lee implied that the ability of the United States to operate in the Indonesian and Malaysian milieu in a way that would provide protection for Singapore was crucial to U.S.-Singapore relations.[77]

Lee was worried that the end of *Konfrontasi* and the Malays' fear of the Chinese would "drive Malaysia and Indonesia closer together, to the detriment of Singapore".[78] It was possible to provide a greater US military presence in Singapore since the US Navy was already utilising the Singapore naval dockyards with British permission.[79] But because the relations of the US with Indonesia and Malaysia were more politically important than those with Singapore, Bundy did not wish to give Lee the impression that the United States was, in any way, committed to protecting Singapore.[80] Lee's preoccupation with the impending British withdrawal was noticeable throughout the trip. Before leaving Los Angeles for Hawaii, on the way back to Singapore, Lee "emphasize[d] again the importance of the United States helping, 'in both our interests', to keep some of the air and naval facilities and the trained personnel who operate them intact and the British in the habit of using them".[81] Still, Lee's final appeal did not yield any verbal commitment from the US that it would guarantee Singapore's security.

Whereas Lee Kuan Yew's political aim of securing American protection over Singapore achieved mixed results, he was more successful in attracting US investors into Singapore. Speaking with 50 Chicago businessmen at a luncheon, Lee touted Singapore's "good schools, excellent communications and transportation, Western standards of sanitation and

---

[77] Ibid.

[78] Ang, "Singapore and the Vietnam War", p. 363.

[79] Captain J.O. Mayo, "Possible Uses for Singapore's Ship and Aircraft Repair", 2 October 1967, in Malaysia/Singapore [Lot File 71D3], 1967, Box 21, Bureau of East Asian and Pacific Affairs. Office of the Country Director for Australia, New Zealand, and Pacific Islands, 1969–74, RG 59, NACP.

[80] Galbraith, "Lee's Visit to US", November 1967.

[81] Ibid.

safe drinking water".[82] Citing Caterpillar Tractor Company and Japanese investors who had already established offices and plants in Singapore,

> [Lee] described Singapore as a good base camp where businessmen could 'leave their expensive machines' and their families in confidence while they sallied forth into the less certain surrounding areas. He amused his listeners with statements such as 'you can get a telephone connection with any place in the world in 5 minutes and if you can't let me know and I'll chop someone's head off'. With such statements he also created an image of a 'no-nonsense' Singapore Government and a people willing and able to work—as was obviously his purpose.[83]

Lee's pitch to the American business communities turned out to be highly effective, bringing in millions of dollars in investments for Singapore beginning in 1968.[84]

In London, the American Department of the British Foreign Office and the Far Eastern and Pacific Department of the Commonwealth Office received a report of Lee's visit from a British diplomat stationed in Washington, Peter R. Spendlove, on 31 October 1967. Spendlove reported that Lee had created a favourable impression of himself in Washington during the visit and was more interested in the security than the economic aspect of the British withdrawal from Singapore.[85] The British diplomat pointed out that Lee's attempts to "avoid controversial tangles" had caused some contradictions in his statements, and Spendlove asserted that there was "no reason to doubt that what [Lee] ... said privately differs very much from ... more public utterance".[86] Lee publicly claimed that he was not seeking any US security guarantee. "I'm not

---

[82] "When the guns are silent", *The Straits Times*, 26 October 1967, p. 1.

[83] Ibid.

[84] Francis J. Galbraith, "Official-Informal Letter to William P. Bundy, Assistant Secretary, Bureau of East Asian and Pacific Affairs", 18 September 1968, in POL 15–1 Amb. Galbraith's Off.-Inf. Lets. 1968, Box 4, Subject Files of the Office of Indonesia, Malaysia and Singapore Affairs, 1965–74, RG 59, NACP.

[85] FCO 7/875, Peter R. Spendlove, "Lee Kuan Yew – Visit to the United States", 31 October 1967, TNA.

[86] Ibid.

seeking American aid," Lee told his audience at the Overseas Writers Luncheon on 18 October, "nor am I in receipt of any. I do not have an American guarantee of my security, nor am I seeking any."[87] Based on Ambassador Galbraith's report, however, Lee had in fact requested for American military presence in Singapore during his private meetings with President Johnson and Secretary Rusk.[88]

Lee's speeches in the meeting rooms and public halls demonstrated his attempts to balance Singapore's non-aligned position with the need for American economic and military support. With respect to Lee's position on American involvement in Vietnam, the British Embassy in Washington reported that at some points during the visit, Lee tried to balance his ardent support for the US by labelling American actions in Vietnam as "inept intervention".[89] Lee opined that the US had missed several opportunities in the past to leave Vietnam, and the best option left was to hold the line until other Southeast Asian countries developed some form of resistance against communism.[90] "Of course Lee does not go 'all the way with L.B.J.'," explained another British Embassy official, "but on the whole he understands why the Americans are in Vietnam and hopes that they will be able to find a way out which will 'enhance the prospects of peace and security for the rest of South and South-East Asia'."[91] Lee asserted that the US should consider a withdrawal from Vietnam only if the stability of the region would be assured after the Americans disengaged themselves. Lee also used his speeches to stress the poor timing of Britain's plan to withdraw from Southeast Asia, which would come at a time when the People's

---

[87] FCO 24/291, "Address and Responses to Questions by His Excellency Lee Kuan Yew, Prime Minister of the Republic of Singapore, to the Overseas Writers at Luncheon on October 18, 1967, Sheraton Carlton Hotel, Washington, D.C.", 18 October 1967, TNA.

[88] Galbraith, "Lee's Visit to US", November 1967.

[89] FCO 24/291, Michael Wilford, "Memorandum from Michael Wilford, British Embassy, Washington D.C., to A.H. Reed, Far East and Pacific Department, Commonwealth Office", 2 November 1967, TNA.

[90] FCO 24/291, "Lee's Responses to Questions to Overseas Writers, 18 October 1967, Washington, D.C.", 18 October 1967.

[91] FCO 24/291, Wilford, "Memo: Wilford to Reed", 2 November 1967.

Republic of China was expected to have around fifty Intercontinental Ballistic Missiles at their disposal by the 1970s.[92]

Perhaps carrying the analysis too far, Spendlove surmised that "there may be a factor related to [Lee's] domestic political situation and to the West Malaysian political situation where he calculates that American support, if plausible and discreet, would be a valuable asset for him in his pursuit of wider objectives than simply remaining the Premier of his Island state".[93] Without further evidence, it is difficult to acquiesce in Spendlove's subtle assertion that Lee's overtures towards the Americans stemmed from his ambitions to lead a political entity larger than Singapore. It was nonetheless clear that Lee wanted US support for himself and Singapore to be discreet, if it was indeed forthcoming. Spendlove concluded that

> [a]lthough [Lee] described himself on arrival [to the US] as being neither a dove nor a hawk but as an owl, his tour has tended to produce the image of one who is a somewhat hawkish owl.... It is not clear to us here how far this is Lee himself or Lee the tactician in the United States.... He may well argue that regardless of his differences with the United States, if they are the only plausible force from without, which could back the weak governments of South East Asia, he would be prepared to do business with them.[94]

Lee's US visit earned him high compliments from American newspapers, demonstrated by *The Straits Times*' reporting of an editorial in a Hawaiian newspaper, which praised the Prime Minister as "one of Asia's most remarkable leaders" who "understands realities that escape others".[95]

Aftermath of Lee's October 1967 Visit

Back in Singapore, Lee's enthusiasm for America faded rather abruptly. In a meeting with Ambassador Galbraith's deputy, John Dexter,

---

[92] FCO 24/291, "Lee's Responses to Questions to Overseas Writers, 18 October 1967, Washington, D.C.", 18 October 1967.

[93] FCO 7/875, Spendlove, "Lee – Visit to US", 31 October 1967.

[94] Ibid.

[95] "Lee 'understands realities that escapes others'", *The Straits Times*, 31 October 1967, p. 7.

[Lee] alluded again to the theme of the United States as an organ-grinder dealing with its client-states as if they were monkeys.... One American shortcoming [Lee] then noted was our tendency to seek short-term advantages rather than looking to long-range objectives.... Despite the shortcomings he finds in American style and policy, ... what [Lee] sought was not ephemeral friendship but an enduring relationship based upon real national interests.[96]

The October 1967 visit had erased Lee's prior suspicions about the United States' intentions towards Singapore. Lee made clear to the American Embassy that he was intent on building a partnership with the US that would last.

Despite efforts by the Singapore government to avoid giving the impression that Lee Kuan Yew was given the "red carpet" and "VIP treatment" in Washington,[97] sections of Singapore's local media held the view that Lee had received special treatment by the Americans during his trip.[98] The editor of *The Straits Times* newspaper, Wee Kim Wee, met Ambassador Galbraith in late 1967 and discussed local impressions that Lee's Washington trip had created. Galbraith was interested in hearing Wee's assessment of the trip because of the close relationship between *The Straits Times* editor and the Prime Minister of Singapore. Wee also commented that he would have accompanied Lee to Washington if his travel plans had coincided with that of the Prime Minister's.[99] During the conversation, Wee asked the US ambassador, "Did the President often spend as much time with visiting Prime Ministers as he had with Lee?"[100]

[96] John B. Dexter, "Prime Minister's Current Foreign Relations Preoccupations", 17 November 1967, in Lee Kuan Yew (1 of 2), Box 2, Subject Files of the Office of Indonesia, Malaysia and Singapore Affairs, 1965–74, RG 59, NACP.

[97] Galbraith, "Letter to Bundy", 7 July 1967.

[98] Francis J. Galbraith, "Memorandum of Conversation between Francis J. Galbraith and Mr. Wee Kim Wee, Editor, Straits Times: Aftermath of Lee Kuan Yew's Trip to the United States", 11 December 1967, in POL 15–1 Ambassador Galbraith's Official-Informals, Box 5, Subject Files of the Office of Indonesia, Malaysia and Singapore Affairs, 1965–74, RG 59, NACP.

[99] Wee Kim Wee returned to Singapore from Europe on 5 October 1967 and "had found out about the possibility of going to the United States too late to do anything about it". Ibid.

[100] Ibid.

Galbraith replied that Lee was an "interesting" visitor but "wouldn't have been the only one to whom the President had devoted that much attention".[101] Wee, as well as some Chinese-educated members within the PAP, thought that Lee "had taken a sharp turn away from nonalignment while he was in the United States" and "[c]oncerted efforts were being mounted by Party workers to repair the damage".[102] Wee also thought that "it was clear" that Lee was seeking American assurance of "protection for Singapore" after the British withdrawal.[103]

Just as Singapore's local newspapers were able to conclude that Lee's visit was a sign that he was leaning too closely towards the United States, foreign media reports too made similar observations. Australian newspapers emphasised the *volte face* of Lee's 1965 anti-American comments to his October 1967 statements of support for the US in Vietnam and long-term military presence in Southeast Asia.[104] *The Australian* newspaper reported that the Singapore Prime Minister made deliberate efforts to avoid commenting on US policies in Vietnam during the Washington visit.[105] Other Australian newspapers also noted that Lee was keeping a balancing act with his comments made during the visit, observing that Lee had to show some level of solidarity with the United States, while at the same time not appear to be an American stooge.

In a televised interview with four foreign correspondents on 5 November 1967, Lee insisted that he had not been backtracking on any of his statements since his return from Washington. Halfway through the programme, Lee's interviewer from the *Melbourne Age*, John Bennetts, queried him with this observation:

---

[101] Ibid.

[102] Ibid.

[103] Ibid.

[104] Australian newspapers, such as *Sydney Morning Herald, The Age, The Australian,* and *The Financial Review*, featured Lee's visit shortly after his visit to Washington in October 1967. The Far Eastern and Pacific Department of the British Commonwealth Office compiled sections of these articles on Lee's visit. See FCO 7/875, Far Eastern and Pacific Department, "Australian Foreign Affairs - Digest of Press Opinion 25.10.67", 25 October 1967, TNA.

[105] Ibid.

Prime Minister, it seems to me, in this interview, you have been at some point to moderate a rather pro-American image of yourself that was projected while you were abroad [in the US]. Is this because you have found some criticism back home of what you said over there?[106]

Lee replied by expressing confidence that he could correct any "slanted reporting" in Singapore newspapers within a fortnight because he could "get through to [his] own people".[107] Lee explained that he was expecting "a very abrasive time" with American journalists who might "rake up the old feuds", probably alluding to Lee's anti-American criticisms in late 1965. "But they decided that they would adopt me and say, 'What a great champion of American policy',," Lee told his interviewers with a tinge of irritation. "I thought it was a very cunning line, because I am the only chap in the whole of Southeast Asia that is not on the American payroll and therefore, credible to the American people."[108] Fred Emery of *The Times*, London, interjected by pointing out that the American press were rightly surprised by Lee's pro-American statements "[b]ecause you [Lee] said things publicly ... that you haven't said before or, shall we say, that have not been heard in America before".[109] Lee insisted that he had been very careful with his statements, and that the newspapers in America and Singapore had not interpreted his position accurately.[110]

Still anxious about public opinions of his statements made in the US, Lee asked the British High Commission in Singapore for an assessment on British press coverage of Lee's US visit.[111] The Singapore

---

[106] FCO 24/291, Lee Kuan Yew, "Transcript of a Television interview with the Prime Minister, Mr. Lee Kuan Yew, and four Foreign Correspondents, recorded at the studios of Television Singapura on 5th November, 1967", 5 November 1967, TNA.

[107] Ibid.

[108] Ibid.

[109] Ibid.

[110] Ibid. Lee also mentioned that he was going to take the editor of *Nanyang Siang Pau* to task for using words which Lee had not personally used such as "fight on" in a caption.

[111] FCO 24/291, Paul C.H. Holmer, "Telegram: HC. Singapore to Commonwealth Office", 15 November 1967, TNA.

Prime Minister's press officer requested the British High Commission to "keep him informed of any indication of British reactions".[112] The British press coverage of Lee's statements made in the US had nonetheless been "sparse, and editorial comment largely absent".[113] The Commonwealth Office and Deputy High Commissioner, Paul Holmer, observed that "there have been no official reactions here" in London.[114] Without much to report, Holmer was somewhat hesitant to meet Lee, who would surely try to extract a British response towards his trip to the US. But Lee was not interested anymore with response to his US trip; he spent the entire meeting with Holmer discussing aid for Singapore after the British withdrew.[115] Ang Cheng Guan notes that Lee used his trip to Cambodia in December 1967, meetings with the North Korean and North Vietnamese officials, as well as "disparaging remarks" about America's Asian allies, to shore up his non-aligned image.[116]

The US Department of State was equally careful not to contradict Lee's efforts to salvage his non-aligned position and undo the political damage caused by his Washington visit. According to Washington, Lee's credibility as a neutralist was his most valuable quality. Hence, the Officer-in-Charge of Malaysian and Singapore Affairs at the State Department, Albert D. Moscotti, cautioned in April 1968 that the US should not hasten to arrange any visits of senior US military officers to Singapore because it "might be seen as evidence of US military interest in Singapore and its bases".[117] Both Singapore and the United States sought to maintain a distance in the public sphere so that Singapore's non-alignment and America's containment policy could complement each other.

---

[112] Ibid.

[113] Ibid.

[114] FCO 24/291, "Telegram: Commonwealth Office to B.H.C. Singapore", 15 November 1967, TNA.

[115] FCO 24/291, Paul C.H. Holmer, "Telegram: BHC Singapore to Commonwealth Office", 17 November 1967, TNA.

[116] Ang, "Singapore and the Vietnam War", p. 372.

[117] Albert D. Moscotti, "Letter to Norman B. Hannah, Political adviser to CINCPAC", 28 April 1968, in POL 7 Visits. Meetings (Malaysia 1966), Box 1, Subject Files of the Office of Indonesia, Malaysia and Singapore Affairs, 1965–74, RG 59, NACP.

CONCLUSION

In March 1966, William Bundy's clarification on US policies towards overseas Chinese and Singapore removed a layer of suspicion through which Lee saw the American administration. Lee was satisfied with Bundy's assurance that there was no American promise to support the Malaysian government if conflicts between the Malays and Chinese came to a head in Malaysia and Singapore. The visit to Washington in October 1967 was Lee's attempt to move Singapore close enough to the United States, without sacrificing Singapore's non-aligned policy, which Washington had come to see as a valuable quality. Once Washington and the Singapore government were able to develop mutual trust, non-alignment and containment became complementary towards achieving common goals. To the British government, the entente between Singapore and Washington was an immensely positive development. While British Deputy High Commissioner, Paul Holmer, expected Lee Kuan Yew to discuss Britain's reaction to his October visit to Washington, it was really the British withdrawal that preoccupied Lee. In some sense, the British withdrawal was a catalyst for strategic cooperation between Singapore and the United States.

PART 2
Keeping at Arm's Length
Securing Singapore's Future

CHAPTER 4

Resolving the British Withdrawal

US-Singapore Defence Cooperation After East of Suez

After a rocky start in 1965, the United States and Singapore began to develop mutual understanding and found a stronger basis for cooperation during the height of the Cold War in Southeast Asia. The British withdrawal from Singapore, announced in July 1967 and accelerated in January 1968, became a catalyst for closer relations between Singapore and the US. Britain's military presence in the region had played a key role in the American strategy of containment in Asia and had also ensured Singapore's security. The retreat of the British armed forces from Singapore opened new platforms for US-Singapore cooperation in the maintenance of peace and stability in the region. The United States, although not part of the Five Power Defence Arrangements (FPDA), was able to influence the negotiations of the FPDA through its alliances with Britain, Australia and New Zealand, and the provision of military assistance to Singapore and Malaysia. With the withdrawal of the British forces from the subregion, Singapore gravitated towards Washington for its security needs, which had previously depended heavily on the British.

BRITISH TROOPS IN SINGAPORE

Under Britain's colonial rule, from 1819 to 1963, Singapore had been under Britain's military protection. When Singapore, Malaya, Sarawak and North Borneo (later renamed Sabah) merged to form the Federation of Malaysia in 1963, the Anglo-Malayan Defence Agreement (AMDA) expanded its coverage to the whole of Malaysia, becoming the Anglo-Malaysian Defence Agreement. Britain's military presence became crucial to the security of Malaysia and Singapore between 1963 and 1966. The formation of the Federation of Malaysia in 1963 triggered the Indonesian-Malaysian *Konfrontasi*, which led to skirmishes between Indonesia and Malaysia, occurring along the border between Indonesia and Malaysia's Borneo states, and parts of the Malay Peninsula. Even after Singapore was separated from Malaysia in 1965, the AMDA remained in effect over Singapore under the Separation Agreement.[1]

Apart from defence, the Singapore economy, too, depended on Britain's military presence on the island. In July 1967, the British troops stationed on the island contributed almost 25 per cent of Singapore's Gross National Product.[2] A briefing report prepared by the Far East and Pacific Department of the British Commonwealth Office in September 1967 noted that until about 1963, one quarter of the income and employment of Singapore was derived from the presence of British bases in Singapore.[3] The remaining quarter was contributed by other sources such as manufacturing. The separation of Singapore from Malaysia and Indonesia's *Konfrontasi* sharply reduced trade between Singapore and its two top trading partners from 1963 to 1966.[4] During that period, Singapore's economy barely maintained some stability largely because of revenue and employment linked to the British military presence on the island. In a National Policy Paper (NPP) on the Indonesia, Malaysia and Singapore subregion drafted by the US State Department in May 1968,

---

[1] Commonwealth Relations Office (UK), "Quadripartite Talks: The Repercussions in South East Asia of the Separation of Singapore (Copy No. 10 – to United States Delegation)", 2 September 1965, in POL–Political Aff. & Rel. United Kingdom, 1965, Box 2, Bureau of Far Eastern Affairs. Office of the Country Director for Malaysia and Singapore. Records Relating to Malaysia and Singapore, compiled 1963–66, RG 59, NACP.

[2] Paul C. Warnke, "Memorandum: Possible Australian Management of British Naval Base at Singapore", 3 October 1967, in POL Singapore, Box 17, Bureau of East Asian and Pacific Affairs. Office of the Country Director for Australia, New Zealand, and Pacific Islands, 1969–74, RG 59, NACP.

[3] FCO 24/292, "Visit of Mr. Lee Kuan Yew, Prime Minister of Singapore: Brief for the Secretary of State", 29 September 1967, TNA.

[4] Ibid.

a comprehensive study on the economic impact of the British military withdrawal noted that

> British bases in Singapore contribute directly or indirectly to the livelihood of 22% of the country's labor force and account for 20% of its national income, 17% of its foreign exchange and 14% of its government revenues. Because of rapid population growth, the number of additional persons seeking work each year is increasing rapidly. The release over the next 3–4 years of some 30,000 civilians from base or base-related jobs will aggravate Singapore's chronic unemployment problem and possibly affect political stability.[5]

Hence, both American and British analysts predicted that a British military withdrawal from Singapore could greatly jeopardise Singapore's security and economy. Nevertheless, Britain's economic woes were too severe to afford the luxury of prolonged overseas deployment of British troops.

In July 1967, the Harold Wilson government announced that British forces based in Singapore and Malaysia would be reduced to half by 1971, and would be completely pulled out from the subregion by mid-1970s. Six months later, the Wilson government cut the timeline by half and brought the date of full withdrawal forward to 31 March 1971. Under pressure from Singapore, the US and its ANZUK allies, Britain eventually set the deadline for withdrawal as 31 December 1971. With the British military scheduled to leave the subregion, defence cooperation between the Singapore and Malaysian governments, which had only recently parted ways in 1965, became more unattainable. The Royal Malayan Navy had been based in Singapore since 1957 with the intention of protecting the island against communist subversion and internal unrest.[6] The Singapore government now saw the Malaysian troops on the island as a

---

[5] "National Policy Paper: Indonesia, Malaysia and Singapore Subregion", 6 May 1968, in Malaysia/Singapore [Lot File 71D3], 1967, Box 21, Bureau of East Asian and Pacific Affairs. Office of the Country Director for Australia, New Zealand, and Pacific Islands, 1969–74, RG 59, NACP.

[6] Chin Kin Wah, *The Defence of Malaysia and Singapore: The Transformation of a Security System 1957–1971* (Cambridge: Cambridge University Press, 1983), p. 42.

contradiction to its sovereignty and a threat to its security.[7] Huxley argues that the presence of Malaysian forces in Singapore "had the potential to compromise or at least complicate" Singapore's efforts to "establish a separate national identity", especially when these forces were responsible for guarding key installations such as Singapore's water supply.[8] Malaysian government officials, on the other hand, claimed that the newly independent Singapore posed a threat to the security of its troops stationed in Singapore. Zainal Sulong from the Malaysian Ministry of Foreign Affairs argued that if the Singapore government became "hostile to Malaysia … Malaysian defence facilities located on the island … would be indefensible against attack by Singapore forces."[9] Malaysia was, therefore, determined to develop separate and independent naval capabilities.[10] Eddie Teo, who joined the Singapore Defence Ministry in 1970, recounted that a major security concern for Singapore was the spill-over of racial problems in Malaysia.[11] There was also a fear that Chinese refugees who were disgruntled with Kuala Lumpur would flee en masse to Singapore.

The British withdrawal from the Singapore-Malaysia subregion altered the security structure of Southeast Asia and the defence arrangements of the two Southeast Asian countries. Most significantly, Britain, Australia, New Zealand, Malaysia and Singapore conferred to update the AMDA with the FPDA, which was an agreement to consult instead of a commitment for mutual defence. The FPDA reflected reduced commitment among the

---

[7] The author's interview with former Permanent Secretary of Singapore's Ministry of Foreign Affairs, S.R. Nathan, revealed that the "ultras" in Malaysia's United Malays National Organisation had intentions to arrest Lee Kuan Yew and some PAP ministers for treason. The "ultras" were against the secession of Singapore and could, in extremis, deploy the Malaysian troops in Singapore to re-take Singapore. While recognising that such an operation would be politically difficult to pull off within UMNO, Nathan recalled that the Singapore government preferred to err on the side of caution and was constantly guarded.

[8] Huxley, *Defending the Lion City*, pp. 8–9.

[9] A.R. Parsons, "Malaysia/Singapore Defence Co-operation", 5 March 1968, in British Withdrawal from Singapore and Malaysia (1 of 2), Box 2, Subject Files of the Office of Indonesia, Malaysia and Singapore Affairs, 1965–74, RG 59, NACP.

[10] Ibid.

[11] Author's interview with Eddie Teo, Public Service Commission, Singapore, 6 January 2015.

ANZUK nations for Singapore and Malaysia, and precipitated plans for Singapore and Malaysia to develop their independent defence forces. In fact, the Singapore government had already begun to develop a Singapore defence force shortly after independence. After failing to obtain help from Switzerland, India and Egypt, the Singapore government managed to reach an agreement with the Israeli government for military advisors to be deployed to Singapore. Israeli military advisors assisted Singapore from late 1965 to 1974, and played a crucial part in the training of Singapore's defence personnel and the development of training manuals for the Singapore Armed Forces (SAF).[12] Both countries enjoyed an "extremely close and multifaceted military relationship".[13] Under the guidance of Israeli military advisors, Singapore began to also develop a deterrent capability described as a 'poisoned shrimp' defence strategy that aimed to "register the island's indigestible qualities to any likely predator".[14] Singapore also turned to the United States for assistance. In October 1967, the Singapore government invited the US Navy and Army to utilise the island's dockyards and air bases for repair works. By the end of 1971, the Singapore government had started to strengthen its defence force with purchases of sophisticated military equipment from the US, which had vital strategic interests in the subregion.

EFFECTS OF BRITISH WITHDRAWAL

Importance of British Presence to the US

During the early Cold War, British forces based in Malaya and Singapore were critical to America's overall strategy in Southeast Asia in several aspects. While the US was fighting the communists in Indochina, Britain was responsible for preserving non-communist regimes in Malaya and Singapore. By the mid-1960s, the United States was embroiled in armed conflict in Vietnam and resisted taking on more defence commitments in the region. The British also kept the area under non-communist influence and maintained control over the sea lanes of communication

---

[12] Huxley, *Defending the Lion City*, pp. 11 and 23.
[13] Ibid.
[14] Ibid.; Leifer, *Singapore's Foreign Policy: Coping with Vulnerability*, p. 33.

between the Indian and Pacific Oceans. A base policy study conducted in 1966 by the Strategic Plans Division of the US Chief of Naval Operations (CNO) concluded that "[t]he only major geographic area where the existing US base structure to support the current strategy of containment of Communist China is inadequate is the Indian Ocean".[15] To overcome the inadequacy of America's naval projection in the Indian Ocean, the CNO recommended a strategy of directing US efforts towards "keeping the British in Malaysia and Singapore".[16] A report written in 1971 by the US Department of Defense argued that Britain's military presence was needed "to ensure continued US access and adequate berthing in Singapore" and "deny availability of the yard to USSR ships" that were using Singapore's ship repair facilities more frequently after 1970.[17]

America's interests in Singapore were determined by the containment strategy of the US in the subregion, especially in relation to Indonesia. If the current non-communist governments in Indonesia, Malaysia and Singapore were to be toppled by communist regimes, the strategic impact on US military operations in the area would be detrimental. An NPP prepared by the US State Department in 1968 assessed that if the US military were to be denied access through the Strait of Malacca, US vessels from Manila to the Indian Ocean would need to increase cruising distance by 1,500 nautical miles. If America's Pacific Fleet and Air Force were denied access through the air and sea spaces of Indonesia, cruising distance would increase by 5,000 nautical miles. Furthermore, Australian support for operations in the subregion would also be greatly obstructed.[18] Greater cruising distances would inevitably increase shipping costs to American allies in the Asia-Pacific region. The impact would be particularly felt by Japan since 20 per cent of Japan's

---

[15] Chief of Naval Operations Strategic Plans Division, USA, "Base Policy Study", 14 September 1966, in Malaysia/Singapore [Lot File 71D3] 1967, Box 21, Bureau of East Asian and Pacific Affairs. Office of the Country Director for Australia, New Zealand, and Pacific Islands, 1969–74, RG 59, NACP.

[16] Ibid.

[17] Melvin R. Laird, "Memorandum for the Assistant to the President for National Security Affairs: US Utilization of Singapore Naval and Air Facilities", 3 August 1971, in DEF 15 U.S. Use of Military Facilities (Singapore 1971), Box 8, Subject Files of the Office of Indonesia, Malaysia and Singapore Affairs, 1965–74, RG 59, NACP.

[18] US Department of State, "NPP: Indonesia, Malaysia and Singapore", 6 February 1968.

foreign trade and 90 per cent of its fuel imports passed through the Strait of Malacca.[19] America and its allies, Japan and Britain, also relied on the subregion for its supply of tin and other raw materials. A break in the supply of the subregion's resources would disrupt the economies of the US and its allies. The NPP posited that once Britain withdrew from bases in Malaysia and Singapore, the Indonesia-Malaysia-Singapore subregion would become "no longer negligible".[20]

The US State Department outlined four objectives for the subregion. The chief aim of the US government for the area was to keep the three states free from "domination by a major power hostile to the United States".[21] Of the three Southeast Asian countries, Singapore possessed the least political significance within the context of the United States' global conflict with the Sino-Soviet bloc. Nevertheless, since Singapore could become a potent asset against the US if aligned with the communist bloc, ensuring that Singapore remained close to the western powers, or at least non-aligned, became an important objective in US policy towards Singapore. Second, the United States aimed to promote economic growth, political stability and communal harmony of each state within the subregion.[22] Third, in order to promote stability, American planners and diplomats sought to reduce conflict and encourage cooperation among the countries within the area, and with other neighbouring states in the broader region.[23] Finally, the NPP stressed that the US government must ensure "[c]ontinued maritime access by the U.S. and other states to the international waters of the area".[24] Because Singapore's naval dockyards had begun to play a critical role in US military operations in Vietnam by 1968, the US Department of Defense kept abreast of the negotiations for the FPDA to ensure that the ANZUK powers retained control over the berthing areas used by the US military for repairs and maintenance of its ships.[25]

---

[19] Ibid.
[20] Ibid.
[21] Ibid.
[22] Ibid.
[23] Ibid.
[24] Ibid.
[25] Laird, "US Utilization of Singapore Naval and Air Facilities", 3 August 1971.

Beyond the four objectives, the 1968 National Policy Paper on the subregion also identified at least four key issues that needed consideration once Britain completed its withdrawal operations:

1. Should the U.S. participate directly in new defense arrangements for the subregion, following the British withdrawal?
2. If the U.S. decides not to participate directly in new defense arrangements, what position should the U.S. take toward new arrangements…?
3. What should be the US attitude toward providing or increasing economic or military aid to each of the three states?
4. To what extent is it feasible and desirable for the US to urge Japan to increase its responsibilities in the subregion?[26]

Direct American involvement in Singapore-Malaysian security was considered undesirable. Within the second question, the State Department explored a range of options, such as encouraging the UK to remain in the subregion, supporting a Commonwealth defence arrangement that linked with ASEAN, and inducing Australia to play a greater role in the defence of the subregion through American assurance under the Australia-New Zealand-United States (ANZUS) Treaty.[27] The NPP followed with three proposed strategies: US deployment of troops to replace British forces stationed in the subregion; minimal US involvement; and a strategy that could strike a "proper balance between intervention and aloofness".[28] The third strategy was preferred since it took into account emerging regional conditions and would protect American interests. Ultimately, US policy in the subregion had to be one that could promote cooperation among Indonesia, Malaysia and Singapore and reduce intra-regional conflict.

Needless to say, the American priority for the region was to maintain the stability of the non-communist governments in the subregion. The NPP discussed at length "serious increase in Communist subversion in Singapore" as one of the contingencies that might arise in the review period of 1968–73.[29] The State Department expected the People's

---

[26] US Department of State, "NPP: Indonesia, Malaysia and Singapore", 6 February 1968.
[27] Ibid.
[28] Ibid.
[29] Ibid. The National Policy Paper had an effective review period of five years.

Action Party government to remain dominant in Singapore but feared that an unsatisfactory settlement in Vietnam and high unemployment, aggravated by Britain's withdrawal, would weaken the PAP's hold on power.[30] If the spectre of a pro-communist party toppling the PAP government arose,

> the United States should be prepared to provide emergency bilateral economic assistance. If public order and security were threatened, we should, if asked, also be prepared to provide assistance to Singapore's internal security apparatus.[31]

To prevent a direct US intervention in Singapore, the US government would "follow closely the situation in Singapore, urge its Commonwealth partners to supply adequate aid, and be prepared to consider U.S. economic aid, should help from other donors be inadequate".[32]

The retreat of British forces back to Europe not only forced the United States government to revise its strategic estimates in Southeast Asia, but had the potential to create domestic political problems in the United States. The US Secretary of State, Dean Rusk, expressed concern about the possible reactions of the American public towards the British withdrawal. By 1967, public dissent against the war in Vietnam had escalated within America. Secretary Rusk feared that the announcement of the UK withdrawal would strengthen voices that demanded a corresponding American withdrawal from Southeast Asia. Britain's exit from the area had put the "validity of and necessity for [American] presence in Vietnam" in question.[33] Furthermore, there could be pressure from the US Congress for the United States to reduce its military commitment in Europe, since Britain was going to deploy forces back to the continent.[34] Rusk's primary concern was never the risk of political instability in Malaysia and Singapore

---

[30] Ibid.

[31] Ibid.

[32] Ibid.

[33] "NATO Ministerial Meeting, British Presence East of Suez", Spring 1967, in United Kingdom East of Suez, Box 17, Bureau of East Asian and Pacific Affairs. Office of the Country Director for Australia, New Zealand, and Pacific Islands, 1969–74, RG 59, NACP.

[34] Ibid.

after the departure of British forces from the subregion in 1971.[35] Instead, his main protest was that Britain's decision to retreat from Southeast Asia had been made without consultation with the US and had been shrouded in secrecy. Since Britain's unilateral decision had made a staged Anglo-American withdrawal from Southeast Asia no longer possible, Rusk complained that it had become more difficult for the US to pull out of Vietnam without destabilising the region. Furthermore, Rusk was worried that the British withdrawal would compel the American government to take on additional commitments in Southeast Asia.[36]

To maintain the credibility of the containment strategy in Southeast Asia without Britain's military presence, the United States adopted a two-pronged approach: first, to ensure the viability of the Five Power Defence Arrangements as a mechanism for preserving stability in the region; and second, to assist Singapore and Malaysia in developing their respective armed forces.[37] In a bid to ensure continued Commonwealth involvement in the security of the subregion, the US government embarked on a strategy that would push Australia towards the leadership of the FPDA.

Australia and the FPDA

With the retreat of British forces from Southeast Asia, the US State Department considered Australia to be the natural successor to Britain's leadership in the security of the Malaysia-Singapore subregion, and pushed for Canberra to accept the role. Shortly after the first announcement of withdrawal in July 1967,[38] US Secretary of Defense, Robert McNamara, met with Australian Minister for External Affairs, Paul Hasluck, in October 1967 to discuss the likelihood of Australia taking over the British bases in Singapore. If Australia would agree to take over the Singapore naval bases,

---

[35] Ibid.

[36] Ibid.

[37] To a large extent, the British withdrawal also enhanced US-Malaysian defence cooperation and military sales. See Sodhy, *The US-Malaysian Nexus*, pp. 277–86.

[38] The Harold Wilson government first announced the British withdrawal east of Suez in July 1967 with the withdrawal planned to be completed between 1973 and 1977. After a series of financial setbacks in late 1967, including the devaluation of the British pound sterling, the British government announced the military withdrawal east of Suez again in January 1968, shortening the timeline of withdrawal for December 1971.

the United States would share the cost of managing the bases.[39] The US government was prepared to shoulder "approximately 70 percent of the Singapore naval base berthing area upkeep costs ($1–2 million), under Australian Navy management".[40] In a briefing memorandum before the meeting, the US State Department argued that Australia was best suited to take over the Singapore bases. Based on historical factors, Australian management of the bases "would maintain Singapore as a Commonwealth responsibility and [avoid] having the United States assume a commitment to defend Singapore (or Malaysia)".[41] Politically, Australia was a part of the Commonwealth and had gained acceptance among Southeast Asian governments. Given this, the US believed that the Australian military forces based in Malaysia and Singapore would raise fewer objections compared to the American troops. Strategically, "[i]t would provide the U.S. Navy with an alternate facility to Yokosuka and Subic, in the event that either of these bases is not available, or if restrictions on their use limit their capability, in the 1970s".[42] Finally, the State Department opined that the strength of the US alliance with Australia surpassed that of any other American allies in the region. State officials tried to argue that the transfer of British bases to an Australian administration would serve both American and Australian interests in the region.

Even if Canberra was willing to replace Britain in the region, it did not have the military capacity to fill the security and economic vacuum left behind by the British forces. Australia's force level in Southeast Asia was meant to complement rather than substitute the deployment of troops from Britain and the United Sates. In fact, the Australian Defence Force had not had a significant presence in Malaysia and Singapore after *Konfrontasi*. Australia had a total of 2,750 military personnel in Malaysia and Singapore, including about 1,000 army personnel stationed at Terendak, Malacca,

---

[39] Warnke, "Possible Australian Management of British Naval Base at Singapore", 3 October 1967.

[40] Interagency Singapore Study Group, "Singapore Study", August 1972, in POL – Policy Study (Singapore) 1972, Box 10, Subject Files of the Office of Indonesia, Malaysia and Singapore Affairs, 1965–74, RG 59, NACP.

[41] Warnke, "Possible Australian Management of British Naval Base at Singapore", 3 October 1967.

[42] Ibid.

another 1,050 Air Force personnel at Butterworth, Penang, and 500 Navy personnel in Singapore.[43] UK military forces in Malaysia and Singapore, on the other hand, comprised about 33,000 British personnel and 10,000 Gurkhas. In total, the British bases employed approximately 80,000 British and local personnel in the subregion.[44] Although these estimates reflected the forces at much-reduced, post-*Konfrontasi* levels, it was still far beyond what Australia, with contributions from New Zealand, could expect to match. Furthermore, in view of Britain's leadership among the ANZUK powers, the Americans were cognizant that the British were "now removing the peg on which Australia hung its participation" in regional security.[45] Thus, the likelihood of Australian forces retreating from the subregion along with the British was high because of Australia's subordinate role in the British-led Commonwealth Strategic Reserve.[46] Still, the US State Department hoped that whatever shortfall Australia experienced would be overcomed by strengthening the local forces in Malaysia and Singapore.

Until late 1967, the Australian government was willing to consider a leading role in the defence of the subregion after Britain had pulled out. According to a State Department report, the Australian government announced in October 1967 that even though Australia could not fully take over from the British, it would participate in the FPDA talks and "be prepared to discuss the size and role of an Australian contribution to combined defense arrangements which embrace a joint Singapore-Malaysia defense effort".[47] But Australia's acquiescence in the plan was short-

---

[43] Colonel H.J. McChrystal, "British Strength and Plans for East of Suez (Singapore-Malaysia Area)", 20 April 1967, in United Kingdom East of Suez, Box 17, Bureau of East Asian and Pacific Affairs. Office of the Country Director for Australia, New Zealand, and Pacific Islands, 1969–74, RG 59, NACP.

[44] "NATO Meeting: East of Suez", Spring 1967.

[45] "The President's trip to Australia (Holt Funeral): Future Defense Arrangements in Singapore-Malaysia", December 1967, in Malaysia/Singapore [Lot File 71D3], 1967, Box 21, Bureau of East Asian and Pacific Affairs. Office of the Country Director for Australia, New Zealand, and Pacific Islands, 1969–74, RG 59, NACP.

[46] Chin, *The Defence of Malaysia and Singapore*, Chapter 4.

[47] Carleton C. Brower, "Background paper: U.K. Withdrawal from Malaysia/Singapore", May 1968, in Malaysia/Singapore [Lot File 71D3], 1967, Box 21, Bureau of East Asian and Pacific Affairs. Office of the Country Director for Australia, New Zealand, and Pacific Islands, 1969–74, RG 59, NACP.

lived. After John Gorton became the Prime Minister of Australia, State Department officials observed that "there have been strong indications that Prime Minister Gorton is backing away from the GOA's [Government of Australia's] previously announced, tentative decision to station forces in Singapore/Malaysia after 1971".[48] Australia's defence thinking during the Gorton administration was increasingly divided between supporters of a "forward defence" strategy, including Minister for Defence Malcolm Fraser and Minister for External Affairs William McMahon, and the Prime Minister himself, who was afraid that Australia's troop deployments in Malaysia and Singapore would be implicated if conflicts arose between Malaysia and either the Philippines or Indonesia.[49] The Australian government was nonetheless in accord on the need to keep the United States engaged in Asia "at all costs".[50] Australia's deployment of troops to fight alongside the US during the Korean War and the Vietnam War was considered "a kind of premium which Australia must pay on its ANZUS insurance policy".[51]

Shortly after the first Five Power Talks held in June 1968, US Ambassador to Singapore, Francis Galbraith, wrote to William Bundy about Australia's ambivalence towards the FPDA, and stressed that America's "presence and activity" was the key to "encourage the Australians to play a security role in Singapore/Malaysia".[52] In a 1969 study on

---

[48] Ibid.

[49] Andrea Benvenuti and Moreen Dee, "The Five Power Defence Arrangements and the Reappraisal of the British and Australian Policy Interests in Southeast Asia, 1970–75", *Journal of Southeast Asian Studies* 41, no. 1 (2010): 113–4. In an article published in *Foreign Affairs* in 1969, Australian diplomat Bruce Grant explains that "forward defence" had been Australia's defence policy since the end of World War II. "The objective of forward defense," according to Grant, "was to keep conflict as far as possible from Australia." Grant contends that because Australia's commitments in Southeast Asia was "predicated on the prior commitment of either or both Britain and America", the withdrawal of the British and the impending retreat of the United States from Vietnam would cause the Australian government to "abandon" forward defence and "withdraw" from the region. See Bruce Grant, "Toward a New Balance in Asia: An Australian View", *Foreign Affairs* 47, no. 4 (1969): 712.

[50] Grant, "Toward a New Balance in Asia", p. 711.

[51] Justus M. van der Kroef, "The Gorton Manner: Australia, Southeast Asia, and the U.S.", *Pacific Affairs* 42, no. 3 (1969): 313.

[52] Galbraith, "Letter to Bundy", 24 June 1968.

Australia's strategy in Southeast Asia, the US State Department reported that

> [a]fter the British begin to phase out, the Australians will be asked to take up a portion of the burden in Malaysia and Singapore; they currently seem disposed to undertake such tasks. How far they go, and how consistently they will carry such burdens will be in part dependent upon the policy of the United States. American encouragement and support will greatly influence the future course of Australian policy and involvement.[53]

Inasmuch as Washington aimed to encourage the Australian government to retain Australian forces in the region, Canberra, too, hoped to "strengthen Washington's resolve" to keep US forces in Southeast Asia.[54]

Recently elected US President Richard Nixon attempted to assure Prime Minister John Gorton of US backing when they met in the beginning of 1969. Robert Moore from the US State Department advised the President that Gorton "could not run the risk of involvement, particularly of his ground forces, in a local crisis in Malaysia/Singapore until he knew in advance who would 'back him up'. He therefore planned to make no decision on post-1971 deployment of ground forces until he had talked to President Nixon."[55] In the same memo, Moore added that "Gorton himself said his main purpose was to obtain assurances from the United States that it would back Australia up if her troops got into trouble in Malaysia defending it against attack from the north—Red China or North Viet-Nam."[56] Gorton needed to know how far the ANZUS Pact would cover Australia's involvement in Malaysia and Singapore, and left Washington on 31 March 1969 with Nixon's commitment that "the United States

---

[53] Richard N. Rosecrance, "Australian Strategies in Southeast Asia", 15 May 1968, in Malaysia/Singapore [Lot File 71D3], 1967, Box 21, Bureau of East Asian and Pacific Affairs. Office of the Country Director for Australia, New Zealand, and Pacific Islands, 1969–74, RG 59, NACP.

[54] Grant, "Toward a New Balance in Asia", p. 713.

[55] Robert W. Moore, "Applicability of ANZUS to Australian Forces in Malaysia/Singapore", 14 February 1969, in DEF 15.9 Malaysia/Singapore (Infrastructure)–NZ/Aust [Lot File 71D3], 1969–69, Box 25, Bureau of East Asian and Pacific Affairs. Office of the Country Director for Australia, New Zealand, and Pacific Islands, 1969–74, RG 59, NACP.

[56] Ibid.

would act under Articles IV and V of the [ANZUS] Treaty" to support Australian forces in Malaysia and Singapore in the event of an overt attack by a communist country.[57]

Nevertheless, President Nixon's assurance of support for Australia's involvement in Malaysia and Singapore lacked substance. It was calculated by planners in Washington, Canberra and London that a communist attack in the subregion would most probably take the form of subversion; an overt communist attack on Malaysia and Singapore would only occur in the most extreme circumstances. Furthermore, the US added that their treaty obligations were bound by the "constitutional processes of the United States, as specified by the ANZUS Treaty".[58] The United States would not be able to come to the aid of their ANZUS allies if the US Congress did not sanction the move. With American troops already heavily committed to the war in Vietnam, it was difficult to foresee Congress supporting further US involvement in other parts of Southeast Asia. After the promulgation of the Nixon Doctrine in July 1969 and the "Vietnamization" of the war in Vietnam, the value of Australia's troop deployments in Southeast Asia came into question among Australia's policymakers.[59]

By late 1969, the US State Department observed Australia's waning commitment towards the establishment of the FPDA. The US Embassy in Singapore followed the developments of the Five Power Defence Talks closely and conducted a series of three studies on the security prospects of the subregion after Britain's military withdrawal.[60] Following the 13 May 1969 racial riots in Malaysia, the Australian government, not wanting to be entangled in the internal security problems in Malaysia and Singapore, showed "marked reluctance to take the lead among the Five Powers".[61] Worried that "this embryo[nic] alliance", the FPDA, would lose its "great

---

[57] Ibid.

[58] Ibid.

[59] Benvenuti and Dee, "The Five Power Defence Arrangements and the Reappraisal of the British and Australian Policy Interests in Southeast Asia, 1970–75", p. 118.

[60] Charles T. Cross, "Letter to Honorable Marshall Green, Assistant Secretary of State for East Asian and Pacific Affairs", 12 December 1969, in POL 15–1 Ambassador's Corres. 1970, Box 8, Subject Files of the Office of Indonesia, Malaysia and Singapore Affairs, 1965–74, RG 59, NACP.

[61] Ibid.

psychological and symbolic value", the US Ambassador to Singapore, Charles Cross, recommended to the Assistant Secretary of State for East Asian Affairs, Marshall Green, that the US should encourage the Australians to take a more vigorous approach to the Five Power arrangements than they had so far. Ambassador Cross reported that the Australian government had been reluctant to "allow the joint Five Power air commander to employ Australian aircraft in combat without specific prior approval from Canberra".[62] The Five Power Integrated Air Defence was only viable if the Australian government was cooperative. Commenting on the impact that the Australians had on joint air defence, Cross added that

> [o]n the nuts and bolts level there is much that Canberra could do to bolster the Five Power arrangements.... [I]f realistic air defense planning is to take place, some sort of commitment by the Australians for the instant repulsion of an external attack against the Malayan peninsula must be worked out.[63]

Cross concluded that a commitment by Canberra to joint air defence would be "the most graphic possible indication" to both the Singapore and the Malaysian governments of Canberra's serious involvement in the defence of the Malaysia-Singapore area.[64]

Ambassador Cross was also concerned because contrary to US opinion, the Five Powers had decided in November 1969 that a Five Power Maritime Defence headquarters was not necessary.[65] In a study conducted in 1969, the US Embassy in Singapore "believed" that maritime defence was integral to a joint air defence system and concluded that such a facility was "useful" because "any air attack against this area would almost certainly be followed by a naval threat".[66] Moreover, establishing the Five Power Maritime Defence headquarters in the subregion "might help in combatting piracy and in patrolling the Straits of Malacca".[67] Hence,

---

[62] Ibid.
[63] Ibid.
[64] Ibid.
[65] Ibid.
[66] Ibid.
[67] Ibid.

in view of the importance of joint naval defence, Cross recommended that the American Embassy in Canberra should hector the Australian government towards developing the Maritime Defence headquarters in the subregion. And if that did not work, "[a]nother possibility might be to raise this [joint Five Power Maritime defence] as a subject for discussion in Washington within the ANZUS forum".[68] Cross suggested that Washington should pull the full extent of its weight to bring about greater commitment in FPDA from the Gorton government. Cross's letter to Marshall Green concluded sombrely: "If Canberra does not assume this [leadership] role, and does not act vigorously within the next several months, we fear that the Five Power alliance will never really amount to anything."[69]

Nevertheless, Cross had overestimated the US government's willingness and capacity to be proactive in the FPDA. Although Washington shared the ambassador's view that the Australians needed to show "leadership and activism" in the Five Power Defence Talks,[70] State Department officials, Maurice Bean and Jonathan Moore, disagreed that the US could "prod the Australians effectively without [the US] assuming a more explicit commitment under ANZUS".[71] Moore doubted that the US should do any more than "subtly and periodically" remind the Australians that the US remained interested in FPDA matters.[72] Deputy Assistant Secretary of State for International Trade Policy, Edwin Cronk, who previously worked with the Australian government suggested that the US could "make the Singapore/Malaysian defense question a key topic on the agenda" for the next ANZUS

---

[68] Ibid.

[69] Ibid.

[70] Jonathan Moore, "Routing slip attached to Charles Cross's Letter to Honorable Marshall Green, Assistant Secretary of State for East Asian and Pacific Affairs", 3 January 1970, in POL 15–1 Ambassador's Corres. 1970, Box 8, Subject Files of the Office of Indonesia, Malaysia and Singapore Affairs, 1965–74, RG 59, NACP.

[71] Maurice D. Bean, "Routing slip attached to Charles Cross's Letter to Honorable Marshall Green, Assistant Secretary of State for East Asian and Pacific Affairs", 30 December 1969, in POL 15–1 Ambassador's Corres. 1970, Box 8, Subject Files of the Office of Indonesia, Malaysia and Singapore Affairs, 1965–74, RG 59, NACP.

[72] Moore, "Routing Slip: Cross to Green", 3 January 1970.

Council meeting with the Australians.[73] Cronk proposed that the best way to get Australia more involved in FPDA was to work with the Australian Prime Minister. Cronk's letter described Gorton's concerns about the FPDA:

> As you know, Gorton is the real problem on this. He has always been cool to the Five Power defense arrangements and even finds it difficult to be civil to the Malaysians and Singaporeans.... He looks on the Five Power arrangement as a very risky business which might accidentally involve Australia in an intra-regional dispute. He wants to keep his options loose so he can extricate the Australian forces if anything like this materializes.[74]

Cronk suggested that the US could encourage Gorton through a personal letter from President Nixon, exhorting the Australian government to do more in the FPDA and indicating US commitments in Southeast Asia in the post-Vietnam period.[75] Cronk also felt that "some careful work" could be done on key members of the Gorton administration to nudge the Australian government towards greater involvement in the FPDA that "would be more acceptable to the Singaporeans and Malaysians".[76] In exchange for Australian leadership of the FPDA, the Nixon administration agreed to shoulder part of the costs of running the Singapore naval dockyards. Nevertheless, President Nixon's pledge that the US would share the cost of running the Singapore bases with Australia became void when the US Congress rejected the US State Department's proposal to bear 70 per cent of the running costs for Singapore naval dockyards under Australian management.[77] Hence, in Assistant Secretary of State Marshall Green's response to Ambassador Cross, Green explained that:

---

[73] Edwin M. Cronk, "Letter to Marshall Green, Assistant Secretary of State for East Asia and Pacific Affairs", 31 December 1969, in POL 15–1 Ambassador's Corres. 1970, Box 8, Subject Files of the Office of Indonesia, Malaysia and Singapore Affairs, 1965–74, RG 59, NACP.

[74] Ibid.

[75] Ibid.

[76] Ibid.

[77] Interagency Singapore Study Group, "Singapore Study", August 1972.

We just do not have the possibility of an additional commitment to use as a bargaining counter in negotiating with the Australians to do those things which might strengthen the Five Power arrangement. Perhaps Prime Minister Lee [Kuan Yew] is correct in feeling that "over the long run…the best way the United States can assist the burgeoning Five Power arrangement is to maintain some presence in Thailand".[78]

The Nixon administration would continue to be interested in the developments of the FPDA but refrained from interfering with the planning of the defence arrangement.

By August 1971, four months before the withdrawal of British troops was completed, it was no longer a question of Australian leadership in the FPDA, but whether or not Australia would abandon the Five Power Defence framework. Washington had to "find ways of providing greater support to the Australians or see them pull out" as well.[79] Gorton's successor, William McMahon, also showed little commitment to the FPDA. In a June 1972 interview with the Australian Broadcasting Corporation when visiting Jakarta, Prime Minister McMahon was asked if Australia would like to have a defence agreement with Indonesia of the same nature as the FPDA. In his attempt to offer a reply acceptable to the Indonesians, McMahon told the interviewer that the FPDA was unnecessary and was "only an obligation to consult".[80] His comments alarmed the US State Department and offended the Malaysian and Singapore governments. The following day, while in Singapore, McMahon issued a statement saying that "the Five Power arrangements with Singapore, Malaysia, New Zealand and the United Kingdom are of great importance".[81] He explained that "what is vital in any relationship

---

[78] Marshall Green, "Official-Informal Letter to The Honorable Charles T. Cross, American Ambassador, Singapore", 13 January 1970, in POL 15–1 Ambassador's Corres. 1970, Box 8, Subject Files of the Office of Indonesia, Malaysia and Singapore Affairs, 1965–74, RG 59, NACP.

[79] Heavner, "Heavner to Shaid", 17 August 1971.

[80] "Untitled document", June 1972, in DEF 4 Collective Defense (FPDA) 1972, Box 10, Subject Files of the Office of Indonesia, Malaysia and Singapore Affairs, 1965–74, RG 59, NACP.

[81] Ibid.

is the totality of it and that pacts and agreements are less important than the goodwill and mutual trust on which they must be based if they are to be effective".[82] After McMahon's visit, the Australian High Commissioner to Singapore, Nicholas F. Parkinson, told the American Deputy Chief of Mission to Singapore, John J. O'Neill, Jr, that

> none of the ranking Singapore officials paid any serious attention to the story [carried in the Indonesian English language newspaper], and in fact when Mr. McMahon rather nervously broached the subject of the interview in his first meeting with the Foreign and Defense Ministers [of Singapore] they both laughed and put the subject aside.[83]

Perhaps the lack of reaction from the Singapore government implied that Singapore no longer looked to the ANZUK powers for security. Indeed, by 1971, Singapore had begun to develop the Singapore Armed Forces with the assistance of the United States.

USING SINGAPORE'S NAVAL DOCKYARDS

In October 1967, US Defense Secretary, Robert McNamara, agreed to send an exploratory team to assess the feasibility of using Singapore's bases after the British withdrawal. Less than two months later, the Commander-in-Chief of the United States Pacific Command (CINCPAC), Admiral Ulysses Simpson Grant Sharp, Jr, visited the Singapore naval dockyards with US Ambassador, Francis Galbraith. When the CINCPAC evaluated Singapore's naval dockyards, he recognised that the dockyards could become a suitable repair facility for the US Pacific Command. After the tour, Ambassador Galbraith reported that the British naval base in Singapore was

---

[82] Ibid.
[83] John J. O'Neill, Jr, "Memorandum of Conversation between Nicholas F. Parkinson, Australian High Commissioner and John J. O'Neill, Jr., American Chargé d'Affaires: Visit to Singapore by Australian Prime Minister", 21 June 1972, in POL Australia 1972, Box 10, Subject Files of the Office of Indonesia, Malaysia and Singapore Affairs, 1965–74, RG 59, NACP.

an absolute first-class installation with a great deal of heavy equipment and about 2500 highly skilled workers who handle the electronics equipment (sonar, radar, radio, etc.) and do the machining on propellers, propeller shafts, gears, etc., and keep the motor equipment in shape. They are also equipped for the heavy work and can fit (as the Navy calls it) any ship up to the size of a frigate.[84]

Admiral Sharp and Ambassador Galbraith recommended that ship repair operations in Singapore needed to commence immediately. Admiral Sharp "seemed to think that an immediate possibility, and one in fact of answering a rather urgent need in Vietnam, would be the repair of small landing craft and river boats of all types".[85] Admiral Sharp told the ambassador that the shipyards in Japan were "overloaded" with orders that the Singapore dockyards could take over.[86] The dockyards in Japan were handling repair orders for both large and small vessels, but were giving priority to larger craft because no other facilities were available to service the larger vessels. As a result, repair works on smaller craft were delayed. Galbraith proposed that representatives from Singapore should be invited to visit the CINCPAC to acquire more details from the US Navy on the type of repairs that may be needed in the future, and that small craft from Vietnam that were being held up could be sent for repair work at Singapore "almost immediately".[87] By December 1967, however, Whitehall had not yet announced the accelerated British troops' withdrawal date of 31 December 1971. Hence, US State Department's reply to the ambassador was, "No point at this time".[88]

In January 1968, soon after Britain had announced its plans for an earlier withdrawal, a delegation from the US Department of Defense set off on a mission to discuss the technicalities of sending US military vessels for maintenance and repair in Singapore. Ambassador Galbraith commented that

---

[84] Francis J. Galbraith, "Official-Informal Letter to Maurice D. Bean, Country Director of Malaysia/Singapore", 8 December 1967, in POL 15–1 Ambassador Galbraith's Official-Informals, Box 5, Subject Files of the Office of Indonesia, Malaysia and Singapore Affairs, 1965–74, RG 59, NACP.

[85] Ibid.

[86] Ibid.

[87] Ibid.

[88] Ibid.

how we [the US government] respond to the GOS interest in engaging us in Singapore as the British withdraw is a question of profound importance in our relations with Singapore and that no aspects of it should be treated as purely technical or outside the immediate concerns of the State Department.... I am apprehensive that DOD may have a tendency to let its interests run beyond technical questions...and into political and economic questions for which the Embassy and State Department ought to have primary responsibility.[89]

Galbraith suggested that Washington and the embassy must work in close consultation with each other at every point of the discussion with the Singapore government to avoid sending conflicting signals to the Singapore government.[90]

The plans of the US Navy to use Singapore for repairs were initiated with haste, but were soon halted because both the US and Singapore governments were still weighing the effects of an increased visibility of US military vessels and personnel in Singapore. In March 1968, the US Department of Defense approved plans for US ships to be repaired at the Singapore dockyards.[91] A month later, the Second Logistical Command Field Office was established to coordinate the repair of vessels from the US Army and Navy. The US military's use of the Singapore ship repair facilities seemed to cohere well with Lee Kuan Yew's request. Ambassador Galbraith reported that

if we [the US] should utilize these facilities and find them valuable to us, we would, even without a permanent "presence", have that much more stake in Singapore and be that much more interested in its fate.[92]

[89] Francis J. Galbraith, "Official-Informal Letter to Maurice D. Bean, Country Director of Malaysia/Singapore", 12 January 1968, in POL 15–1 Amb. Galbraith's Off.-Inf. Lets. 1968, Box 4, Subject Files of the Office of Indonesia, Malaysia and Singapore Affairs, 1965–74, RG 59, NACP.

[90] Ibid.

[91] "Study of Non-Embassy U.S. Government Presence in Singapore", 23 November 1969, in POL 15–1 Ambassador's Correspondence 1969, Box 3, Subject Files of the Office of Indonesia, Malaysia and Singapore Affairs, 1965–74, RG 59, NACP.

[92] Francis J. Galbraith, "Official-Informal Letter to Maurice D. Bean, Country Director of Malaysia/Singapore: US Department of Defense Study Team to Singapore", 14 March 1968, in POL 15–1 Amb. Galbraith's Off.-Inf. Lets. 1968, Box 4, Subject Files of the Office of Indonesia, Malaysia and Singapore Affairs, 1965–74, RG 59, NACP.

Nevertheless, the impression of an alliance with Singapore would affect America's relations with other countries in the region. Singapore's assertion that its immediate threat came from within the subregion raised Malaysia's and Indonesia's concerns over American presence in Singapore.[93] Ambassador Galbraith therefore qualified his "wholehearted backing" for the use of Singapore's shipbuilding and repair facilities by US naval forces with the warning that the US military should not establish a "sizeable, permanent 'presence'" in Singapore.[94]

Singapore and Washington decided and agreed that a cautious start in the ship repair operations was needed.[95] In its first month of the ship repair operation, Singapore gave up US$1 million worth of repair contracts with the US because it was uncertain about local and regional reactions to American warships arriving at the island in large numbers. One ship repair contract that was given up involved the repair of a nuclear-powered US frigate, *Enterprise*, which was too large to berth at the naval base in Sembawang.[96] It could, however, fit the man-of-war anchorage situated at the commercial shipping area off downtown Singapore.[97] The conspicuous arrival of the massive US Navy warship would be followed by 6,000 US military personnel going ashore on the city's waterfront. It was a spectacle that might be misinterpreted as American soldiers landing in Singapore to take over from the British. Lee Kuan Yew's initial response was to allow the *Enterprise* to berth at the man-of-war anchorage, but he was dissuaded by Rajaratnam, who considered the deal ill-timed due to the recent British announcement of withdrawal and the uncertainty of how the FPDA might take shape.[98]

---

[93] Ibid.

[94] Ibid.

[95] Francis J. Galbraith, "Official-Informal Letter to William P. Bundy, Assistant Secretary, Bureau of East Asian and Pacific Affairs", 9 April 1968, in POL 15–1 Amb. Galbraith's Off.-Inf. Lets. 1968, Box 4, Subject Files of the Office of Indonesia, Malaysia and Singapore Affairs, 1965–74, RG 59, NACP.

[96] For a map on the location of Sembawang, see p. xviii of this book.

[97] Francis J. Galbraith, "Official-Informal Letter to William P. Bundy, Assistant Secretary, Bureau of East Asian and Pacific Affairs", 24 May 1968, in POL 15–1 Amb. Galbraith's Off.-Inf. Lets. 1968, Box 4, Subject Files of the Office of Indonesia, Malaysia and Singapore Affairs, 1965–74, RG 59, NACP.

[98] Galbraith, "Letter to Bundy", 9 April 1968.

Ambassador Galbraith shared Rajaratnam's assessment in a report to State Department after the deal fell through, expressing that

> I'm inclined to think this [decision to reject the US$1 million ship repair contract] also turned out well for us.... Their [Singapore government] decision justifies our [US government] continued low posture and even aloofness while they're negotiating their new defense arrangements with their Commonwealth allies.[99]

Galbraith also stressed that Lee should not be encouraged to make the US a "first point of reference for any and all assistance" in the future, especially with the Five Power Defence Conference still at a rudimentary stage.[100]

Despite the false start in ship repair contracts between Washington and Singapore, the volume of US military vessels using the repair facilities in Singapore soon increased because ship repairs in Singapore were cheaper than they were in Japan, Taiwan, Hong Kong and the Philippines. The Officer-in-Charge of repair contracts for the US Seventh Fleet, Admiral Ward, told Ambassador Galbraith that the use of Singapore repair facilities would take the pressure off the dockyards in Subic Bay, located in the Philippines, and Sasebo, in Japan.[101] In May 1968, the Singapore government had yet to recognise "the full potential" of the business that could be generated, and the US government had yet to realise the "extent to which Singapore's convenience and usefulness as a military 'service station'" could become "a desirable, if not indispensable, asset from the standpoint of [the US] Navy and Air Force".[102]

Before the British withdrawal was completed in December 1971, the Singapore government instructed US Navy ships to arrive in Singapore "quietly and with little fanfare".[103] In 1972, Rajaratnam informed John J. O'Neill, Jr that Singapore was no longer anxious about the visibility of US military vessels on the island. The deterioration of Sino-Soviet relations

---

[99] Ibid.

[100] Ibid.

[101] Galbraith, "Letter to Bundy", 24 May 1968.

[102] Ibid.

[103] John J. O'Neill, Jr, "US Policy in East Asia, US Aid, Regionalism, US Military Presence in SEA, Indian Ocean, Malaysia", 20 June 1972, in POL 1 General Policy and Background 1972, Box 10, Subject Files of the Office of Indonesia, Malaysia and Singapore Affairs, 1965–74, RG 59, NACP.

partially accounted for Singapore's newfound ease towards a greater US military presence in Singapore. Rajaratnam believed that the Sino-Soviet split had worsened to the extent that "any Russian moves in the area are similar in a way to the Dulles policy of containment of China and designed to keep [the PRC] worried on its entire periphery".[104] Hence, when the *Enterprise*, which was denied access in 1968, arrived at the man-of-war anchorage off downtown Singapore, the Singapore Foreign Ministry observed no PRC reaction. Rajaratnam concluded that the PRC's lack of protest for US military presence in Singapore could stem from Beijing's preference for America's presence in Singapore over the Soviet Union.

Although Lee Kuan Yew invited US military presence in October 1967, he no longer deemed it beneficial for USN ships to be permanently based in Singapore after the British withdrawal. In 1972, an Interagency Study Group formed by the US State and Defense Departments concluded that the US should maintain some military presence in Singapore after US forces withdrew from Vietnam.[105] The Singapore government would allow more USN ships to use the island's naval dockyards for repairs, but rejected a USN proposal to homeport several American destroyers in Singapore.[106] Homeporting US warships in Singapore would make Singapore the port of origin for US vessels, thereby increasing the number of US military personnel and their families residing in Singapore. Acceptance of the homeporting arrangement would, in fact, make Singapore a host to US military bases and put Singapore's non-aligned credentials at risk. Singapore could also become a target for anti-American attacks, which might involve the use of nuclear weapons. Considering these factors, the Singapore government rejected the homeporting proposal but hoped to preserve the current arrangement since Singapore would continue to enjoy both the economic benefits from US ship repairs and the psychological assurance that the visiting US warships would provide. After the withdrawal of American troops from South Vietnam in March 1973, the number of USN ships visiting

---

[104] Ibid.
[105] Interagency Singapore Study Group, "Singapore Study", August 1972.
[106] Ibid.

Singapore's ship repair facilities increased sharply. From an average of seventeen visits per quarter previously, the US Seventh Fleet increased the number of ships scheduled to visit Singapore's naval dockyards by 65 per cent from June to September of 1973.[107] American use of Singapore's naval dockyards from 1968 to 1973 was a major contribution by the US to mitigate the economic impact and the loss of confidence caused by the British withdrawal.

USING SINGAPORE'S AIR BASES

Along with the commercialisation of Singapore's naval dockyards, the air bases handed over to the Singapore government by the British were converted to perform maintenance and repair services on military aircraft. After Lee's visit to Washington in October 1967, an Air Force Study Team was sent by the US Department of Defense to Singapore in early 1968. Like the study team despatched by the US Navy, the US Air Force Study Team observed keen interest by the Singapore government to establish aircraft repair facilities after the British withdrew.[108] Singapore's Defence Minister, Lim Kim San, soon held talks with US companies interested to establish aircraft repair and maintenance facilities in Singapore.[109] In April 1969, two American companies, Lockheed Aircraft Services and Lear Siegler, proposed to set up aircraft repair facilities in Singapore.[110] On 23 September 1969, the Singapore government awarded Lockheed a contract to establish an aviation maintenance facility at Paya Lebar International Airport.[111] The contract

---

[107] Edwin M. Cronk, "Official-Informal Letter to Theodore J.C. Heavner, Country Director for Indonesia, Malaysia and Singapore", 26 July 1973, in DEF 15 U.S. Use of Military Facilities 1973, Box 11, Subject Files of the Office of Indonesia, Malaysia and Singapore Affairs, 1965–74, RG 59, NACP.

[108] Galbraith, "Letter to Bundy", 24 May 1968.

[109] Ibid.

[110] Albert K. Ludy, "Ambassador's Visit to Washington", 9 April 1969, in POL 15–1 Ambassador's Correspondence 1969, Box 3, Subject Files of the Office of Indonesia, Malaysia and Singapore Affairs, 1965–74, RG 59, NACP.

[111] "Telegram from USDAO/Singapore to CINCPAC: Lockheed Air Services (LAS) - GOS Aviation Maintenance Agreement", September 1969, in FN 9 Grumman International (Singapore 1970), Box 8, Subject Files of the Office of Indonesia, Malaysia and

granted Lockheed exclusive permission to establish and develop facilities to perform "third and fourth line" service, maintenance, repair, overhaul and modification of US military aircraft and large civilian aircraft in Singapore for six years, with a possible five-year extension.[112] The Defense Attaché Office of the US Embassy in Singapore observed that the deal with Lockheed might have been struck too hastily. The Singapore government was so eager to perform maintenance for US DOD aircraft in Singapore over a long term that it was willing to offer significant concessions to Lockheed by providing facilities and equipment under lease.[113] In return, the contract required Lockheed to obtain sufficient DOD maintenance contracts for the Paya Lebar facilities, apart from supporting the maintenance of the Singapore Air Defence Command.[114] But Lockheed did not have control over the award of DOD contracts, and certainly could not give the Singapore government any assurance that the aircraft repair facility would be profitable. The Defense Attaché Office reported that "an American owned and operated, first class facility in this Republic is strategically of long term advantage to the U.S. in view of the political stability of the government and the strategic geographic location of Singapore".[115] Hence, it was important for the project to work out since any fallout resulting from a failure in this venture risked damaging US-Singapore relationship. Three days after signing the contract with

---

Singapore Affairs, 1965–74, RG 59, NACP. For a map on the location of Paya Lebar International Airport, see p. xviii of this book.

[112] Ibid. Third and fourth line maintenance of aircraft include work that requires major parts of aircraft to be changed.

[113] Ibid.

[114] "Memorandum of Understanding Between the Government of Singapore and Lockheed Aircraft Service Company of U.S.A. dated this 23rd September, 1969", 23 September 1969, in FN 9 Grumman International (Singapore 1970), Box 8, Subject Files of the Office of Indonesia, Malaysia and Singapore Affairs, 1965–74, RG 59, NACP. Lockheed's exclusivity to operate in Singapore was put at risk in late 1970 when it had difficulties competing with Australia and China Air Lines of Taiwan for US DOD contracts. See Josiah W. Bennett, "Memorandum for the Files: Lockheed in Singapore", 23 November 1970, in FN-9 Lockheed (Singapore 1970), Box 8, Subject Files of the Office of Indonesia, Malaysia and Singapore Affairs, 1965–74, RG 59, NACP.

[115] William G. von Platen, "Aviation Maintenance Facility for Singapore Air Force", 25 September 1969, in FN 9 Grumman International (Singapore 1970), Box 8, Subject Files of the Office of Indonesia, Malaysia and Singapore Affairs, 1965–74, RG 59, NACP.

the Singapore government, representatives from Lockheed kept to their promise and met the Commander-in-Chief of the US Pacific Fleet "to start [the] ball rolling".[116]

The major contract between Singapore and Lockheed was soon followed by an exploratory visit by a third US aviation company, Grumman Corporation. In November 1969, Grumman Corporation's President, Thomas P. Cheatham, Jr, met Lee Kuan Yew and other Singapore government officials to express interest in taking over the air bases at Seletar and Changi from the British Royal Air Force and establishing an aerospace complex. The complex managed by Grumman would be used for manufacturing aircraft, as well as maintaining helicopters, generators and aircraft equipment such as Airborne Early Warning Systems.[117] To gain US State and Defense Departments' approval, Cheatham wrote to the Deputy Commanding General of the US Army Materiel Command, Lieutenant-General Henry A. Miley, and visited Assistant Secretary of State for East Asian Affairs Marshall Green in December 1969. Cheatham highlighted that Grumman's facilities in Singapore would solve the logistical problems arising from a future US withdrawal from South Vietnam and would also contribute to Singapore's air defence after the British withdrawal. He foresaw an impending need for a staging facility for sorting, cataloguing, overhauling, repairing, protecting and repackaging military equipment when US troops would eventually withdraw from South Vietnam.[118] Cheatham argued that Singapore was the most suitable location for staging US withdrawal operations because it was situated at "strategic cross-roads of importance to Southeast Asia and the Indian Ocean".[119] Moreover, Singapore was run by an "honest government", which

---

[116] "Telegram: USDAO/Singapore to CINCPAC", September 1969.

[117] Thomas P. Cheatham, Jr, "Letter to Dr. Goh Keng Swee, Minister of Finance, Republic of Singapore", 31 January 1970, in FN 9 Grumman International (Singapore 1970), Box 8, Subject Files of the Office of Indonesia, Malaysia and Singapore Affairs, 1965–74, RG 59, NACP.

[118] Thomas P. Cheatham, Jr, "Letter to Lt. General Henry A. Miley, USA", 2 December 1969, in POL 15–1 Ambassador's Corres. 1970, Box 8, Subject Files of the Office of Indonesia, Malaysia and Singapore Affairs, 1965–74, RG 59, NACP.

[119] Ibid.

maintained Singapore's "low cost and cooperative environment".[120] At the same time, Cheatham pointed out that current staging areas that the US military had access to, such as Okinawa, Manila, Taiwan and Japan, were experiencing "rising political, psychological, and financial problems".[121] "By comparison," Cheatham opined, "I feel Singapore has much to offer."[122]

The US State Department accepted Cheatham's proposal but was concerned that competition between Lockheed and Grumman would damage diplomatic relations between Singapore and the US. Cheatham assured Assistant Secretary Marshall Green that Grumman's aviation complex would not duplicate the functions of Lockheed's aircraft maintenance facilities.[123] Cheatham stressed that Grumman's main objective was "to form a consortium with British, Japanese and Australian firms to establish a facility for rehabilitating millions of dollars worth of goods to be taken out of Viet-Nam upon the completion of hostilities".[124] Grumman intended to begin operations within six months and had committed to train and employ 2,000 locals while injecting capital investment of an aggregate of US$31.5 million over five years.[125] The Grumman training facility in Singapore would be of exceptional value to Singapore, as it would provide training for Singapore and other Southeast Asian air forces in the maintenance of military aircraft. In fact, Grumman's proposal was so enticing that the Singapore government requested an "early release" of the facilities by the British in July 1970.[126] Given that Lee Kuan Yew had reacted with such vehemence against Britain's announcement to accelerate its military withdrawal in January

---

[120] Ibid.

[121] Ibid.

[122] Ibid.

[123] Marshall Green, "Memorandum of Conversation: Grumman Investment in Singapore", 14 January 1970, in FN 9 Grumman International (Singapore 1970), Box 8, Subject Files of the Office of Indonesia, Malaysia and Singapore Affairs, 1965–74, RG 59, NACP.

[124] Ibid.

[125] Cheatham, "Letter to Goh", 31 January 1970.

[126] John J. O'Neill, Jr, "Memorandum of Conversation between John J. O'Neill, Jr., American Embassy, Singapore and Walter Schnederbeck, Grumman Aerospace", 28 July 1970, in FN 9 Grumman International (Singapore 1970), Box 8, Subject Files of the Office of Indonesia, Malaysia and Singapore Affairs, 1965–74, RG 59, NACP.

1968, the Singapore government's request for a speedy withdrawal at this point reaffirmed a significant shift in Singapore's strategic calculations.

GOS AND THE AMERICAN EMBASSY

The United States-Singapore cooperation in defence was strengthened at both government and personal levels during the years leading to the British withdrawal. In 1968 and 1969, Lee Kuan Yew and Defence Minister, Lim Kim San, made courtesy calls to the headquarters of the US Pacific Fleet at Hawaii. During these visits, the Commander-in-Chief, Admiral McCain, and Lee "sized each other up" favourably.[127] Along with the political leadership, officials from Singapore's Ministry of the Interior and Defence (MID) and several senior US military personnel also developed affable personal and professional relationship with each other.[128] By 1969, the American Embassy had cemented strong ties with the government of Singapore. The "special nature of the relationship" between the US and Singapore was apparent from the correspondence between George Bogaars, the Permanent Secretary of Singapore's MID, and Colonel James Larkin, the Army Attaché at the US Embassy.[129] In 1969, the MID issued a document outlining the protocol that governed the interaction between MID and foreign military attachés accredited to Singapore. The document, entitled "Procedure for Military Attachés Accredited to the Republic of Singapore", provided pedantic instructions on how newly assigned military attachés should distribute their calling cards within the MID, on whom they should make formal calls, and how they should make appointments to meet senior officials in the MID. After sending a copy to the US Embassy, Bogaars followed with a note to Colonel Larkin stating that

---

[127] William H. Bruns, "Official-Informal Letter to Maurice D. Bean, Country Director of Malaysia-Singapore Affairs", 7 August 1969, in POL 7 Visits. Prime Minister Lee 1968, Box 4, Subject Files of the Office of Indonesia, Malaysia and Singapore Affairs, 1965–74, RG 59, NACP.

[128] Ibid.

[129] George Bogaars, "Letter to Colonel Larkin, Army Attache, Embassy of the United States of America", 15 May 1969, in POL 15–1 Ambassador's Correspondence 1969, Box 3, Subject Files of the Office of Indonesia, Malaysia and Singapore Affairs, 1965–74, RG 59, NACP.

[w]ith a view to maintaining the present close and full co-operation between yourself and the Ministry of the Interior and Defence, I propose exempting you from the procedures laid down for 'Military Attaches accredited to the Republic of Singapore'. I enclose herewith a copy of those established procedures which because of the special nature of the relationship existing between our two organisations especially on defence matters will not apply.[130]

The tone of the letter and special exemption given by the MID to the US Army Attaché demonstrated the goodwill between Singapore and the United States. Marshall Brement, First Secretary of the US Embassy in Singapore, described the MID document as "a rather lovely example of the sledgehammer way with which the GOS sometimes operates" and expressed delight that "the sledgehammer" was not meant for the US, but "only for those other guys".[131]

After the British withdrew in December 1971, US-Singapore defence relations grew closer. In 1972, when Defence Minister Goh Keng Swee found out that the Singapore Foreign Ministry had refused the landing rights of a US military aircraft without consulting the Ministry of Defence,[132] Goh "was sufficiently distressed to write a letter to the Foreign Minister [Rajaratnam] in which he took him to task, using some sharp language, for not cooperating with the USG".[133] Reporting the incident to Theodore Heavner in the US State Department, John J. O'Neill, Jr added that "the Defense Minister is an extremely important individual in this Government and I think it worthwhile for you and others in the Department to have this as background."[134] Hence, it became apparent

---

[130] Ibid.

[131] Marshall Brement, "Letter to Maurice D. Bean, Country Director, East Asia/Malaysia-Singapore", 8 July 1969, in POL 15–1 Ambassador's Correspondence 1969, Box 3, Subject Files of the Office of Indonesia, Malaysia and Singapore Affairs, 1965–74, RG 59, NACP.

[132] Singapore's Ministry of Interior and Defence (MID) was split to two separate ministries, the Ministry of Defence and the Ministry of Home Affairs, in August 1970.

[133] John J. O'Neill, Jr, "Official-Informal Letter to Theodore J.C. Heavner, Country Director for Indonesia, Malaysia and Singapore", 16 May 1972, in DEF 15 US Use of Military Facilities 1972, Box 10, Subject Files of the Office of Indonesia, Malaysia and Singapore Affairs, 1965–74, RG 59, NACP.

[134] Ibid.

within the US government that Singapore was no longer a distant Southeast Asian country that rejected American influence, but a country run by a government that valued close relations with the United States. Nevertheless, a formal defence alliance between the US and Singapore did not serve the interests of the two countries because Singapore was deemed more valuable to the United States if it maintained a non-aligned image. Hence, Washington showed its support for the Singapore government by quietly supplying military equipment to Singapore's defence force.

"POISON SHRIMP" STRATEGY

In response to the British withdrawal from east of Suez, the Singapore government devised what it called a "poison shrimp" defence strategy.[135] The 'poisoned shrimp' concept was articulated by Lee Kuan Yew as early as October 1967, during his first official visit to Washington, where he pledged to "give anyone a bloody nose who [was] going to rob the house and take [his] jade pieces".[136] "The idea" behind the poisoned shrimp defence concept, according to Tim Huxley, "was that any aggressor would find that the costs of attempting to invade and occupy Singapore outweighed any conceivable benefits."[137] Singapore's 'poisoned shrimp' defence strategy, which was developed under the guidance of Israeli military advisors, was "intended to register the island's indigestible qualities to any likely predator".[138] In order to develop a strong deterrent force, the Singapore defence ministry invested heavily in sophisticated US military equipment. Together, with the acquisition of weapons, the Singapore government introduced the conscription of male citizens into the Singapore Armed Forces.[139] Foreign Minister Rajaratnam highlighted the importance of conscription in a 1972 speech:

---

[135] Charles T. Cross, "Embassy Conference, April 9, 1970, American Embassy, Singapore, Ambassador's Briefing", 9 April 1970, in POL 1 General Policy (Political Affairs & Relations 1970), Box 8, Subject Files of the Office of Indonesia, Malaysia and Singapore Affairs, 1965–74, RG 59, NACP.

[136] Galbraith, "Lee's Visit to US", November 1967.

[137] Huxley, *Defending the Lion City*, p. 56.

[138] Leifer, *Singapore's Foreign Policy: Coping with Vulnerability*, pp. 33–4.

[139] Huxley, *Defending the Lion City*, pp. 12–4.

[A]n effective defence policy should make the probable invader aware before he invades the country that this would be the situation in which he will find himself. He is more likely then to keep out. This should be done not by bluffing or posturing but by convincing him by deeds rather than words that occupation would be costly; that he would get none of the benefits of occupation. This is one reason why we have instituted National Service.[140]

Whereas Washington acquiesced in the logic behind Singapore's 'poisoned shrimp' strategy, State Department officials doubted if Singapore could afford the expensive military hardware. Since the economic impact of the British withdrawal was predicted to be severe, the Singapore government's high defence spending was particularly worrying for London and Washington. Still, the Singapore government muted calls for caution and pursued the 'poisoned shrimp' strategy with single-mindedness. In mid-1971, the American Embassy in Singapore estimated that the Singapore government's 'poisoned shrimp' strategy had cost the island 32 per cent of its budget in 1970 and would increase to 37 per cent in 1971.[141] Technological superiority was seen as a "force multiplier" that compensated for Singapore's lack of strategic depth and manpower.[142] A comparison between Singapore's defence and welfare expenditures reveals that the Singapore government spent 100 per cent more on welfare than defence in 1968, but ended up spending 30 per cent more on defence than welfare in 1971 and 1972.[143] The reversal of spending patterns signalled a clear shift in Singapore's priorities. The US and Britain were

---

[140] S. Rajaratnam, "Speech by Mr. S. Rajaratnam, Minister for Foreign Affairs, to the Singapore Institute of International Affairs at the Queen's Hotel, 24 Mt. Elizabeth, on Monday 3rd January, 1972: Davids in a World of Goliaths", 3 January 1972, in POL 1 General Policy and Background 1972, Box 10, Subject Files of the Office of Indonesia, Malaysia and Singapore Affairs, 1965–74, RG 59, NACP.

[141] Charles T. Cross, "Official-Informal Letter to Marshall Green, Assistant Secretary of State for East Asian and Pacific Affairs", 11 April 1971, in POL 1.1 Incoming Official-Informal Correspondence (Singapore 1971), Box 8, Subject Files of the Office of Indonesia, Malaysia and Singapore Affairs, 1965–74, RG 59, NACP.

[142] Huxley, *Defending the Lion City*, p. 30.

[143] Hafiz Mirza, *Multinationals and the Growth of the Singapore Economy* (Sydney: Croom Helm, 1986), p. 50. In Haifz Mirza's study, defence includes justice and police, and welfare comprises education, health, social and community services.

compelled to supply Singapore with American and British military equipment because if they were overly obstructive, Singapore could turn to the Soviet Union for military equipment.[144]

Singapore's 'poisoned shrimp' strategy was intended to work hand-in-hand with the FPDA after the British withdrawal. Ambassador Cross observed that Singapore's Ministry of Defence had gradually become less dependent on Israeli defence advisors and was beginning to work closer with Commonwealth and American advisors.[145] Cross reported that Singapore needed to rely on the "possible stabilizing effect" of the FPDA on Singapore-Malaysian relations and take advantage of the FPDA's potential to "discourage aggressive acts by Indonesia".[146] Hence, after the signing of the FPDA, Singapore aligned its military equipment with partners of the FPDA by matching aircraft technology with Britain, Australia and New Zealand. Between 1970 and 1972, the Singapore government acquired 47 Hunter fighter ground-attack aircraft from Britain.[147] In mid-1972, Singapore acquired 40 A4B ground support aircraft to complement the A4M aircraft that Australia and New Zealand used in their air force fleets.[148] The US Department of State reported that Singapore's decision to align its air defence technology with that of Australia and New Zealand was a sign that Singapore's air defence would be complementary to the FPDA. The State Department concluded that Singapore's acquisition of 40 A4B aircraft could also be a response to its threat perception. Since the A4B had "considerable potential to defend against seaborne attack", the Country Director for Indonesia, Malaysia and Singapore, Theodore Heavner, thought the Singapore government would have intended to use it against a naval attack from or through Indonesia.[149]

---

[144] Galbraith, "Letter to Bundy", 24 June 1968.

[145] Cross, "Letter to Green", 11 April 1971.

[146] Ibid.

[147] Huxley, *Defending the Lion City*, p. 21.

[148] Theodore J.C. Heavner, "Supplementary Briefing Material for your talks with the British and French", 17 May 1972, in Briefing Papers 1972, Box 10, Subject Files of the Office of Indonesia, Malaysia and Singapore Affairs, 1965–74, RG 59, NACP.

[149] Ibid.

US MILITARY SALES

The US State Department did not probe into the reason for Singapore's need of the A4B aircraft. It was concerned, however, that Singapore was building its defence at the expense of economic prudence. Theodore Heavner reported that "Singapore is arming itself to the teeth with a variety of modern weapons in the absence of any very sophisticated external threat. The only potential aggressors are close to home and they are not armed with sophisticated weapons."[150] Hence, Washington would become less responsive when the Singapore government expressed interest in purchasing expensive and highly sophisticated military equipment. Furthermore, Singapore's non-aligned foreign policy and Lee's earlier anti-Americanism still evoked negative sentiments among American politicians and government officials who did not support the selling of military equipment to Singapore. At almost every stage of negotiating US-Singapore military sales, sections of American government officials and members of the US Congress questioned the sagacity of supplying arms to a non-aligned country that used to be highly critical of the US. Nevertheless, the US State Department managed to follow through with the arms sales, albeit with some resistance from the US Congress from time to time. Between 1967 and 1975, the US government supplied Singapore with a range of equipment, which included small arms, armoured vehicles, air defence equipment and naval vessels.

Supply of AR-15 Rifles

During Lee Kuan Yew's visit to Washington in October 1967, William Bundy assured Lee that the US government would supply Singapore with the AR-15 rifles needed to equip Singapore's conscripted defence force.[151] The supply of the rifles turned out to be more problematic than either Washington or Singapore had anticipated. In 1967, and

---

[150] Theodore J.C. Heavner, "Memorandum from Ted Heavner to John W. Sipes: F-4Es for Singapore", 23 April 1973, in DEF 19 Air F-4 1973, Box 11, Subject Files of the Office of Indonesia, Malaysia and Singapore Affairs, 1965–74, RG 59, NACP.

[151] Galbraith, "Lee's Visit to US", November 1967. The AR-15 rifle that Colt produced in Singapore was called the M-16. Both models were almost identical and differentiated mainly by manufacturing locations.

again in early 1968, shipment of the rifles to Singapore was disrupted because of concerns raised by the US Congress that Singapore might re-export the rifles to North Vietnam and North Korea, which had trade relations with Singapore. Moreover, Colt Company, the company that was producing the rifles, was handling large orders from the US Department of Defense, which needed the rifles for American troops in South Vietnam.[152] The view of Congress was that DOD's purchase orders should be of higher priority than Singapore's order, and should not be delayed because of Singapore. In May 1967, US State Department officials Maurice Bean and Samuel Berger, together with Defense Department representatives Richard Steadman and Frank Fede, testified before the House Armed Services Committee Special Sub-committee that was investigating the sale of AR-15 rifles to Singapore.[153] One of the questions raised by the sub-committee was:

> Why DOD had not raised objections to the proposed sale in view of the "shortage" of the rifle for our [US] troops in Viet-Nam or in training for Viet-Nam.[154]

Richard Steadman from DOD clarified that there was no shortage of rifles for American troops and that Colt was meeting delivery schedule for its contract with the US Department of Defense.[155] After much questioning, the sub-committee eventually approved the sale of AR-15 rifles to Singapore.

To avoid future obstruction from the US Congress, the Singapore government requested for Colt to set up a factory in Singapore to produce rifles for the Singapore military. In August 1968, the Director of Logistics in MID, Ong Kah Koh, "complained bitterly at the continued slowdown

---

[152] Francis J. Galbraith, "Letter to Maurice D. Bean, Country Director of Malaysia/Singapore", 14 April 1969, in POL 15–1 Ambassador's Correspondence 1969, Box 3, Subject Files of the Office of Indonesia, Malaysia and Singapore Affairs, 1965–74, RG 59, NACP.

[153] Maurice D. Bean, "Briefing Memorandum: House Armed Services Committee Special Sub-committee - Investigation of M-16 Rifles", 31 May 1967, in DEF 19 Military Assistance (Defense Affairs), Box 4, Subject Files of the Office of Indonesia, Malaysia and Singapore Affairs, 1965–74, RG 59, NACP.

[154] Ibid.

[155] Ibid.

in AR-15 rifle deliveries to Singapore".[156] After listening to recurrent explanations for the delays, Ong pointedly told the US Embassy Army Attaché, Colonel James Larkin, that "the real reason for curtailment of deliveries" for the shortfall of 12,000 AR-15 rifles was the "lack of trust" on the part of Washington.[157] In December 1968, Ong visited the US to negotiate the building of a rifle manufacturing factory in Singapore.[158] State Department officials advised that building the factory was "not economically viable", but worried that US refusal might cause the Singapore government to seek help from another country, and potentially damage US-Singapore relations.[159] Despite an offer by Washington to "expedite delivery of the current rifle order and to guarantee minimum annual deliveries of future orders with soft financing", Singapore insisted on making its own AR-15 rifles.[160] Earlier in 1968, Ambassador Galbraith had written to Washington, explaining the strategic significance of supplying the rifles to Singapore:

> I would regard it as contrary to our interests if Singapore, failing to satisfy its security requirements, including procurement of a certain amount of weaponry from either a combination of Commonwealth powers or from the U.S., should turn to the Soviets with all that might mean for the availability of Singapore as a service center for our ships, sailors and any fighting men we might have in this part of the world at any time. This contingency seems rather remote today but it is not out of the question in the long run. If effective Commonwealth security arrangements do not materialize, if Singapore loses confidence in the future American role in this area and if communist China resumes its progress toward superpower status, we are likely to see a growing

---

[156] Francis J. Galbraith, "Official-Informal Letter to Maurice D. Bean, Country Director of Malaysia/Singapore", 30 August 1968, in POL 15–1 Amb. Galbraith's Off.-Inf. Lets. 1968, Box 4, Subject Files of the Office of Indonesia, Malaysia and Singapore Affairs, 1965–74, RG 59, NACP.

[157] Ibid.

[158] Louis N. Cavanaugh, "Visit to United States of Mr. Ong, Director of Logistics, Singapore's Ministry of Defence", 11 December 1968, in DEF 19 Military Assistance 1968, Box 4, Subject Files of the Office of Indonesia, Malaysia and Singapore Affairs, 1965–74, RG 59, NACP.

[159] Ibid.

[160] Ibid.

Singapore desire to involve the Soviet Union here to help maintain the power balance.[161]

With broader strategic interests at stake, approval was granted for Colt to set up a factory in Singapore. More significantly, Ambassador Galbraith remarked that the Singapore government would consider the United States and the Soviet Union as viable partners who could be used to balance China's influence in the region.

Within two months, a contract was signed between the Singapore government and Colt.[162] One key element of the contract that Singapore's negotiator, Ong Kah Kok, might have missed was that Washington would retain control over the pace of rifle production in Singapore by maintaining the option to withhold export licenses for key parts from the US.[163] Washington could stop Colt-Singapore from obtaining key parts by citing that the US "needed the parts" for its "own defense".[164] In his letter to the Country Director for Malaysia and Singapore, Maurice Bean, Galbraith pointed out that the contract signed between Colt and the Singapore government to produce 200,000 AR-15 rifles involved the Singapore government paying Colt a total of US$350,000 plus a 10 per cent royalty on the rifles produced. Galbraith remarked that Singapore was making a hasty decision by "paying a heavy price" for "an assured source of AR-15 rifles" and might not have considered the full effect of Washington's rights if the US government restricted the export of the parts.[165] Hence, he urged Washington to spell out the "pitfalls" to the Singapore government "in as much detail as possible in order to avoid possible future accusations of bad faith" on the part of the US.[166]

---

[161] Galbraith, "Letter to Bundy", 24 June 1968.

[162] Francis J. Galbraith, "Letter to Maurice D. Bean, Country Director of Malaysia/Singapore", 20 February 1969, in POL 15–1 Ambassador's Correspondence 1969, Box 3, Subject Files of the Office of Indonesia, Malaysia and Singapore Affairs, 1965–74, RG 59, NACP.

[163] Ibid.

[164] Louis N. Cavanaugh, "Letter to Francis Galbraith, US Ambassador to Singapore", 10 March 1969, in POL 15–1 Ambassador's Correspondence 1969, Box 3, Subject Files of the Office of Indonesia, Malaysia and Singapore Affairs, 1965–74, RG 59, NACP.

[165] Galbraith, "Letter to Bean", 20 February 1969.

[166] Ibid.

The US Congress queried the Department of State over the approval of the Colt-Singapore contract shortly after the Colt factory had gone into operation in Singapore. The Director of Survey and Investigations Staff under the House Appropriations Committee, Paul Mohr, met with State Department officials in April 1970 to conduct a general investigation on "the establishment of small arms production facilities abroad utilizing U.S. manufactured and/or patented components or technology".[167] The State Department assured the investigators that careful consultation had been made between the State and Defense Departments throughout the negotiations, and the political and economic factors were considered before approving the deal between Colt and the Singapore government. Maurice Bean informed Paul Mohr that the US government retained two forms of control over the production of the rifles: the right to reject the Singapore government's request if it wanted to sell the rifles to a third country; and the right to disapprove licensing for most of the parts from the US that were needed to produce the rifles.[168] Bean also dismissed the likelihood that Singapore would export any of the rifles since the Singapore military greatly needed to make up for its shortage in those weapons.[169]

One year later, the United States government began to contemplate lifting the restriction on the export of Singapore-produced rifles to third countries. Colt Company in Singapore and South Korea were the only two Asian countries authorised by the US government to manufacture M-16 rifles. In 1971, Colt requested to export Singapore-made M-16s to Laos, Cambodia and Thailand. The request was rejected at the time by the US Defense Department, which deemed the arrangement "not in the best interest of the US Government and [might] endanger US security".[170] The security environment in Asia had nonetheless evolved to a point where it had become strategically attractive for Washington to approve

---

[167] Maurice D. Bean, "Memorandum of Conversation: HAC/S&IS Inquiry Concerning the Establishment of an AR-15 Rifle Production Facility in Singapore", 21 April 1970, in DEF 19 Military Assistance (Defense Affairs 1970), Box 7, Subject Files of the Office of Indonesia, Malaysia and Singapore Affairs, 1965–74, RG 59, NACP.

[168] Ibid.

[169] Ibid.

[170] John W. Sipes, "Colt's Efforts in Malaysia", 17 November 1971, in DEF 19 Military Assistance–Army 1973, Box 11, Subject Files of the Office of Indonesia, Malaysia and Singapore Affairs, 1965–74, RG 59, NACP.

Colt-Singapore's request to export rifles to third countries. The Munitions Control Office and the State Department feared that Southeast Asian countries would try to produce their own rifles, which was an "expensive as well as uneconomic utilization of resources".[171] The US government was therefore willing to "encourage the Malaysian[s] and others to buy from either Singapore or South Korea".[172]

Colt-Singapore was eventually allowed to export M-16 rifles made in Singapore to regional countries, under the condition that every transaction had to attain prior approval from the US government. The Singapore government, however, shipped M-16 rifles for the Philippines and Thailand in 1974 and 1975, respectively, without waiting for the approval from the US government.[173] Although US Secretary of State, Henry Kissinger, empathised that the Singapore government was trying to be "forthcoming with the Thai" and that he did not foresee difficulties in approving the export licences, he was concerned that the conditions set in the M-16 Manufacturing License Agreement signed in 1969 were blatantly ignored by the Singapore government.[174] Kissinger urged the US Embassy in Singapore to remind the Singapore government that the agreement could be suspended if there was further breach.[175] When US Ambassador to Singapore, John Holdridge, met with Singapore Defence Minister, Goh Keng Swee, to discuss the matter, Goh explained that "GOS had been under tremendous pressure from the Thai to make the shipment".[176] Holdridge informed the State Department that Goh was under the impression that Colt had submitted a complete set of documents to the US government that were only pending approval. Seeing no likely

---

[171] Ibid.

[172] Ibid.

[173] Henry A. Kissinger, "Singapore Shipment M16 Rifles to Thailand", September 1975, in Singapore–State Department Telegrams: From SECSTATE–EXDIS, Box 16, National Security Adviser. Presidential Country Files for East Asia and the Pacific, 1974–77, GRFL.

[174] Ibid.

[175] Ibid.

[176] John H. Holdridge, "Singapore Shipment of M-16 Rifles to Thailand", September 1975, in Singapore–State Department Telegrams: To SECSTATE–EXDIS, Box 16, National Security Adviser. Presidential Country Files for East Asia and the Pacific, 1974–77, GRFL.

restrictions on the deal, the Singapore government made the delivery before the approval was formally given. Goh "appeared surprised" to learn from Holdridge that Colt had not completed the paperwork needed.[177]

Supply of M-109 Howitzers

There were other instances where military sales almost created diplomatic problems between Singapore and the US. Whereas the supply of rifles to Singapore eventually went smoothly, the Singapore government's attempt to purchase M-109 Howitzers Self-Propelled artillery vehicles from the United States turned out to be a "fiasco".[178] The Singapore government showed interest in buying M-109s and tanks from the US in October 1969. In November, the US government authorised the American Embassy in Singapore to inform the Singapore government of the price and availability of the M-109s.[179] But on 17 March 1970, after delays in correspondence, the US Embassy was put in an awkward position when it had to inform the Singapore government that the M-109s were "out of production" and would no longer be available.[180] The Singapore government was "greatly disappointed" that the US government had reversed its "earlier commitment" to supply the M-109s.[181] Furthermore, news that a new shipment of M-109s that had recently arrived in Israel caused the Defence Ministry to question American intentions for not supplying Singapore with the M-109 artillery vehicles.[182] The US government offered the "105" or "8" Self-Propelled artillery vehicles instead, but Singapore remained solely interested in the M-109 and urged the US government

---

[177] Ibid.
[178] Colonel Canham, "Chronology on M-109 Fiasco", 17 July 1970, in DEF 19 Military Assistance (Defense Affairs 1970), Box 7, Subject Files of the Office of Indonesia, Malaysia and Singapore Affairs, 1965–74, RG 59, NACP.
[179] Ibid.
[180] Ibid.
[181] William H. Bruns, "Official-Informal Letter to Josiah W. Bennett, Country Director for Malaysia/Singapore", 21 July 1970, in DEF 19 Military Assistance (Defense Affairs 1970), Box 7, Subject Files of the Office of Indonesia, Malaysia and Singapore Affairs, 1965–74, RG 59, NACP.
[182] Ibid.

to find supplies from South Vietnam.[183] After the affair blew over, US Ambassador Cross reflected that: "It is only a small consolation that they [the Singapore government] lay the blame on our [US government] incompetence rather than on some malevolent motive."[184] The M-109 fiasco demonstrated the negative effects that unsuccessful military sales had on US-Singapore relations.

Supply of M60 Tanks

From the M-109 episode, the Singapore government learnt to go through less formal channels to test the response of the US government before making formal requests and risking embarrassment in case of rejection by Washington. In 1973, the Singapore Defence Ministry was interested in buying 40 M60 tanks from the United States. Ted Mataxis, a retired Brigadier General from the US Army and consultant to the MID, relayed Singapore's intentions to the US Ambassador, Edwin Cronk. The peculiarity of the request lay in the locations where the Singapore government intended to store the tanks. Mataxis told the ambassador that the MID planned to store the 40 M60 tanks in Taiwan or Thailand. When Ambassador Cronk conveyed the request to the US State Department on behalf of the Singapore government, he remarked: "I don't know what to make of the idea of storing the tanks in Taiwan or Thailand, but it does show some sensitivity to the political implications of parading these tanks around Singapore."[185] Cronk speculated that Singapore might be planning to use Taiwan and Thailand as training facilities for the SAF.

The US government was planning to reject Singapore's request to store the M60 tanks in a third country, but tried to hold back a response and delay the process. In a reply to Ambassador Cronk's letter, Arthur W.

---

[183] Canham, "M-109 Fiasco", 17 July 1970.

[184] Charles T. Cross, "Official-Informal Letter to Maurice D. Bean, Country Director of Malaysia-Singapore Affairs", 6 May 1970, in POL 1 General Policy (Political Affairs & Relations 1970), Box 8, Subject Files of the Office of Indonesia, Malaysia and Singapore Affairs, 1965–74, RG 59, NACP.

[185] Edwin M. Cronk, "Official-Informal Letter to Theodore J.C. Heavner, Country Director for Malaysia/Singapore", 10 May 1973, in DEF 19 Military Assistance–Army 1973, Box 11, Subject Files of the Office of Indonesia, Malaysia and Singapore Affairs, 1965–74, RG 59, NACP.

Hummel, Jr from the State Department instructed the American Embassy in Singapore to make clear that a formal request needed to be made by the Singapore government before any consideration was given. Hummel advised Cronk to "reserve judgment" on Singapore's proposal to store the tanks in Taiwan or Thailand until a formal request for the M60 tanks had been tendered.[186] By prolonging the process of acquiring the M60 tanks, the US government hoped that the Singapore government would eventually lose interest. After two months of silence from the Singapore government regarding the tanks, Cronk concluded that the faded interest for the M60 tanks was a "pipe dream" of the logistics director at Singapore's Defence Ministry, Ong Kah Kok, as well as Defence Minister, Goh Keng Swee.[187] It seemed that the US State Department and embassy in Singapore had averted another diplomatic imbroglio.

Apart from artillery vehicles, the Singapore government also expressed intentions to purchase the improved Hawk (I-Hawk) Air Defence system. Singapore's interest to buy two batteries, or 32 I-Hawk missiles, alarmed US State Department officials because it would cost the Singapore government over US$10 million.[188] Furthermore, Singapore's acquisition of the "very sophisticated" missiles would "cause envy and resentment in neighboring countries".[189] As a consequence, the US government introduced a guideline stating that

> [n]o offensive weapon which might threaten political repercussions or jeopardize SEA [Southeast Asian] stability should be considered for sale to Singapore unless we and/or the GOS have discussed it with other appropriate governments in the ASEAN and FPDA contexts.[190]

---

[186] Arthur W. Hummel, Jr, "For Ambassador from Hummel: Singapore Military Requests", May 1973, in DEF 19 Military Assistance–Army 1973, Box 11, Subject Files of the Office of Indonesia, Malaysia and Singapore Affairs, 1965–74, RG 59, NACP.

[187] Edwin M. Cronk, "Official-Informal Letter to Theodore J.C. Heavner, Country Director for Indonesia, Malaysia and Singapore", 9 July 1973, in DEF 19 Military Assistance General 1973, Box 11, Subject Files of the Office of Indonesia, Malaysia and Singapore Affairs, 1965–74, RG 59, NACP.

[188] Theodore J.C. Heavner, "Improved Hawk Missiles for Singapore", 30 November 1972, in DEF 19 Military Assistance–Army 1973, Box 11, Subject Files of the Office of Indonesia, Malaysia and Singapore Affairs, 1965–74, RG 59, NACP.

[189] Ibid.

[190] Ibid.

Hence, in order to block the purchase, the US government restricted the I-Hawk manufacturer, Raytheon Company, from disclosing classified information on the missiles to the Singapore Ministry of Defence. Nonetheless, Washington had no control over Singapore's attempts to purchase costly and advanced military equipment from other countries. Other than expressing interest for the I-Hawk Air Defence system, Singapore's Defence Ministry was also in talks with the British about the "Rapier" and conferring with the French about the "Crotale" Air Defence system.[191] Seeing that Singapore would acquire weapons from other sources anyway, the National Disclosure Committee of the US Defense Department eventually authorised Raytheon Company to disclose related 'Secret' information to the Defence Ministry during sales negotiations.[192] The State Department nonetheless emphasised that Raytheon needed to stress to the Singapore government that sharing of classified information should not be interpreted as "a commitment, express or implied, for the USG to approve eventual sale".[193] A separate request would still need to be submitted, should the Singapore government decide to purchase the missiles.

Supply of F-4

From 1971 to 1974, the Singapore government intermittently expressed the desire to purchase supersonic military aircraft, the F-4, from the United States.[194] The US government was hesitant to supply the advanced aircraft to Singapore for fear of setting off a regional arms race in Southeast Asia. If Singapore acquired the F-4 from the United States, it would be less able to integrate its air defence with the Five Power Integrated Air Defence

---

[191] Ibid.

[192] Norman E. Eliasson, "Exception to Policy - Singapore (NDPC Case No. 8010-72)", 17 November 1972, in DEF 19 Military Assistance–Army 1973, Box 11, Subject Files of the Office of Indonesia, Malaysia and Singapore Affairs, 1965–74, RG 59, NACP.

[193] Theodore J.C. Heavner, "Exception to Policy - Singapore (NPDC Case No. 8010-72)", 5 December 1972, in DEF 19 Military Assistance–Army 1973, Box 11, Subject Files of the Office of Indonesia, Malaysia and Singapore Affairs, 1965–74, RG 59, NACP.

[194] Theodore J.C. Heavner, "Singaporean Interest in F-4 Aircraft", 18 August 1972, in DEF 19 Air F-4 1973, Box 11, Subject Files of the Office of Indonesia, Malaysia and Singapore Affairs, 1965–74, RG 59, NACP.

system and thus undermine the cohesiveness of the FPDA. Eventually, Singapore dropped plans to buy the F-4s and decided to match its fleet with the Australian and New Zealand fleets of A4M aircraft at the signing of the FPDA. Ambassador Edwin Cronk reported in July 1973 that the Singapore government had ceased to talk about buying the F-4 aircraft, and surmised that the F-4s were "more of a gleam in Ong Kah Kok's eye than an active subject of defense planning in the Ministry".[195]

Plans to purchase the F-4 supersonic aircraft were revived in 1974, however, when Singapore's Ambassador to the US, Ernest Steven Monteiro, wrote to the Deputy Assistant Secretary for East Asia and Pacific Affairs, Richard Sneider, to request permission for a Singapore delegation to obtain classified information on the F-4 from McDonnell-Douglas.[196] The State Department decided not to obstruct Singapore's purchase of the F-4 any further because "if the GOS [had] decided to go supersonic, [the US government] should try to give the U.S. supplier ample opportunity to close the sale".[197] Hence, the State Department acceded to Ambassador Monteiro's request to allow the Singapore delegates access to information related to the F-4 aircraft from McDonnell-Douglas, but only after consultation with the US Embassies in Kuala Lumpur and Jakarta.[198]

REDUCING REGIONAL TENSIONS

Apart from supplying arms and providing training to the SAF, perhaps the most direct way the US contributed to Singapore's security was to keep fighting in Vietnam. The US Secretary of State during President Nixon's first term, William P. Rogers, described Lee's expectations of the US in the following way:

---

[195] Cronk, "Letter to Heavner", 9 July 1973.

[196] Ernest S. Monteiro, "Letter to Richard L. Sneider, Deputy Assistant Secretary, Bureau of East Asia and Pacific Affairs", 26 July 1974, in DEF 19 F4S, Box 12, Subject Files of the Office of Indonesia, Malaysia and Singapore Affairs, 1965–74, RG 59, NACP.

[197] Philip C. Gill, "F4s for Singapore", 12 August 1974, in DEF F4S, Box 12, Subject Files of the Office of Indonesia, Malaysia and Singapore Affairs, 1965–74, RG 59, NACP.

[198] Ibid.

[Lee] has come to realize that British disengagement in Southeast Asia is real and imminent. The realization has led him to two related beliefs:

1. That a <u>continuing American role</u> in Viet-Nam and in support of national and regional economic development programs <u>is vitally important</u> to <u>all of the nations of Southeast Asia</u>; and

2. that <u>the nations of the region</u> must use the time we have bought for them in Viet-Nam (his [Lee's] own formulation) to <u>strengthen themselves and to cooperate much more closely and effectively</u>.[199]

Of the many roles played by the United States in Singapore and the region, the government of Singapore regarded the most crucial role to be America's military engagement in Vietnam. According to Cross,

Singapore believes that only the United States can instill that confidence [that the spread of communism would not eventuate] and we [the US] cannot do so by words or even vast amounts of economic assistance and military equipment but only by our coolness and steadiness in settling Viet-Nam. Therein lies the greatest implication for American policy in terms of this tiny republic [Singapore].[200]

In a less direct but significant way, American ties with Singapore's neighbours, Malaysia and Indonesia, also contributed to Singapore's security in the subregion. Being a major supplier of military equipment to Singapore, the US government worked in concert with its embassies in Singapore, Kuala Lumpur and Jakarta to "enhance the FPDA and to minimize alarm among Singapore's neighbors".[201] Timely and opportune counsel from US ambassadors in Kuala Lumpur and Jakarta played down Singapore's 'poisoned shrimp' defence posture, as well as sources of tension between Singapore and its two neighbours. Differences in positions regarding Singapore's use of the Jungle Warfare School in Malaysia, water supply agreement between Singapore and Malaysia, and the Malaysian government's "overtures" to China were issues that hindered

---

[199] Rogers, "President's Meeting with Lee", 2 May 1969. Emphasis in original.
[200] Cross, "Letter to Green", 11 April 1971.
[201] Ibid.

Malaysia-Singapore rapprochement.[202] According to Ambassador Cross, Indonesia-Singapore cooperation lacked depth largely because Jakarta held the view that "Singapore's little navy and air force" were designed for defence against an Indonesian attack.[203] American mediation from the background not only benefited regional cooperation but also reduced the perception that Singapore was a threat to its larger neighbours. In April 1971, Ambassador Cross told US Assistant Secretary of State Marshall Green that there were probably some "diplomatic efforts" the US could make to help improve relations between Singapore and its neighbours but these should be "quiet and behind-the-scenes".[204]

CONCLUSION

The United States attempted to maintain the security of the Malaysia-Singapore subregion after the British withdrawal by pushing the Australian government to lead the FPDA. But diplomatic pressures from Washington failed to move Canberra towards greater engagement in the subregion. The US government then resorted to supplying US military equipment to the armed forces of Singapore and Malaysia. By 1973, the Singapore Armed Forces had grown considerably. Singapore's achievement was owed largely to American support in supplying the island with equipment and training, while enhancing Singapore's ship and aircraft repair industries by utilising Singapore's repair facilities. The SAF had established two infantry brigades, one reserve infantry brigade, one armoured brigade, one artillery command, two engineering battalions and one signal battalion, comprising a total of 14,500 personnel in its land forces.[205] Singapore's Navy consisted of approximately 1,000 personnel who received training at military schools in New Zealand and the US Naval War College.[206] The Republic of Singapore Air Force, staffed by approximately 1,400

---

[202] Ibid.

[203] Ibid.

[204] Ibid.

[205] "Singapore Armed Forces", February 1973, in Background (Singapore 1973), Box 11, Subject Files of the Office of Indonesia, Malaysia and Singapore Affairs, 1965–74, RG 59, NACP.

[206] Ibid.

personnel, 130 pilots, operated two Hawker Hunter squadrons, two flying training squadrons, two A4B squadrons, one Short Skyvan search and rescue team, one Bloodhound Air Defence Missile squadron and one anti-aircraft gun battalion.[207] Yet America's role in Singapore's defence was only one part of Washington's strategy in Singapore. Another indispensable contribution of the United States government to Singapore's survival was American economic support towards Singapore.

---

[207] Ibid.

CHAPTER 5

Activating Singapore's Economy

US Economic Diplomacy in Singapore

At the height of the Cold War in Southeast Asia, the American policy towards Singapore constituted a crucial part of a larger Southeast Asian strategy, which was to contain communist influence in the region by strengthening diplomatic relations among Indonesia, Malaysia and Singapore. The policy of the United States towards Singapore between 1965 and 1975 was to maintain Singapore's stability through economic assistance. From the beginning of 1966, after Singapore Prime Minister Lee Kuan Yew stopped criticising the US government in public, American trade with Singapore expanded. In less than a decade, the United States replaced Malaysia to become Singapore's top trading partner.[1] Accelerated growth in US-Singapore trade was the result of American investors expanding their operations into Southeast Asia through Singapore. Furthermore, the American military campaign in Vietnam benefitted Singapore through the use of the island's ship and aircraft repair facilities, as well as the transhipment of sundry supplies needed for the war. As American involvement in the Vietnam War escalated,

---

[1] Republic of Singapore Ministry of Finance, *Economic Survey of Singapore 1978* (Singapore: Ministry of Finance, 1978), p. 69. In 1975, Singapore's trade with the US reached S$4.8 billion, Singapore's trade with Malaysia hit S$4.4 billion, and trade with Japan was S$4.3 billion. Comparing the 1975 figures with the figures in 1970, Singapore's trade with Malaysia was S$2 billion, with Japan S$1.8 billion, and the United States S$1.3 billion.

war-related trade between Singapore and the US grew apace. By the time the American Embassy in Saigon closed in 1975, Singapore had evolved into an industrialised economy, and had begun to play a role in regional cooperation.[2] During the Johnson administration, the United States and Singapore strengthened diplomatic ties and laid the foundation for increased US-Singapore trade.

THE US FACTOR IN THE SUBREGION

American economic assistance to Singapore formed part of the US government's overall strategy towards Asia, and specifically what it designated as the Indonesia-Malaysia-Singapore subregion. The aim of the US government in the subregion was to reduce competition and enhance cooperation among Singapore, Malaysia and Indonesia. To be sure, it was not easy for an outside power to smoothen existing tensions among the three Southeast Asian governments. Relations between Singapore and Malaysia remained strained and acrimonious after the secession of Singapore from the Federation on 9 August 1965. Singapore-Indonesian relations did improve slightly after the end of *Konfrontasi* (1966) but deteriorated in 1968 when the Singapore government executed two Indonesian marines, who had been convicted of bombing attacks in Singapore during *Konfrontasi*.[3] When engaging with Singapore and Kuala Lumpur, the US government navigated carefully between the sensitivities of both governments, not wanting to appear partial to any side in its policies. Washington, however, did not adopt a policy of passivity towards Singapore-Malaysian relations. When American interests were at stake, the US government exerted its influence diplomatically, often working in the background. The US government aimed to induce the Singapore government not just to embrace regionalism, but to also contribute towards regional stability.

The improvement of diplomatic ties between Singapore and the United States after Lee Kuan Yew's meeting with William Bundy in March 1966 marked the start of trade and economic assistance from

---

[2] Huxley, *Defending the Lion City*, p. 35.
[3] Ibid.; Lee, *From Third World to First*, p. 264.

the US to Singapore. Lee's personal rapport with Bundy contributed greatly to the warming of US-Singapore relations. In his memoir, Lee referred to Bundy fondly, as someone he could "trust" and who "had an air of quiet confidence".[4] Reporting on his successful visit to Singapore, Bundy informed the State Department that his meeting with Lee

> found him more mellow, and may have opened the way to a more serious and deep relationship than we have ever had. He committed himself to accept an Ambassador, but was evasive on timing.[5]

US Consul General in Singapore, Richard Donald, similarly reported that Lee's attitude towards the elevation of the American consulate general to an embassy seemed to have changed, stating that Lee "had already decided in principle that this should take place but that it must be done in a 'very wily fashion' and on his own timing, on which he gave no clear indication".[6] The US Embassy in Singapore was established in April 1966 and Singapore's Embassy was set up a year later in Washington, D.C., in April 1967.[7] Shortly after Bundy ended his Singapore visit, the Singapore government and the United States established new platforms for trade and investments that catalysed Singapore's industrialisation and resolved the unemployment problem in Singapore.

When Lee met Bundy in 1966, he urged the American government not to take sides on Singapore-Malaysian affairs. He particularly warned Bundy that if the US government showed support for Malays in the communal conflicts between Malays and Chinese populations in Malaysia, the possibility of an accommodation between the Malays and Chinese in Malaysia would be gone.[8] Lee also warned Bundy that American attempts to interfere in racial conflicts in the subregion would be counter-productive. Bundy agreed that Washington ought to steer clear of racial matters in the subregion.[9] But other than on communal issues, the US

---

[4] Lee, *From Third World to First*, p. 453.
[5] Bundy, "Lee to Chiang", 14 March 1966.
[6] Richard Donald, "Memorandum of conversation: Lee Kuan Yew and William Bundy", 8 March 1966, in Lee Kuan Yew (2 of 2), Box 2, Subject Files of the Office of Indonesia, Malaysia and Singapore Affairs, 1965–74, RG 59, NACP.
[7] Berger, "Chargé in Singapore", 11 April 1966.
[8] "Memcon: PM Lee and Bundy", 8 March 1966.
[9] Ibid.

administration played an active role whenever opportunities arose for US diplomats in Singapore and Kuala Lumpur to facilitate positive relations between the two Southeast Asian countries.

Correspondence between the US Embassies in Singapore and Malaysia revealed that efforts were made by American diplomats to reduce the level of suspicion between the governments of Singapore and Malaysia. In March 1971, the US Ambassador to Singapore from 1969 to 1971, Charles Cross, wrote to his counterpart in Kuala Lumpur, Ambassador Jack Lydman. Commenting on unspecified and "largely unfounded" complaints against Singapore by Malaysia's Minister for Home Affairs, Ghazali Shafie, Cross told Lydman that he had not observed "anything recently that might have upset the Malaysians".[10] Cross suggested that it would be "useful" for Lydman to discuss "GOM's concerns about Singapore" with Ghazali, in the hope that

> [i]f you [Lydman] can get him [Ghazali] on this subject more frequently, it is possible that we might be able to do something in a quiet way about one or another of his complaints without of course getting in the middle or serving as a channel for him to the GOS.[11]

It is unclear how actively Ambassadors Cross and Lydman played peacemakers between Malaysia and Singapore, but their correspondence suggested that the American diplomats saw the former's usefulness as mediators. Former Singapore diplomat Mushahid Ali reveals another element in US-Singapore relations. He observed that the US diplomats would ask Singapore officials about the Malaysian government because the US diplomats "found that Singaporeans have an insight into what was going on in Malaysia which they did not have and ... the Malaysians were not prepared to share with them".[12]

The United States government adopted the same approach towards Singapore-Indonesian relations. The US government promoted Singapore-

---

[10] Charles T. Cross, "Official-Informal Letter Honorable Jack W. Lydman, American Ambassador, Malaysia", 25 March 1971, in POL 1.1 Incoming Official-Informal Correspondence (Singapore 1971), Box 8, Subject Files of the Office of Indonesia, Malaysia and Singapore Affairs, 1965–74, RG 59, NACP.

[11] Ibid.

[12] Interview with Mushahid Ali, 27 November 2014.

Indonesian ties by encouraging the Singapore government to invest more in the Indonesian economy in 1970. The Singapore government intended to develop cordial relations with Indonesia on the condition that neither country would interfere in each other's domestic affairs.[13] Whereas Singapore and Malaysia explicitly acknowledged the indivisibility of their mutual security, which compelled each country not to take any action that would threaten the other, the case of Indonesian-Singapore security was more subtle. Mushahid Ali recalls that it took some time before Singapore and Indonesia tacitly understood the indivisibility of their security.[14] When Marshall Green was US Ambassador to Indonesia in 1969, he met Singapore Finance Minister, Goh Keng Swee, to discuss investment possibilities in Indonesia.[15] One year later, Goh wrote to Green, who had become Assistant Secretary of State for East Asia and Pacific Affairs at the State Department, to inform Green of the progress Singapore investments had made since the beginning of 1970. Under the inducement of US diplomats posted to Singapore and Jakarta, the Singapore government encouraged Singapore businessmen to develop tourism and hospitality in the Indonesian island of Bali, providing 49 per cent of the finances used to build hotels in Bali.[16] Singaporean investors were involved in several industries—rubber production, logging, flour milling, banking, iron and steel production, electrical products, food making, and hospitality. For the first three months of 1970, these companies invested approximately $50 million in Indonesia.[17]

The Singapore government's economic links with Indonesia were not only aimed at enhancing regional economic cooperation, but were also in response to the US government's reluctance to offer direct economic

---

[13] Ang, *Lee Kuan Yew's Strategic Thought*, p. 20.

[14] Interview with Mushahid Ali, 27 November 2014. A case in point would be formal relations with the PRC. Singapore established formal diplomatic ties with the PRC only after Indonesia had done so in 1990.

[15] Goh Keng Swee, "Letter to Marshall Green, Assistant Secretary of State for East Asia and Pacific Affairs", 8 June 1970, in POL Indonesia 1970, Box 8, Subject Files of the Office of Indonesia, Malaysia and Singapore Affairs, 1965–74, RG 59, NACP.

[16] Ibid.

[17] Ibid. Figures are derived from a table appended in Goh Keng Swee's report to Marshall Green. Some figures are quoted in US dollars and converted to Singapore dollars here with an approximate exchange rate of US$1 to S$3.

aid to the Singapore government. Despite the US State Department's recommendation for more economic assistance to Singapore, the American economic policy towards Singapore excluded direct grants for subsidising Singapore's economic plans. In November 1966, the Adviser to the President on Southeast Asia Economic and Social Development, Eugene Black, led an economic mission to Thailand, Indonesia, Malaysia and Singapore to explore ways in which the United States could support the region's economic development.[18] The Black mission held talks with Singapore's prime minister, defence and finance ministers, the Economic Development Board (EDB) and the Port of Singapore Authority (PSA) to explore areas where the United States could assist Singapore.

In a meeting with delegates of the Black mission, Singapore Finance Minister Lim Kim San and Defence Minister Goh Keng Swee spoke of how Singapore's economy was in need of urgent help from the US.[19] In particular, Lim attempted to convince the American delegates of the severity of Singapore's unemployment problem. Despite Singapore's high growth rate of almost 10 per cent per annum,[20] Lim asserted, Singapore lacked new industries to provide enough jobs for its citizens.[21] Positing a worst-case scenario, Lim stressed that prolonged high unemployment in Singapore would lead to political instability, which would result in a loss of confidence by foreign investors. If foreign investors were to withdraw their businesses from the island one after another, Singapore's economy would be in crisis.[22] Lim noted that the lack of skilled workers

---

[18] Robert W. Barnett, "Black Visit to Singapore", December 1966, in Aid–General (Singapore 1966), Box 3, Bureau of Far Eastern Affairs. Office of the Country Director for Malaysia and Singapore. Records Relating to Malaysia and Singapore, compiled 1963–66, RG 59, NACP.

[19] Goh Keng Swee held the post of Defence Minister from 9 August 1965 to August 1967. He exchanged portfolio with Lim Kim San in August 1967 and became Finance Minister. See "Morning Briefing–Malaysia-Singapore, Indonesia", 21 August 1967, in POL 7 Visits. Meetings (POL–Political Aff. and Rel.), Box 1, Subject Files of the Office of Indonesia, Malaysia and Singapore Affairs, 1965–74, RG 59, NACP.

[20] Republic of Singapore Ministry of Trade and Industry, *Economic Survey of Singapore 1988* (Singapore: Ministry of Trade and Industry, 1988), p. ix. Singapore's Gross Domestic Product expanded at approximately 9.9 per cent per year in 1960 and 14.9 per cent per year in 1970.

[21] Barnett, "Black Visit to Singapore", December 1966.

[22] Ibid.

in Singapore was a hurdle that needed to be tackled in order to attract foreign manufacturing companies. To deal with the problem, the Singapore government developed a five-year training plan that would cost the government US$60–70 million. Lim asked if the US government could offer some form of assistance for the training plan. The Black mission acquiesced in Lim's analysis but told the minister that country-specific projects were less likely to gain US Congressional approval than multi-lateral Asian initiatives for regional development.[23] The Singapore ministers shifted the discussion from seeking monetary aid to soliciting ways in which the US could open its market to Singapore's exports. Nevertheless, the Black mission was unable to offer tangible assistance, apart from advising that the Singapore government "should survey the entire United States market, identify products for which relatively free access was traditional, and then encourage their production in Singapore".[24] All in all, the Black mission did not result in concrete solutions for Singapore's economic difficulties. Nonetheless, Eugene Black's economic mission led the Singapore Prime Minister, Lee Kuan Yew, to commend the calibre of American officials. In Lee's letter to Black, he wrote:

> I thought you and your team would like to know that my colleagues and I were agreeably impressed by the calibre of the men that the President sent out.… It was … reassuring that now Americans in high places who decide policies which will shape the destinies of hundreds of millions of people in this region are men of ability, whose approach to the complex problems of this area are both subtle and sophisticated.[25]

America's economic assistance towards Indonesia, Malaysia and Singapore took varied forms. According to a 1968 National Policy Paper on the Indonesia, Malaysia and Singapore subregion, Malaysia received approximately US$58 million in loans from the Export-Import Bank

---

[23] Ibid. As early as 1965, the American Ambassador to Malaysia, James Bell, had spoken about "more emphasis on a multi-lateral rather than a bi-lateral approach" for US economic aid to less developed countries. See "Economic Aid: Bell explains", *The Straits Times*, 18 October 1965, p.1.

[24] Barnett, "Black Visit to Singapore", December 1966.

[25] Lee, "Letter to Eugene Black", 6 December 1966, in Memos - Singapore (Vol. I) 8/65–7/67, Box 281, National Security File. Country File. Asia and the Pacific, LBJL.

of the United States.[26] Since April 1966, the US government had provided the Indonesian government with US$76 million in loans and aids, and added a further US$27 million in 1968.[27] Instead of generous loans and grants, however, US economic assistance to Singapore came in the form of US-Singapore trade. Apart from direct US-Singapore trade, the US State Department also increased Singapore's trade with regional countries through aid agreements signed between the US and other Southeast Asian countries—Indonesia and Thailand. A US$10 million loan agreement signed between the US government and the Indonesian government facilitated the sale of goods produced by American companies in Singapore into Indonesia.[28] Following the same model, American-funded construction projects in Thailand increased demand for supplies from US manufacturers based in Singapore.[29] These arrangements provided jobs for Singaporeans and a ready market for products manufactured in Singapore. From 1966 to 1968, US Ambassador to Singapore, Francis Galbraith, promoted Singapore as a regional hub with favourable financial and labour conditions for US investments. Ambassador Galbraith urged the State Department to encourage US diplomats posted to the region to base their families in Singapore.[30] Although American interests were foremost in his considerations, Galbraith served not just as America's ambassador to Singapore, but at times also as Singapore's spokesman to American investors. During the Johnson administration, Galbraith's dual role contributed towards a better understanding of America with regard to Singapore.

During the late 1960s, the Singapore government began developing regional initiatives to complement its domestic economic projects. Besides

---

[26] US Department of State, "NPP: Indonesia, Malaysia and Singapore", 6 February 1968.

[27] Ibid.

[28] Francis J. Galbraith, "Official-Informal Letter to Maurice D. Bean, Country Director of Malaysia/Singapore: Procurement for Singapore", 14 April 1967, in POL 15–1 Ambassador Galbraith's Official-Informals, Box 5, Subject Files of the Office of Indonesia, Malaysia and Singapore Affairs, 1965–74, RG 59, NACP.

[29] Ibid.

[30] John B. Dexter, "Official-Informal Letter to Maurice D. Bean, Country Director of Malaysia/Singapore", 12 May 1967, in POL 15–1 Ambassador Galbraith's Official-Informals, Box 5, Subject Files of the Office of Indonesia, Malaysia and Singapore Affairs, 1965–74, RG 59, NACP.

rapid industrialisation of its domestic economy, the Singapore government concurrently developed its credentials as a Southeast Asian regional centre. Singapore's regionalisation strategy was a response to Eugene Black's advice given in November 1966, when he explained to Goh Keng Swee and Lim Kim San that the US Congress was more likely to support projects that involved more than one country.[31] Having understood that aid was more likely to be granted for regional projects, the Singapore government initiated regional projects so that US grants would indirectly flow into Singapore. In 1969, the US Embassy in Singapore reported that

> [i]n a recent speech GOS Minister for Science and Technology Dr. Toh Chin Chye gave cogent and illuminating reasons for Singapore's support for regionalism. "We cannot regard Singapore's economic development in isolation," said Dr. Toh. "There is no doubting the need for Singapore to involve itself in cooperative projects which will bring economic and social benefits to countries in this region. A more active participation by Singapore in such projects will build us a reserve of goodwill and also help towards establishing our political position in Southeast Asia."[32]

Since the establishment of regional centres in Singapore attracted sponsorship from the United Nations and the US Agency for International Development (USAID), the Singapore government accelerated the drive towards regionalism. In addition to increased funding, the UN and USAID also committed facilities and staff that developed the executive and management skills of local employees. To ensure a steady flow of sponsorships, the Singapore government maintained a track record of effective regional projects that it played an active role in, such as the Asian Development Bank (ADB) and the Southeast Asian Ministers of Education Organization (SEAMEO).[33]

Singapore's economic strategy of initiating regional projects complemented US Congress' preference for funding regional projects rather than country-specific proposals. Charles Cross, proposed that the US

---

[31] Barnett, "Black Visit to Singapore", December 1966.

[32] Donald F. Meyers, "Singapore and Regionalism", 8 April 1969, in POL 15–1 Ambassador's Correspondence 1969, Box 3, Subject Files of the Office of Indonesia, Malaysia and Singapore Affairs, 1965–74, RG 59, NACP.

[33] Meyers, "Singapore and Regionalism", 8 April 1969.

government should utilise "American economic presence in Singapore" to help Singapore play a role in regional development.[34] He felt that Singapore should be a "thinking center" and that the US Embassy should strive to "fit Singapore into existing USG plans and programs in the area so that Singapore's contributions can be complementary" to overall US approach towards Southeast Asia.[35] Inheriting Galbraith's enthusiasm in promoting Singapore, Cross attempted to elevate Singapore's importance in Washington's containment strategy in Southeast Asia. Cross commented that Singapore's development as a prosperous new nation with a growing regional role could be cited as a product of the success and patience of American strategy in the region. Furthermore, the Singapore example also reflected the importance of effective local governance since US support for projects led by other Southeast Asian states were not always successful.

The United States Embassy in Singapore concluded that regional projects mooted by the Singapore government seemed "destined to develop with reasonable assurance of success".[36] Singapore-initiated regional projects that USAID supported included the Regional English Language Centre (RELC), Southeast Asian Fisheries Development Centre, and regional transportation and communications surveys. The RELC, which opened in February 1968, was involved in organising seminars, facilitating research projects, and attracting professional visitors into Singapore. The Centre, a joint venture between USAID and the Singapore government, began with a five-year budget of US$4 million, of which USAID sponsored half of the funds.[37] The Southeast Asian Fisheries Development Centre that was based in Singapore received a US$60,000 sponsorship. Other regional projects such as regional surveys for transportation and communications, which included aeronautical telecommunications, flight inspection, air sea rescue, and marine navigational aids in the Strait of Malacca, received US$202,000 from USAID.[38] The survey of marine navigational aids along the Strait of Malacca also attracted Japanese interest and received an additional sponsorship of US$250,000 from the Japanese government, as well as the

---

[34] Cross, "Embassy Conference 1970", 9 April 1970.
[35] Ibid.
[36] Meyers, "Singapore and Regionalism", 8 April 1969.
[37] Ibid.
[38] Ibid.

participation of a Japanese team of surveyors.[39] The coordination of regional projects not only gave the Singapore government the aid it needed from the US, but also attracted other sources of support, most evident in the Strait of Malacca project.

There was, however, one exception to US refusal to finance Singapore-based projects. In August 1966, a recommendation was made for a US$15 million loan to the Port of Singapore Authority to finance the building of four deep water berths, a new port engineer's plant yard and workshop, replacement and provision of additional floating craft and cargo handling equipment, and provision of data processing equipment.[40] The loan enabled Singapore to develop its port—one of its most vital economic assets—and came with generous financing terms of 6 per cent interest per annum, repayable over 25 years.[41] American assistance to the PSA was exceptional because it complemented Washington's plans to increase US-Singapore trade and served the interests of both the United States and Singapore. Although substantial, the economic aid received through Singapore's regional projects could not match the US-Singapore trade that expanded exponentially from 1966.

UNITED STATES-SINGAPORE ECONOMIC PARTNERSHIP DURING THE VIETNAM WAR

It was perhaps Singapore's good fortune that the United States' military involvement in Vietnam had escalated after March 1965. The US government needed a suitable procurement office for war supplies and Singapore fitted the bill. In January 1966, the State Department and the consulate general in Singapore made "vigorous" recommendations "to improve the export

---

[39] Ibid.

[40] Bernard Zagorin, "Letter from Bernard Zagorin, U.S. Alternate Executive Director, to the Secretary, National Advisory Council on International Monetary and Financial Policies, U.S. Department of Treasury", 5 August 1966, in Aid - General (Singapore 1966), Box 3, Bureau of Far Eastern Affairs. Office of the Country Director for Malaysia and Singapore. Records Relating to Malaysia and Singapore, compiled 1963–66, RG 59, NACP.

[41] Ibid.

opportunities for Singapore by any legitimate means available".[42] The
State Department listed attributes that supported Singapore's suitability
as the main procurement centre for the US military based in Vietnam.
In an action memorandum calling for more US economic assistance
to Singapore, Rutherford Poats from the USAID argued that because
of Singapore's location, it was in an "advantageous position to supply
rapidly to Vietnam".[43] Also, Singapore could often supply at a cheaper
price because of efficiency in manufacturing and handling shipments.[44]
Furthermore, Singapore was becoming an "increasingly substantial supplier
under U.S. Government-financed procurement for Vietnam".[45] Hence, on
15 March 1966, days after Bundy's meeting with Lee Kuan Yew, the
United States government designated Singapore "as a 'developing country'
and [therefore] given priority status in the United States Procurement
Program".[46] Vietnam War-related trade with Singapore expanded rapidly
after the US government included Singapore into the Vietnam procurement
program, which "sparked a modest consumer boom".[47] Singapore Finance
Minister, Goh Keng Swee, reported in his budgetary statement in 1967
that Singapore took export orders amounting to S$300 million from
South Vietnam in 1966.[48] Goh also reported revenue from the business
brought by American troops on combat leave in Singapore.[49]

Shortly after the Lee-Bundy meeting, American servicemen from
Vietnam arrived on the island for combat leave. Lee described it as

---

[42] Rutherford M. Poats, "Action Memorandum for the Deputy Administrator: To
determine the eligibility of Singapore under Program Determination 31, concerning
restriction of procurement to the U.S. or LDCs meeting certain conditions", 18 January
1966, in Aid–General (Singapore 1966), Box 3, Bureau of Far Eastern Affairs. Office
of the Country Director for Malaysia and Singapore. Records Relating to Malaysia and
Singapore, compiled 1963–66, RG 59, NACP.

[43] Ibid.

[44] Ibid.

[45] Ibid.

[46] Albert N. Abajian, "Letter from Albert N. Abajian, Associate Director of International
Marketing Institute, to Lim Ho Hup, Director of Economic Development Board of
Singapore", 31 May 1966, in Aid - General (Singapore, 1966), Box 3, Bureau of Far
Eastern Affairs. Office of the Country Director for Malaysia and Singapore. Records
Relating to Malaysia and Singapore, compiled 1963–66, RG 59, NACP.

[47] McMahon, *The Limits of Empire*, p. 142.

[48] Chan, *Singapore: The Politics of Survival*, p. 46.

[49] Ibid.

"a quiet way of showing support for America's effort in Vietnam".[50] He recalled that about 20,000 US military personnel arrived in Singapore in a year, making up 7 per cent of the total number of tourists of that time.[51] The Rest and Recuperation Program, which began in 1966, was an impetus for Singapore's tourism and hospitality boom during the late 1960s.[52] Tourist traffic in Singapore grew by 30.7 per cent in 1966 to 59.2 per cent, 22.5 per cent and 62.7 per cent in 1967, 1968 and 1969 respectively.[53] In 1967, 39 US Navy ships and more than 11,000 American sailors and officers took their shore leave in Singapore.[54] The number of US military personnel on R&R increased the following year, and in 1969, the US Embassy in Singapore reported that an average of 1,600 US servicemen arrived in Singapore each month, and about US$300 was spent by each person visiting Singapore on R&R totalling in excess of US$500,000 per month.[55] According to a letter by Ambassador Cross written in 1970, Singapore had become a destination for "the enormous number of high brass military visitors who seem[ed] to have discovered Singapore as the most likeable R&R center in the area".[56] Singapore was such a popular site for the US Rest and Recuperation Program that, in early 1971, the US Embassy in Singapore sought permission from the Singapore government to allow American servicemen stationed in Thailand to also use Singapore as "a site for environmental and morale leave".[57]

---

[50] Lee, *From Third World to First*, p. 453.

[51] Ibid.

[52] "Non-embassy USG Presence in Singapore", 23 November 1969. See also Ang, "Singapore and the Vietnam War", p. 364.

[53] Lim Chong Yah and Ow Chwee Huay, "The Economic Development of Singapore in the Sixties and Beyond", in *The Singapore Economy*, ed. You Poh Seng and Lim Chong Yah (Singapore: Eastern Universities Press, 1971), p. 30.

[54] Galbraith, "Letter to Bundy", 24 June 1968.

[55] "Non-embassy USG Presence in Singapore", 23 November 1969.

[56] Cross, "Letter to Bean", 6 May 1970.

[57] William H. Bruns, "Letter to Stanley Stewart, Permanent Secretary, Ministry of Foreign Affairs, Singapore", 19 January 1971, in POL 1.1 Incoming Official-Informal Correspondence (Singapore 1971), Box 8, Subject Files of the Office of Indonesia, Malaysia and Singapore Affairs, 1965–74, RG 59, NACP. Malaysia was also used for the R&R Program but the Malaysian government had to terminate the Program because of strong domestic outcry. See Sodhy, *The US-Malaysian Nexus*, pp. 282–3.

The Singapore government's approval was granted shortly.[58] The tourism and hospitality boom in Singapore not only contributed to Singapore's GDP and foreign exchange earnings, but the growing industry also absorbed many of the workers previously employed on the British military base.[59]

Perhaps the most critical contribution the United States government made to the Singapore economy was the utilisation of Singapore's naval dockyards that were vacated by the British. After the British withdrawal was announced in July 1967 and January 1968, the growing presence of the US Seventh Fleet demonstrated US interest in Singapore's security and boosted US investors' confidence in Singapore.[60] In 1966, British military spending amounted to S$550 million, or 16.3 per cent of Singapore's Gross Domestic Product. After the announcement of Britain's military withdrawal, Britain's military expenditure in Singapore shrank to 8.6 per cent of Singapore's GDP in 1969.[61] In addition, Britain's military withdrawal directly led to the unemployment of 40,000 civilian workers.

During this period, the profitability of the ship repair business for Singapore gradually became apparent. The American Embassy reported that US Army and Navy repair contracts brought in revenue of close to US$3.25 million for Singapore in 1969, and signed contracts worth up to US$7.4 million in 1970.[62] The average number of ships stopping for repairs between 1968 and 1970 was 52 visits per year.[63] By the first half of 1971, the number of ships arriving in Singapore for repairs

[58] William H. Bruns, "Official-Informal Letter to John P. Heimann, Country Officer for Malaysia and Singapore", 9 February 1971, in POL 1.1 Incoming Official-Informal Correspondence (Singapore 1971), Box 8, Subject Files of the Office of Indonesia, Malaysia and Singapore Affairs, 1965–74, RG 59, NACP.

[59] Lim and Ow, "The Economic Development of Singapore", pp. 31–2.

[60] For an analysis of how the US Seventh Fleet began utilising Singapore's naval dockyard and the political and security aspects of US presence in Singapore, see Chapter 4.

[61] Lim and Ow, "The Economic Development of Singapore", pp. 12–3. The figure of S$550 million is in 1970 terms, and approximately US$180 million.

[62] "Non-embassy USG Presence in Singapore", 23 November 1969.

[63] Laird, "US Utilization of Singapore Naval and Air Facilities", 3 August 1971.

already exceeded the total number of ship visits in the previous year. The more days US military vessels berthed in Singapore for repairs, the more revenue was generated. In 1971, the US vessels stayed a total of 29 days longer in Singapore compared with 1970, and brought in more tourist revenue from the thousands of US Navy servicemen who waited for the repairs to be completed.[64] The number of ship visits had to be reduced in November 1971 when the British Navy deployed three large ships to carry out withdrawal operations.[65] That year, the number of ship visits reached 90 and dropped slightly to 86 visits in 1972.[66] In the first quarter of 1973, the US Seventh Fleet made 35 visits to the Singapore naval dockyard and signed contracts indicated that US ship visits would exceed 100 that year.[67] From 1969, Singapore supplied US$200 million of petroleum products annually to American military vessels repaired in Singapore, or to those that had stopped for refuelling.[68]

By the end of 1969, Singapore's concerns over the economic impact of the British withdrawal had been substantially overcome by the commercialisation of former British bases to repair US vessels and the trade brought about by the involvement of American troops in the Vietnam War. The Vietnam War ensured Singapore's economic viability. Increases in repair contracts for US ships and aircraft in Singapore created corresponding reductions in repair contracts at Sasebo, Japan, and Guam because Singapore was able to offer repair contracts that were cheaper and met repair schedules more efficiently than the other Western Pacific repair facilities used by the US.[69] According to the Country Director for Indonesia, Malaysia and Singapore Affairs at the US State Department, Theodore Heavner, in 1971–72 the "level of aircraft and ship repairs in Singapore [was] the result in part of a White

---

[64] Ibid.

[65] Ibid.

[66] "US Naval Presence", 1 February 1973, in Background (Singapore 1973), Box 11, Subject Files of the Office of Indonesia, Malaysia and Singapore Affairs, 1965–74, RG 59, NACP.

[67] Ibid.

[68] "Non-embassy USG Presence in Singapore", 23 November 1969.

[69] Laird, "US Utilization of Singapore Naval and Air Facilities", 3 August 1971.

House directive to increase [America's] use of Singapore facilities".[70] The directive to increase the number of USN ship visits to Singapore aimed to minimise the chance of Soviet Union warships utilising vacant berths in the Singapore dockyard.[71] Lee Kuan Yew's appeal to US Ambassador Charles Cross in February 1971 to increase US repair contracts, as well as Cross' persistence in getting a decision "at the highest level to make such increases", contributed to the rise in number of ship repair contracts in Singapore.[72]

Both Washington and the Singapore governments welcomed the increase of repair contracts for US military vessels and aircraft in Singapore. According to Ambassador Cross, increased visits by US military vessels were an indication of "a continuing American interest in the area, thus serving as a deterrent to China".[73] In 1971, Ambassador Cross argued that the US could benefit from maintaining a military presence in Singapore while withdrawing troops from Vietnam: "[W]e can underline the fact that we are not retreating from Southeast Asia by the use of Singapore facilities for the repair and maintenance of US naval vessels and aircraft and by low key but frequent ship visits."[74] The psychological boost provided by visits of American military vessels and personnel was significant to Singapore, and only overshadowed by the substantial economic benefits that the repair contracts brought. Although the US government had been careful not to give any commitment to protect Singapore against external attacks, an American military presence facilitated the development of Singapore's defence and confidence in a post-British withdrawal security environment.[75] According to Ambassador Cross' successor, Edwin Cronk, Sembawang naval dockyard in Singapore

---

[70] Theodore J.C. Heavner, "US and Soviet Use of Singapore", 15 February 1972, in DEF 13 Logistics Matters (Soviet Navy) 1972, Box 10, Subject Files of the Office of Indonesia, Malaysia and Singapore Affairs, 1965–74, RG 59, NACP.

[71] Ibid.

[72] Cross, "Memcon: US Repair Program", 24 July 1971.

[73] Cross, "Letter to Green", 11 April 1971.

[74] Ibid.

[75] Ibid.

was "becoming a favorite port of call for the Seventh Fleet" and the Singapore government seemed "delighted" with these ship visits.[76] Ambassador Cronk added that:

> They [the GOS] like the fact that the Seventh Fleet is maintaining a visible presence in the area—and hope it will continue in the post-Viet-Nam period—and, of course, they like the tourist and other income derived. I've [Cronk] told people in the Foreign Ministry and Defense [of Singapore] to let me know if they want to slow this down for any reason, but their attitude seems to be the more the better. So, at the moment at least, the welcome mat is out.[77]

Like the naval dockyards vacated by the British when they withdrew from Singapore, the air bases that the Singapore government took over also provided substantial revenue. The revenue generated by the budding aviation industry in Singapore and the rehiring of workers laid off by the British reduced the negative economic impact of the British withdrawal. US aviation companies, Lockheed Air Services and Grumman Corporation, established aircraft repair operations in Singapore with support from both the US and Singapore governments. In 1971, Lockheed was awarded aircraft repair and maintenance contracts for US Navy C-121s and C-130s, US Air Force C-121s, and T-28 aircraft. These aircraft repair contracts amounted to US$2 million in 1972.[78] The aviation maintenance facilities were also used for regional operations. Lockheed and Grumman used Singapore's repair facilities for repairing helicopters deployed in Vietnam. Lockheed's C-130 repair contracts from Vietnam and Indonesia were also carried out in Singapore.[79] According to the State Department, keeping Lockheed operational in Singapore served "the purpose of retaining U.S. access and denying or minimizing access by the Soviet Union" to

---

[76] Edwin M. Cronk, "Official-Informal Letter to Theodore J.C. Heavner, Country Director for Indonesia, Malaysia and Singapore", 18 December 1972, in DEF 15 U.S. Use of Military Facilities 1972, Box 10, Subject Files of the Office of Indonesia, Malaysia and Singapore Affairs, 1965–74, RG 59, NACP.

[77] Ibid.

[78] Laird, "US Utilization of Singapore Naval and Air Facilities", 3 August 1971; Cross, "Memcon: US Repair Program", 24 July 1971.

[79] Cross, "Memcon: US Repair Program", 24 July 1971.

Singapore's air bases.[80] Hence, to ensure the viability of Lockheed Air Services in Singapore, a White House directive was passed in 1971 to increase the usage of Singapore's "strategic facilities by U.S. military aircraft and naval vessels".[81]

After a promising start, however, inability to attain sufficient contracts from the US Department of Defense gave Lockheed a difficult year in 1973. Lockheed and the DOD disagreed on the volume of contracts needed for Lockheed to be profitable in Singapore. According to the US State Department, DOD would not give Lockheed "as much work as they say they need" because the DOD did not feel that Lockheed had reached the point where it had to "pull-out" of Singapore because of the lack of contracts.[82] In other words, Lockheed had been trying to secure more DOD contracts with the argument that operations were at risk of becoming unsustainable. Country Director Theodore Heavner further remarked that if Lockheed were to pull out of Singapore in the short-term, it would hurt US standing with the Singapore government, "but not to an unacceptable extent".[83] DOD was right to conclude that Lockheed's operations in Singapore were not likely to fold. The Direct Procurement Program initiated by the White House directive exempted Lockheed from a competitive bidding process and guaranteed DOD contracts for Lockheed's facilities in Singapore of up to 300,000 man-hours. By 1974, the Direct Procurement Program had created over US$7 million of business for Lockheed in Singapore.[84]

American involvement in Singapore's economic development was only one side of the story. The Singapore government's implementation of the country's industrialisation plan, starting from 1961, established conditions that made Singapore an attractive investment destination for

---

[80] Theodore J.C. Heavner, "Your 4:00 O'clock Appointment with Mr. Ferraro and Lockheed Air Services Singapore (LASS) (Direct Procurement for FY-75)", 8 April 1974, in DEF 15 U.S. Use of Military Facilities (LASS) 1974, Box 12, Subject Files of the Office of Indonesia, Malaysia and Singapore Affairs, 1965–74, RG 59, NACP.

[81] Ibid.

[82] Theodore J.C. Heavner, "Briefing Book for Mr. Green's Asian Trip - Special Problems", 23 February 1972, in Briefing Papers 1972, Box 10, Subject Files of the Office of Indonesia, Malaysia and Singapore Affairs, 1965–74, RG 59, NACP.

[83] Ibid.

[84] Heavner, "Ferraro and LASS", 8 April 1974.

American companies. The linchpin of Singapore's industrialisation plan was Jurong Industrial Estate.[85] Located in the southwestern part of Singapore's main island, Jurong was considered "absolutely crucial" for Singapore's economic development.[86] "In fact," as geographer Chiang Tao-Chang argues, "the question whether Singapore would survive as a viable and prosperous island Republic would be largely determined by the success or failure of the industrialization of Jurong".[87] Jurong Industrial Estate was part of a plan for the Singapore economy to focus less on entrepôt trade and more on industries. Economists Lim Chong Yah and Ow Chwee Huay attributed the sharp decrease of Singapore's entrepôt trade to the cessation of trade with Indonesia during *Konfrontasi*, where Singapore-Indonesian trade fell by 24.1 per cent in 1964.[88] In addition, the shift towards industrialisation was an attempt to address three economic conditions in the subregion: Singapore's high unemployment rate; the opening of competing ports in Malaysia and Indonesia to avoid dependence on Singapore; and the rapid industrialisation of Singapore's neighbours.[89]

Like Chiang, the World Bank and other economists who conducted economic surveys in Singapore during the 1950s and 60s assessed that Malaya and Singapore should merge to form a federation with "an industrial orientation as its modernisation thrust".[90] In 1961, after a United Nations Survey Mission led by Dutch economist Albert Winsemius visited Singapore, the Singapore government established the Economic Development Board (EDB) and adopted the Winsemius mission's proposals to implement a "radical program of industrial development".[91] The Singapore government took up the recommendations of the Winsemius mission and even hired Winsemius to be Singapore's economic advisor from 1961 to 1984. His

---

[85] Lim and Ow, "The Economic Development of Singapore", p. 7.
[86] Chiang Tao-Chang, *The Jurong Industrial Estate: Present Pattern and Future Prospects* (Singapore: Institute of Southeast Asia, Nanyang University, 1969), p. 8.
[87] Ibid.
[88] Lim and Ow, "The Economic Development of Singapore", p. 10.
[89] Chiang, *Jurong Industrial Estate*, p. 1.
[90] Linda Low, et al., *Challenge and Response: Thirty Years of the Economic Development Board* (Singapore: Times Academic Press, 1993), pp. 4–5.
[91] Chiang, *Jurong Industrial Estate*, p. 5.

assistant, I-Fang Tang, was also employed by the Singapore government and eventually became Chairman of the EDB. In 1963, because of its relative wealth, Singapore possessed almost as large a market as the rest of Malaysia; Malaysia's domestic market thus had the potential to expand faster than Singapore's.[92] Indeed, the incentive for establishing a tariff-free common market with Malaysia was not just the size of the market there, but also the potential that it had for growth. Hence, the success of Jurong had been premised on Singapore's merger with Malaysia, which comprised a growing market of over 11 million people.[93] Furthermore, the common market with Malaya, Sabah and Sarawak would be a great attraction for foreign investors.[94] Nevertheless, optimism about common market with Malaysia fizzled after the separation and Jurong risked being redundant after investments had been made to develop its infrastructure and amenities.[95] It was, therefore, crucial that the Singapore government attracted enough foreign investments into Jurong to justify the resources poured into the Industrial Estate.

During Lee Kuan Yew's first official visit to the United States, he vigorously promoted Singapore to US investors. By then, Singapore had already become part of the USAID Investment Guarantee Program, which insured US capital against losses resulting from political instability in Singapore. Lee and Finance Minister Goh, in a bid to attract more US investors, promised that American investors would be given preferential treatment in Singapore.[96] To the president of General Instrument, Goh said, "Tell us what you want; we'll see that you get it."[97] When the Business Committee of the American Association, comprising the heads of leading American businesses in Singapore, was eager to donate money to build an American school, the Singapore government offered tax exemptions

---

[92] Ibid.

[93] Ibid.

[94] Ibid. Lim and Ow report that manufacturing establishments grew from 548 in 1960 to 1,000 in 1965. See Lim and Ow, "The Economic Development of Singapore", p. 7.

[95] The former Chairman of EDB accounted for how Jurong Industrial Estate was developed. See Chan Chin Bock et al., *Heart Work* (Singapore: Singapore Economic Development Board, 2002), pp. 179–84.

[96] Galbraith, "Letter to Bundy", 18 September 1968.

[97] Ibid.

for the donations.[98] Lee's pitch to American businessmen in October 1967 and the Investment Guarantee Program for Singapore created great momentum for US private investments into Singapore.[99]

During the first ten years of Singapore's independence from Malaysia, American investors in Singapore not only generated revenue, but also reduced Singapore's unemployment rate. In 1967, Mobil Oil established an oil refinery in Singapore, investing about US$35 million.[100] By the end of 1967, Esso, another American oil company, built another refinery off the coast of Jurong that cost US$70 million and brought in orders worth US$100 million.[101] Managers from Mobil Oil who oversaw the implementation of the building projects in Singapore enthusiastically told their visitors how Singaporean workers completed the construction of their facilities "months ahead of the deadline and at less than original cost estimates".[102] By 1969, Mobil had hired 153 employees and was processing 20,800 barrels of crude oil a day.[103] Apart from setting up refineries in Singapore, US oil companies initiating exploration operations in Indonesia, Malaysia, Thailand and Vietnam began to establish their offices in Singapore and housed the families of their employees in Singapore.[104] In June 1970, 142 out of 186 oil exploration companies in Southeast Asia were based in Singapore.[105] American construction and electronics manufacturing companies also started operations in Singapore.

---

[98] Ibid.

[99] For Lee's pitch to the American business community during his October 1967 trip to Washington, see Galbraith, "Lee's Visit to US", November 1967. For mention of the USAID Investment Guarantee Program for Singapore, see Henry L. Heymann, "Topics Ambassador Wong May Raise", 23 May 1967, in POL 17 Ambassador Wong, Box 1, Subject Files of the Office of Indonesia, Malaysia and Singapore Affairs, 1965–74, RG 59, NACP; Donald F. Meyers, "Possible Denial of Aid to Singapore Under Conte-Long Amendment", 11 September 1968, in POL 15–1 Amb. Galbraith's Off.-Inf. Lets. 1968, Box 4, Subject Files of the Office of Indonesia, Malaysia and Singapore Affairs, 1965–74, RG 59, NACP.

[100] Galbraith, "Letter to Bundy", 18 September 1968.

[101] Ibid.

[102] Ibid.

[103] Chiang, *Jurong Industrial Estate*, p. 30.

[104] Galbraith, "Letter to Bundy", 18 September 1968.

[105] Lim and Ow, "The Economic Development of Singapore", p. 33.

In 1967, the American firm, Caterpillar, set up a warehouse in Singapore for distributing spare parts to Asia and Africa with an investment of about US$1.4 million.[106] Manufacturers of electronic products such as General Instrument and Westinghouse began operations in Singapore in 1968, providing jobs for thousands of locals.[107] In 1968, the International Executive Service Corps ran its largest training operation in Singapore, managing 86 projects that equipped Singaporean executives with "knowledge of American methods and know-how".[108] In 1969, the manufacturing sector in Singapore employed more than 96,000 workers, an increase from 34,000 in 1960.[109] The US State Department reported that employment in US plants in Singapore had grown from 1,500 in 1968 to about 10,000 in 1972.[110] Apart from increasing an average of 6,715 jobs per year from 1960 to 1969, the Singapore government also introduced compulsory national service for male citizens above 18 years old and restricted the number of workers from Malaysia through a work permit scheme in order to alleviate the high unemployment problem.[111] From 12–15 per cent unemployment in 1967,[112] Singapore's unemployment rate dropped to 4 per cent in 1972.[113]

United States' investments in Singapore from 1965 to the early 1970s were instrumental to Singapore's economic growth. In the first five years after Singapore's separation from Malaysia, Singapore's gross domestic product had increased by 80 per cent. Even when Britain withdrew from the naval and air bases in Singapore between 1969 and 1972, Singapore's

---

[106] Galbraith, "Letter to Bundy", 18 September 1968.

[107] Ibid.

[108] Ibid.

[109] Lim and Ow, "The Economic Development of Singapore", p. 4.

[110] "Briefing Papers: Singapore", 1972, in Briefing Papers 1972, Box 10, Subject Files of the Office of Indonesia, Malaysia and Singapore Affairs, 1965–74, RG 59, NACP.

[111] Lim and Ow, "The Economic Development of Singapore", p. 20.

[112] Maurice D. Bean, "Material for the Secretary's Year-End Review", 2 November 1967, in POL 1 Gen. Policy. Background., Box 1, Subject Files of the Office of Indonesia, Malaysia and Singapore Affairs, 1965–74, RG 59, NACP.

[113] "Economic Situation–US Investment and Trade", 2 February 1973, in Background (Singapore 1973), Box 11, Subject Files of the Office of Indonesia, Malaysia and Singapore Affairs, 1965–74, RG 59, NACP.

economy was growing at a rate of 14 per cent annually.[114] In 1968, American foreign direct investments (FDI) were US$15 million out of the total FDI inflow of US$23 million into Singapore. The inflow of American FDI into Singapore continued to rise every year until it reached a peak of US$92 million in 1973, when an oil crisis hit the world economy.[115] By 1972, the United States had become the largest foreign investor in Singapore, having poured in US$500 million in private investments; US companies invested only half of that amount in Malaysia.[116] In 1972, Singapore had accumulated reserves of up to US$2 billion, indicating the depth of its financial stability, and trade between Singapore and the United States amounted to US$650 million.[117] Singapore became an export-oriented industrialised country, absorbing 48.6 per cent of the total FDI that flowed into Asia in 1975.[118] Whereas some economists credit the Singapore government with the economic success in Singapore, the economic assistance that the United States government provided should not be easily passed over.[119] The influx of American businesses accelerated Singapore's industrialisation, reduced the severity of unemployment, and established Singapore as a centre for US businesses in the region.

Although Lim Chong Yah and Ow Chwee Huay downplay the significance of the Vietnam War on Singapore's economic development

---

[114] Ministry of Trade and Industry, *Economic Survey of Singapore 1988*, p. ix; "Summary of Singapore-U.S. Relationships", August 1973, in Background (Singapore 1973), Box 11, Subject Files of the Office of Indonesia, Malaysia and Singapore Affairs, 1965–74, RG 59, NACP. In 1968, Singapore's GDP grew by 15.3 per cent, the fastest rate of growth in the 1960s. See Lim and Ow, "The Economic Development of Singapore", p. 2.

[115] Mirza, *Multinationals and Singapore*, p. 8.

[116] "PARA - Malaysia", 1973.

[117] "Singapore-U.S. Relationships", August 1973.

[118] Mirza, *Multinationals and Singapore*, p. 6.

[119] For an example of an analysis of the country's economic success explained as strong governance on the part of the PAP government, see Low, et al., *Challenge and Response*, p. 7. For examples of analyses less enamoured of the role played by the Singapore government, see Mirza, *Multinationals and Singapore*, p. 6; Lawrence B. Krause, et al., *The Singapore Economy Reconsidered* (Singapore: Institute of Southeast Asian Studies, 1987).

from 1965 to 1970,[120] they acknowledge that trade with South Vietnam did increase during the war, such that South Vietnam became one of the largest markets for Singapore exports.[121] Writing in 1971, their analysis was limited to statistics available in the period up to 1970. Furthermore, in the midst of speculations on the pace of US military withdrawal from Vietnam at the time of writing, they might have felt the need to divorce Singapore's economic growth from the Vietnam War, in case a quick withdrawal of American troops created a loss of confidence in the Singapore economy. Lim and Ow note, however, that

> [b]ecause of the war, Singapore's sale of petroleum products to South Vietnam rose tremendously, thus arresting the decline of Singapore's entrepôt trade during this period. In addition, the intensified war brought in more revenue for Singapore's workshops for the repair of equipment and industry for the repair of ships.[122]

They posit that Singapore's economic growth in its first five years was largely a result of strong efforts to promote foreign investment in industries and introduction of laws to attract investors into Singapore. In 1967, the Economic Expansion Incentives Act, which replaced the Pioneer Industries Ordinance of 1959, reduced company tax from 40 per cent to 4 per cent for export-oriented industries for a 15-year period. Discipline in the Singapore labour force was enhanced through the Employment Bill and the Industrial Relations Ordinance, both introduced in 1968.[123] Although Hong Kong, Taiwan, Indonesia and Malaysia provided somewhat similar benefits to attract foreign investments, economists stress upon the efficiency and integrity of the Singapore government, the availability of public utilities and a well-disciplined work force that drew investors to

---

[120] Lim and Ow, "The Singapore Economy and the Vietnam War", pp. 352–69.

[121] Lim and Ow, "The Economic Development of Singapore", p. 10. In 1967, Singapore was South Vietnam's fifth-largest supplier of imports, up from 25th position in 1965. Conversely, in 1969, South Vietnam became the third-largest destination for Singapore's exports, up from 13th place in 1961. See Lim and Ow, "The Singapore Economy and the Vietnam War", p. 354.

[122] Lim and Ow, "The Economic Development of Singapore", p. 34.

[123] Ibid.

Singapore.[124] According to them, the "imprint of the Government was everywhere". Yet even Lim and Ow concede that "[a] baker, however good, cannot make bread without flour, water, yeast, oven, etc".[125] They attribute Singapore's good economic performance in the late 1960s to booms in three key industries: hospitality, ship repair and ship building, and oil prospecting in Southeast Asia.[126] W.G. Huff emphasises the growth of the electronics manufacturing sector as a driving force for Singapore's economic development in the 1970s.[127] American investments and market for Singapore's exports played a key role in the rapid growth in these industries that kept Singapore's economy viable in the midst of Indonesia's *Konfrontasi*, separation from Malaysia and Britain's military withdrawal. According to Huff, Singapore's economic growth from 1966 to 1973 depended on "a combination of external free trade and strong internal economic control".[128] A complete picture of Singapore's economic development must therefore take into account the efforts by the Singapore government as well as external factors, especially the US strategy of economic diplomacy that aimed to bolster Singapore's political stability and economic viability.

CONCLUSION

The United States-Singapore bilateral relationship developed rapidly on multiple levels from 1966 to 1975. The volume of trade between the two countries, and the influx of US investments into Singapore dispelled the anxieties of the Singapore government after the British government announced plans for military withdrawal east of Suez. By 1975, the distance between the non-aligned Singapore and the anti-communist

---

[124] Ibid. W.G. Huff illustrates the point with the move by Texas Instruments from Taiwan to Singapore in 1973, where it "simply got browned off with red tape in Taiwan and revamped its investment plans to centre on Singapore—the company was in operation only 50 days after the investment decision was made". See W.G. Huff, *The Economic Growth of Singapore: Trade and Development in the Twentieth Century* (Cambridge: Cambridge University Press, 1994), p. 325.

[125] Lim and Ow, "The Economic Development of Singapore", p. 27.

[126] Ibid.

[127] Huff, *The Economic Growth of Singapore*, p. 34.

[128] Ibid.

superpower was merely a matter of perception. The Singapore government had defined its policy towards the US as purely commercial, yet enmeshed at so many levels that the fates of American interests in the region was tied to Singapore's political, economic and social stability. But American contribution to the economic developments in Singapore was not altruistic. Decisions made by the US government towards helping Singapore were motivated by America's interests in Southeast Asia, and deemed appropriate within US containment strategy. That being the case, the US government readily refused the Singapore government's requests when the consequences of assisting Singapore would damage American relations with Singapore's larger neighbours. The following section examines the tensions between Singapore and Washington between 1965 and 1975.

PART 3
Strategic Distancing
Balancing Non-Alignment and Containment

CHAPTER 6

Catching the Cold

Obstacles in US-Singapore Relations

By 1966, Singapore and the United States had developed a remarkably close relationship, albeit one that was given the public appearance of being at a distance. Singapore offered strategic and public support for US military operations in Vietnam beginning from the late 1960s. In return, the United States provided economic and military assistance that guaranteed Singapore's security. As the US government began to show signs of military withdrawal from Vietnam in 1968, its strategic interest in Singapore diminished; so, too, did the Singapore government's confidence in the commitment of the US in the region. Although their relations remained strong, Singapore reverted to its earlier strategy of hinting at a possible shift away from western alliance, playing the Soviet Union as an alternative to keep the People's Republic of China in check. The Nixon administration, though keen to maintain close relations with the Singapore government, recognised that Singapore was less significant to US political interests in the region compared to Malaysia and Indonesia. Tensions between the US and Singapore grew as the Singapore government established formal diplomatic engagement with the Soviet Union.

SOVIET-AMERICAN COLD WAR IN SOUTHEAST ASIA

During the early Cold War period, from late 1940s to the 1950s, conflict and competition between the USSR and the US escalated apace and spread to parts of Asia. Large portions of the region were recovering from the trauma of the Second World War and were undergoing decolonisation. In Asia, the Taiwan Strait, the Korean peninsula and Southeast Asia became, in various degrees, military and political battlegrounds for the Soviet-American Cold War. In 1962, deterred by the spectre of nuclear war after the Cuban Missile Crisis, the United States and the Soviet Union entered an interregnum of détente.[1] The US government signed a Limited Test Ban Treaty (LTBT) with the USSR in 1963.[2] Although the LTBT was a step towards reducing the intensity of nuclear arms race between the two superpowers, it did little to reduce the "spirit of competition" and "mutual suspicion" between the United States and the Soviet Union.[3] Three years after the treaty was signed, the US State Department observed that "it is more plausible to believe that the Soviets regarded the test ban as a tactical episode which did not carry with it a significant change in their stance toward the US".[4] In fact, part of Moscow's motivation for signing the LTBT came from the escalating competition between the USSR and the PRC to be the "true champion of liberation movements everywhere".[5] In a policy planning report written in 1966, the US State Department noted that Moscow "defied bitter Chinese opposition" towards the LTBT, and used it mainly as "an opportunity to isolate Peking in the Communist movement and Afro-Asian countries because of [the PRC's] blatant opposition to this popular agreement".[6] Because Russian motivation behind the signing of the treaty might be more a result of a Sino-Soviet split than a détente between Washington and Moscow, the State Department

---

[1] Campbell Craig and Fredrik Logevall argue that "[i]f nations are going to be as terrified by nuclear war as the United States and the Soviet Union were in 1962, then it becomes reasonable to conclude … that war between nuclear states has become effectively impossible". See Campbell Craig and Fredrik Logevall, *America's Cold War: The Politics of Insecurity* (Cambridge, Massachusetts: The Belknap Press of Harvard University Press, 2009), pp. 210–4.

[2] US Department of State Policy Planning Council, "Prospects for Detente with the USSR", 23 March 1966, in State, Department of. Policy Planning, Vol. 7 [1 of 2], Box 53, National Security File. Agency File, LBJL.

[3] Craig and Logevall, *America's Cold War*, pp. 213–4.

[4] Policy Planning Council, "Prospects for Detente", 23 March 1966.

[5] Craig and Logevall, *America's Cold War*, p. 215.

[6] Policy Planning Council, "Prospects for Detente", 23 March 1966.

advised that the US government should recognise the "transient and fragile character of the détente of 1963".[7] The LTBT did not alter the dynamics of the superpower rivalry until the Sino-Soviet split became apparent in the late 1960s.[8]

Vietnam, and the broader Southeast Asia, became geopolitically important to the Soviet Union after the rupture of the Sino-Soviet alliance.[9] An increased Soviet interest in Vietnam not only concerned the PRC, but also drew much attention from the US government. According to the State Department, Soviet involvement in Vietnam was symptomatic of Moscow's competition with Beijing for leadership and influence among communist regimes in Asia. The division of labour observable during the early Cold War period had given way to a struggle for "leadership of world Communism".[10] The State Department foresaw that, in time, Soviet hostilities towards the US would be redirected increasingly to Beijing, which was also competing for greater clout in Vietnam and the Third World.[11] The competition for influence in developing countries in Southeast Asia, such as Singapore, intensified as the Soviet Union vied for strategic leverage in the region.

The 1950s was a period that saw the Soviet Union uninterested in the communist insurrection in Burma and also one that witnessed the country failing to establish superiority over the western powers during

---

[7] Ibid.

[8] Vojtech Mastny argues that the value of the LTBT as a "tool for achieving political goals" was considered low by the US and USSR. Mastny further asserts that the LTBT was a missed opportunity to completely ban nuclear tests and bring the Cold War to an earlier close. See Vojtech Mastny, "The 1963 Nuclear Test Ban Treaty: A Missed Opportunity for Détente?", *Journal of Cold War Studies* 10, no. 1 (Winter 2008): 24–5.

[9] Sophie Quinn-Judge, "Through a Glass Darkly, Reading the History of the Vietnamese Communist Party, 1945–1975", in *Making Sense of the Vietnam Wars: Local, National and Transnational Perspectives*, ed. Bradley and Young (New York: Oxford University Press, 2008), p. 116.

[10] Policy Planning Council, "Prospects for Detente", 23 March 1966.

[11] In the context of the Cold War period, the phrase "Third World" is used to refer to developing countries. Leslie Wolf-Phillips also points out that some scholars attribute non-alignment with the Third World because many of these countries are also developing countries. For the origins of the phrase, see Leslie Wolf-Phillips, "Why 'Third World'?: Origin, Definition and Usage", *Third World Quarterly* 9, no. 4 (1987). This book adopts the first usage.

the Korean War.[12] During this time, Soviet engagement with non-communist Asian states was superficial. Newly independent countries in Southeast Asia were suspicious of the Soviet Union, which was perceived to have intentions of spreading communism in the region by force.[13] Furthermore, communist parties in Southeast Asia were receiving political guidance and military assistance mainly from the PRC, which had the support of Moscow during this period.[14] Hence, Soviet engagements with non-communist governments in Southeast Asia were limited to economic links and diplomatic recognition with some countries in the region. Nevertheless, the Soviet leader from 1953 to 1964, Nikita Khrushchev, was beginning to recognise that relations with newly independent countries in Asia could benefit the Soviet Union.[15] Hence, as a result of 'de-Stalinization' of Soviet policies under Khrushchev, Soviet policy in Southeast Asia shifted from supporting armed insurrections to putting greater emphasis on political and economic relations with newly decolonised Asian states. In fact, at the dawn of the Sino-Soviet split, the Soviet Union avoided association with the communist parties in the region because of the Chinese identification with communist insurgencies in the region.[16] By cultivating state-to-state relations through economic diplomacy in Southeast Asia, Moscow abandoned its coercive image while exploiting the grievances that decolonised states had against the West, which was perceived to be perpetuating an unjust international order.[17] Signs of a Sino-Soviet split were observable through North Vietnamese relations with the Soviet Union and the PRC during the Indochina conflict. The 1964 ninth plenum of the Vietnamese Workers' Party Central Committee introduced a shift in strategy to engage in "a general offensive war"

---

[12] Leszek Buszynski, *Soviet Foreign Policy in Southeast Asia* (Kent: Croom Helm, 1986), p. 12.

[13] Ibid. Muthiah Alagappa argues that Southeast Asian governments continued to hold suspicions against Soviet subversive behaviour in the late 1970s and 1980s. See Muthiah Alagappa, "The Major Powers and Southeast Asia", *International Journal* 44, no. 3 (1989): 555–6.

[14] Kelemen, "Soviet Strategy in Southeast Asia", pp. 335–6.

[15] Buszynski, *Soviet Foreign Policy in Southeast Asia*, p. 13.

[16] Ibid.

[17] Ibid.

in South Vietnam, a departure from the previous approach endorsed by Beijing to focus on "guerrilla warfare ... conducted as part of a social revolution".[18] Hanoi's decision required Soviet assistance, since China could not supply the sophisticated anti-aircraft weapons needed to counter American bombers.[19] Moscow's response to Hanoi's request was positive and immediate. By the mid-1960s, the USSR had become embroiled in Southeast Asian affairs through military support in Vietnam.

Ideologically, Moscow's approach in Southeast Asia aligned with its aim of disseminating socialism in the Third World. To the Soviet Union, non-alignment did not imply "equidistance between socialism and capitalism", but was an "active policy of confronting 'imperialism' or the West".[20] Furthermore, Moscow also aimed to assist Asian states in the achievement of "genuine economic independence, which the Third World is yet to attain, without which a state could not be truly independent".[21] Therefore, the Soviet goal was to draw the newly decolonised countries out of a capitalist system by helping these countries to become politically and economically independent from their former colonisers.[22] Because reduced reliance on the western powers by newly independent states contributed to the Soviet objective, Moscow embraced non-alignment, or neutralism, more readily than the United States.[23] The United States only began to adopt a more accommodating view of neutralism during the Kennedy administration.[24] The Soviet Union was able to utilise its relative success in diplomacy with non-aligned countries "to orchestrate Third World opinion in a way that would place limits upon United States activity".[25] Moscow presented the USSR as an ally to the non-aligned nations against the

---

[18] Kelemen, "Soviet Strategy in Southeast Asia", p. 336.
[19] Ibid.
[20] B.G. Gufarov quoted in Buszynski, *Soviet Foreign Policy in Southeast Asia*, p. 15. See also Note 64, Kelemen, "Soviet Strategy in Southeast Asia".
[21] Ibid.
[22] Ibid.; Alagappa, "The Major Powers and Southeast Asia", p. 553.
[23] Buszynski, *Soviet Foreign Policy in Southeast Asia*, p. 16.
[24] See Chapter 1 of this book for an analysis of the American view towards neutralism.
[25] Buszynski, *Soviet Foreign Policy in Southeast Asia*, p. 27.

United States, which it claimed to be a "predatory" superpower.[26] Even "semi-socialist" governments gained Moscow's "full support" because these regimes "weakened capitalism and thereby strengthened the world position of socialism".[27]

Predictions of an intensifying rivalry between the Soviet Union and the People's Republic of China became a reality in the late 1960s. The veneer of Sino-Soviet solidarity was removed in March 1969 with two border clashes at the Damansky/Zhenbao Island.[28] Following the open clash between the Soviet Union and the PRC, Soviet-American détente became formalised as policy in 1971 when both superpowers recognised the "establishment of nuclear equality".[29] Détente limited the "dangers of escalation" in the US-Soviet conflict and was intended by Moscow to "throw the responsibility of restraint upon the American side".[30] In addition, the Soviet Union capitalised on détente to trumpet that "socialism was indeed expanding and capitalism contracting".[31] Yet it would be delusional to assume that the USSR had achieved its aims because most non-communist Southeast Asian countries still functioned in a capitalist system.

MANAGING THE COLD WAR: THE SINGAPORE APPROACH

Although the Singapore government proclaimed non-alignment when it became independent in 1965, the non-communist People's Action Party government leaned closer to the United States than to the Soviet Union. Lee Kuan Yew left Washington in October 1967 with the assurance that President Lyndon Johnson's administration was committed to preventing the spread of communism south of Vietnam. Lee's visit to the US came a few months after the British government announced plans to withdraw troops from Singapore. One of Lee's chief objectives was to ascertain

---

[26] Ibid.

[27] Clive Christie, *Ideology and Revolution in Southeast Asia, 1900–1980: Political Ideas of the Anti-Colonial Era* (Surrey: Curzon Press, 2001), p. 128.

[28] Buszynski, *Soviet Foreign Policy in Southeast Asia*, p. 44.

[29] Ibid.

[30] Ibid.

[31] Ibid.

whether the US government would play a role in Singapore's security after the British withdrawal. In his memoir, Lee quotes Johnson's reassuring speech during his visit to the White House:

> Yes, America has the resolution and the restraint to see this struggle through in Vietnam.... I cannot put it more clearly or with more confidence. You have a phrase in your part of the world that puts our determination well. You call it 'riding the tiger'. You rode the tiger. We shall.[32]

While conversing with Lee about riding the communist tiger, US Vice President Hubert Humphrey estimated that "70 to 80 percent of the senate supported the president's Vietnam policy".[33] Humphrey urged "people like [Lee], who were nonaligned and known to be politically independent, [to] speak up and stop the erosion of public opinion in the United States".[34] According to Lee, Humphrey had urged the Singapore Prime Minister to "help keep the carpet under Johnson's feet" or "he [Johnson] would be beaten in America, not Vietnam".[35] Lee left the United States in October 1967, heartened by the resolve exhibited by the Johnson administration to hold the line in Vietnam.

Nevertheless, events that ensued after Lee's US visit dampened the Singapore government's confidence in the British and the American governments to resist the expansion of communist influence in Southeast Asia. In November 1967, the British currency was devalued, followed by an announcement made in January 1968 of an accelerated British withdrawal from Malaysia and Singapore.[36] In the same month, the American war effort in Vietnam came under severe domestic opposition after a fierce battle in Vietnam known as the Tet Offensive.[37] President Johnson announced in March 1968 that he would not represent his party to contest the US Presidential Election that year and expressed

---

[32] Lee, *From Third World to First*, p. 456.

[33] Ibid.

[34] Ibid.

[35] Ibid.

[36] The circumstances surrounding Britain's east of Suez policy is analysed in greater depth in Chapter 4.

[37] McMahon, *The Limits of Empire*, pp. 146–9.

willingness to enter into peace talks with Hanoi.[38] After Johnson's shocking announcement, it became clear to Southeast Asian leaders that the American government was looking for an exit strategy in Vietnam.[39] The Singapore government could no longer depend on the Anglo-American powers to resist the military expansion of communism in Southeast Asia and moved quickly to find an alternative power that could contain the PRC in the region. On 1 June 1968, two months after President Johnson's announcement, the Foreign Ministry of Singapore established diplomatic relations with the Soviet Union.[40] Richard Nixon's first year in the White House produced even greater anxieties for Lee and the Singapore government.

Lee made his fourth official visit to the United States as Prime Minister in May 1969. In making his first official call on President Nixon, Lee wanted to know whether the US had "the stamina to see Viet-Nam through, and the subtlety and the will to play the important but, over time, diminishing role" in the Southeast Asia.[41] The US State Secretary, William P. Rogers, commented that Lee might also discuss the future of Southeast Asia and assess American policy in the region.[42] The US Embassy in Singapore advised the new administration to build a close and personal relationship with Lee, cautioning that

> Lee would take offense easily if he felt we [the US government] were merely "tolerating" him rather than welcoming his periodic stopovers…. Because Lee can be prickly and difficult, however, it is vital

---

[38] Ang Cheng Guan offers a comprehensive analysis of the impact of the Tet Offensive on five Southeast Asian countries—Indonesia, Malaysia, the Philippines, Singapore and Thailand. His work highlights the loss of confidence among Southeast Asian leaders towards the Johnson administration after the 31 March 1968 announcement by the US president. See Ang, *Southeast Asia and the Vietnam War*, pp. 54–75.

[39] Ibid.

[40] "Katzenbach Report", 14 June 1968, in POL 3 Organizations & Conferences (General) 1968, Box 1, Subject Files of the Office of Indonesia, Malaysia and Singapore Affairs, 1965–74, RG 59, NACP. Bilveer Singh partly attributes the establishment of USSR-Singapore relations at ambassadorial level to the developments within the US and the UK. See Bilveer Singh, *The Soviet Union in Singapore's Foreign Policy: An Analysis* (Kuala Lumpur: Institute of Strategic and International Studies, 1990), pp. 20–1.

[41] Rogers, "President's Meeting with Lee", 2 May 1969.

[42] Ibid.

that Washington be prepared to handle him and fully understand his purposes and attitudes.[43]

When Lee Kuan Yew met Richard Nixon, he gave President Nixon the similar advice he had offered to Johnson that "no Southeast Asian leader … wanted to see the United States 'pull out' of Viet-Nam".[44] Country Director for Malaysia and Singapore, Maurice D. Bean, who was the control officer for Lee's May 1969 visit, accompanied Lee for most of his meetings in Washington and observed distinct differences in the way Lee behaved since his first state visit to Washington in October 1967. Lee was "relaxed, warm and friendly in every situation" and avoided comparing Americans with their "British cousins".[45] When asked if the United States should resume contacts with the PRC, Lee recommended that Washington should do so.[46] He felt that the PRC government would likely be unresponsive to US rapprochement, but thought the US should still attempt to establish a relationship with the PRC because "a very large community of Chinese" outside mainland China "would welcome a resumption of China's links with the U.S.".[47]

Bean also noted that Lee was now less critical of the Malay leadership in Malaysia than he had been before. Communal violence broke out between Malays and Chinese in Kuala Lumpur on 13 May 1969, bringing the country "to the brink of collapse".[48] When asked to comment on the communal riots, which occurred while Lee was still in Washington, he told reporters that: "Malaysia is our closest neighbor. Her well-being

---

[43] "Memorandum from POL to the Ambassador: Topics to Discuss in Washington", 3 April 1969, in POL 15–1 Ambassador's Correspondence 1969, Box 3, Subject Files of the Office of Indonesia, Malaysia and Singapore Affairs, 1965–74, RG 59, NACP.

[44] Maurice D. Bean, "Memorandum for the Record: Informal Visit of Singapore Prime Minister Lee Kuan Yew, May 10–14, 1969", 4 June 1969, in POL 7 Prime Minister Lee's Visit 1969, Box 3, Subject Files of the Office of Indonesia, Malaysia and Singapore Affairs, 1965–74, RG 59, NACP.

[45] Ibid.

[46] Robert W. Barnett, "Memorandum for the Record: Views of Prime Minister Lee Kuan Yew", 12 May 1969, in POL 15–1 Lee's Speeches 1969, Box 3, Subject Files of the Office of Indonesia, Malaysia and Singapore Affairs, 1965–74, RG 59, NACP.

[47] Ibid.

[48] A.J. Stockwell, "Conceptions of Community in Colonial Southeast Asia", *Transactions of the Royal Historical Society* 8 (1998): 338.

or otherwise must affect us in Singapore."[49] Lee also said that "the United Kingdom, Australia and New Zealand (in that order) were in the best position to offer (and have accepted) useful advice to the GOM [Government of Malaysia]" and "neither Singapore nor the United States could play such a role".[50] Having previously expressed the view that the US had encouraged the Malaysian government to be dependent on American protection, perhaps Lee might have been urging Bean not to appear overly helpful to requests for assistance with communal conflicts in Malaysia.[51]

In addition to the impact on Malaysia's internal instability, the 13 May 1969 riot also affected regional security. Ambassador Cross observed that progress in the development of the FPDA suffered a setback when the Australian government, a key contributor to the FPDA, had shown "a marked reluctance" to play a significant part in the defence arrangement since the May 13 incident.[52] The US government saw Australia as the most likely power to shoulder the defence burden of the Malaysia-Singapore subregion after Britain's military withdrawal. Although the United States had assured Australia that the US would honour its ANZUS treaty obligations and support the Australians and New Zealanders in the subregion if requested, Washington had also stressed to Canberra that ANZUS obligations would not cover Australian involvement in Malaysia's and Singapore's internal security. With the Australian government nervous about getting dragged into the internal conflicts in Malaysia, both the Singapore and Malaysian governments were anxious that the ANZUK powers might delay the establishment of the FPDA. The situation would be graver if the new American President were to pull out US forces hastily from Vietnam.

Lee's rationale for American involvement in Vietnam had not changed since 1965. During media interviews, Lee presented the view

---

[49] "Mr. Lee: I hope the difficulty is soon resolved", *The Straits Times*, 16 May 1969, p. 1.
[50] Bean, "Visit of PM Lee, May 10–14, 1969", 4 June 1969.
[51] From mid-1964 to late 1965, Lee Kuan Yew was led to believe that the US government had an agreement with Malaysian Prime Minister Tunku Abdul Rahman to protect Malay interests in Malaysia. Lee's views changed after William Bundy visited Singapore in March 1966. Details of the Lee-Bundy meeting are discussed in Chapter 3.
[52] Cross, "Letter to Green", 12 December 1969.

that the US had been overcommitted in Vietnam.[53] Having already committed ground forces and incurred "40,000 dead, 200,000 wounded and maimed" and billions of dollars in aid, however, Lee urged the US administration not to "throw it away".[54] Lee argued that the US had more to lose if it pulled out from Vietnam too soon.[55] "So I think," Lee argued, "making the stand in Vietnam was not particularly wise, but a stand having been taken, I think it will be even more unwise to throw it away."[56] After returning from the US in May 1969, in a conversation with William Bruns, Chargé d'Affaires ad interim at the US Embassy in Singapore, Lee was asked for his assessment of Asian leaders concerning the situation in Southeast Asia in the event of the end of the Vietnam War.[57] Lee stressed that the US must not leave South Vietnam before October 1972. He predicted that the US Congressional election in 1970 would increase the "pressures on President [Nixon] to withdraw from Vietnam too soon", and holding on until just before the November 1972 US Presidential elections would be a sound strategy for Nixon to win re-election.[58] If American logistical and military support continued after the US withdrawal and elections were held successfully in South Vietnam that year, Lee opined that the situation would "probably be all right for Southeast Asia".[59] Nevertheless, Lee was less optimistic about the situation if the South Vietnamese government fell, predicting that the Thais would "cave in" and the Malaysians would not be able to contain the communists.[60] In a memorandum of conversation recorded by William Bruns one month later, he highlighted that Lee warned US Commander-

---

[53] "Excerpts from recent statements of Singapore Prime Minister Lee Kuan Yew", 1 March 1969, in POL 7 Prime Minister Lee's Visit 1969, Box 3, Subject Files of the Office of Indonesia, Malaysia and Singapore Affairs, 1965–74, RG 59, NACP.

[54] Ibid.

[55] "Lee calls for 'honourable' settlement in Vietnam", *The Straits Times*, 18 May 1969, p. 8.

[56] "Excerpts from recent statements of Singapore Prime Minister Lee Kuan Yew", 1 March 1969.

[57] William H. Bruns, "Memorandum of Conversation between Lee Kuan Yew and William H. Bruns", 24 July 1969, in POL 15–1 Ambassador's Correspondence 1969, Box 3, Subject Files of the Office of Indonesia, Malaysia and Singapore Affairs, 1965–74, RG 59, NACP.

[58] Ibid.

[59] Ibid.

[60] Ibid.

in-Chief of the Pacific Fleet, Admiral McCain, that US credibility was at stake if it pulled out of Vietnam "as early as 1970 or 1971".[61] Lee's counsel to the US government did not seem to affect the Nixon administration's determination to exit Vietnam.

In July 1969, President Nixon outlined his administration's foreign policy approach during a press conference held in the American military base at Guam.[62] President Nixon's foreign policy pronouncement was commonly referred to as the Nixon, or Guam, Doctrine. President Nixon also announced a withdrawal of 25,000 troops from South Vietnam. The Nixon Doctrine struck Lee Kuan Yew as a preamble for a quick and complete US withdrawal from Vietnam.[63] Weeks later, President Nixon announced that he would double the number of troops to be withdrawn. In late 1969, Ambassador Francis Galbraith reported that Lee's "outlook was as gloomy as [Galbraith] had ever seen it", and Lee "had large doubts about [US] policy in Viet-Nam".[64] Malaysian Prime Minister Tunku Abdul Rahman was equally concerned about "the will and capability of the United States to safeguard the security of the Southeast Asian region", especially when the Malaysian government regarded US involvement in the Vietnam War as an aid to Malaysia.[65] At the Commonwealth Conference, soon after the US withdrawal was announced, Lee observed that the news was a "crushing blow" to the Australians and New Zealanders.[66] Lee heard an Australian government official at the Conference expressing "grave doubts about the dependability of the US".[67] For the Singapore government, the planned US withdrawal from Vietnam, coupled with the British

---

[61] William H. Bruns, "Memorandum of Conversation between Prime Minister Lee Kuan Yew, Admiral McCain, Minister Koren and William H. Bruns: Courtesy Call on Singapore Prime Minister Lee, August 5, 1969", 6 August 1969, in POL 7 Visits. Prime Minister Lee 1968, Box 4, Subject Files of the Office of Indonesia, Malaysia and Singapore Affairs, 1965–74, RG 59, NACP.

[62] Nixon, "Informal Remarks in Guam with Newsmen", 25 July 1969. In November 1969, President Nixon made a speech on US national television and articulated the Nixon Doctrine in three points. For details of the Nixon Doctrine, see Chapter 1 and Nixon, "Nixon Doctrine (1)", 3 November 1969.

[63] Cross, "Embassy Conference 1970", 9 April 1970.

[64] Ibid.

[65] Sodhy, *The US-Malaysian Nexus*, p. 282.

[66] Bruns, "Memocon: PM Lee, McCain, Koren and Bruns", 6 August 1969.

[67] Ibid.

military pull-out from Singapore, warranted a significant re-assessment of Singapore's strategy to rely on powerful western countries for its defence.

The Singapore government consequently developed plans to mitigate the negative impact of the US military withdrawal from Vietnam. A series of studies conducted by the American Embassy in Singapore in late 1969 reported that

1. the GOS is deeply disturbed that the US disengagement in Vietnam and the UK withdrawal from this [Malaysia-Singapore] area are happening at more or less the same time;

2. because of this growing insecurity, the Singaporeans are more determined than ever to implement Lee Kuan Yew's "poison shrimp" defense concept, even if it means going it alone; and

3. little has been accomplished within the Five Power [Defence] framework to ease the worries of the Singaporeans.[68]

It was no wonder then that the Singapore government deepened its relations with the Soviet Union in order to find an alternative power to balance communist Chinese influence in Singapore and the wider region.

The Soviet Union was highly suspicious of the Nixon Doctrine, attributing the doctrine to Sino-American collaboration against the USSR. Russian commentator E.M. Zhukov wrote that

[t]he main task of the [Nixon] doctrine was, accordingly, resolution of the China problem in US foreign policy and in this respect the adjustment demanded the withdrawal of forces in areas close to China and their retention in regions removed from the mainland. The doctrine, therefore, was acknowledgement that the US and China shared interests in Asia against the Soviet Union and consequently was preparation for Nixon's eventual visit to China.[69]

Zhukov argued that the Nixon doctrine paved the way for a US-China "grand design" against the USSR.[70] Now, it was not just the Soviet superpower that was suspicious of the Nixon Doctrine, but Singapore, a small state, also became uncertain of the implications of such a policy.

---

[68] Cross, "Letter to Green", 12 December 1969.
[69] Buszynski, *Soviet Foreign Policy in Southeast Asia*, p. 49.
[70] Ibid.

SINGAPORE'S BALANCE-OF-POWER APPROACH

For the Singapore government, establishing diplomatic relations with both the United States and the Soviet Union was an attempt to balance the two superpowers. As a small state, Singapore possessed little or no freedom of action within a marked sphere of influence of great powers such as the US and the USSR.[71] Hence, a balance of power in Southeast Asia gave Singapore greater freedom of action compared to the presence of one dominant power in the region. For Singapore, "being small and in no way able to prevent the entry of great powers into the region, the next best policy … [was] to invite the presence of all great powers".[72] Singapore Foreign Minister Rajaratnam, in a 1976 speech, defended Singapore's endorsement of a Soviet presence in the region thus:

> Insofar as the Soviet Union is concerned, there is no doubt about the role she intends to play in the region. Her policy in regard to Southeast Asia is activist, consistent and credible…. [W]e will continue to maintain good relations with the Soviet Union but at the same time resist on our own, or through the collective strength that ASEAN provides, any Soviet influence or pressure which we believe would be detrimental to our national interests or to our non-communist way of life. Of course our capacity to resist big power pressure would be greater if there were a multiplicity of powers present in the region. When there are many suns the gravitational pull of each is not only weakened but also, by a judicious use of the pulls and counterpulls of gravitational forces, the minor planets acquire a greater freedom of navigation.[73]

Rajaratnam's speech highlighted the Singapore government's adoption of a balance of power strategy towards the US and the Soviet Union. Since the likelihood of the Soviet Union imposing a "communist way of life" on Singapore was considered to be remote, the Singapore government accepted some level of Soviet presence in the region.[74]

---

[71] Singh, *The Soviet Union in Singapore's Foreign Policy*, p. 4.
[72] Ibid.
[73] Chan and Haq, eds., *S. Rajaratnam*, p. 284.
[74] Ibid.

There were at least three advantages for Singapore to open doors to all major powers. First, no one power would be "too powerful to be in a position to put pressure on the leadership".[75] Nevertheless, in practice, the Singapore government was under pressure to consider the views of both the US and the USSR and had to portray an evenhanded approach. The second advantage for inviting all major powers to the region was a "direct economic spinoff" as a result of investments from the great powers into the Singapore economy.[76] The volume of trade between Singapore and the USSR, nonetheless, suggested that the US was more significant to the Singapore economy than the Soviet Union was, by a large margin. In 1970, Singapore's total trade with the US recorded $1.34 billion while trade with the USSR reached $174 million. In 1975, US-Singapore trade shot to $4.8 billion whereas Soviet-Singapore trade shrank to $144 million.[77] Finally and most significantly, Singapore benefitted from the efforts by the major powers to keep the vital sea lanes of communication open.[78] In November 1971, Indonesia, Malaysia and Singapore issued a statement claiming "exclusive responsibility" over the safety of navigating in the Strait of Malacca.[79] One section of the declaration included by Indonesia and Malaysia asserted that the Malacca and Singapore Straits were not international straits, implying that the Malaysian and Indonesian governments could challenge the right of free passage along the two straits.[80] Singapore did not possess the leverage to prevent Malaysia and Indonesia from 'nationalising' the Strait of Malacca.[81] Since both major power blocs had stakes in the free passage along the Malacca Strait, Singapore could depend on their strong bargaining positions to maintain the status quo in the sea lanes that crossed Singapore.[82] Plans

---

[75] Singh, *The Soviet Union in Singapore's Foreign Policy*, p. 5.

[76] Ibid.

[77] Ministry of Finance, *Economic Survey of Singapore 1978*, p. 69. Figures quoted are in Singapore currency.

[78] Singh, *The Soviet Union in Singapore's Foreign Policy*, p. 5.

[79] Ralf Emmers, "The Five Power Defence Arrangements and Defense Diplomacy in Southeast Asia", *Asian Security* 8, no. 3 (2012): 275; Michael Leifer, "The Soviet Union in South-East Asia", in *The Soviet Union and the Third World*, ed. Feuchtwanger and Nailor (New York: St. Martin's Press, 1981), p. 179.

[80] Emmers, "The Five Power Defence Arrangements", p. 275.

[81] Singh, *The Soviet Union in Singapore's Foreign Policy*, pp. 21–2; "PARA - Malaysia", 1973.

[82] Leifer, "The Soviet Union in South-East Asia", p. 179.

to nationalise the Strait of Malacca were stalled when Malaysia and Indonesia disagreed over Southeast Asia's neutralisation.[83] Eventually, the issue of free passage through the Malacca Strait was resolved at the 'Law of the Sea Conference' in 1977.[84] Hence, the Singapore government preferred the presence of major powers in the region because such a dynamic created a stable balance of influence in Southeast Asia.[85]

Closer Singapore-USSR relations led to the US government's reassessment of the strategic importance of Singapore in the 1970s. Before 1966, the United States had little stake in Singapore's security. But by 1966, Singapore had become an increasingly crucial part of American containment strategy in Asia, chiefly due to America's military entanglement in Vietnam. In 1966, the US Defense Department linked Singapore's strategic importance with US military operations in the Indian Ocean.[86] When the British government announced its policy of withdrawal from the Malaysia-Singapore subregion in 1967, Washington began to view Singapore's importance as part of the American containment strategy against the PRC. A 1972 study conducted by an Interagency Study Group (ISG), formed by various branches within the US State Department and Defense Department, remarked that Singapore was important to American interests because of the "large and growing U.S. investment" in Singapore.[87] The ISG laid out US strategic objectives in Singapore and proposed ways of meeting those objectives in the midst of emerging circumstances such as

> the British decision to withdraw a significant portion of its military forces from Singapore, previous Anglo-Australian difficulties with the Singapore Government in nailing down arrangements for their residual forces, the progressive expansion of Soviet influence in the Indian Ocean, and recent Soviet attempts to increase their influence in Singapore.[88]

---

[83] Emmers, "The Five Power Defence Arrangements", p. 275.
[84] Leifer, "The Soviet Union in South-East Asia", p. 179.
[85] Ang, *Lee Kuan Yew's Strategic Thought*, p. 24; Huxley, *Defending the Lion City*, pp. 33–7.
[86] Strategic Plans Division, "Base Policy Study", 14 September 1966.
[87] Interagency Singapore Study Group, "Singapore Study", August 1972.
[88] Ibid.

AMERICAN STRATEGIC INTERESTS IN SINGAPORE

As reported in the 1972 Singapore Study by the ISG, the US CINCPAC considered the possible loss of America's access to Singapore naval dockyards to be "nearly as critical as losing [US] base rights in the Philippines or Japan".[89] The ISG calculated that a countervailing US Navy presence in the Indian Ocean could be supported from Singapore with "much less cost in terms of ship time and forces required" in comparison with other bases available to the United States.[90] If a USN presence in the east of the Indian Ocean were called for, Singapore would be "commanding an importance far greater than its small size and relatively small population".[91] But CINCPAC's position was not shared by all members of the ISG. Although some "high level planners" considered Singapore to be more significant than US bases in Japan and the Philippines, there were members in the ISG who demurred.[92] Hence, the decision on whether or not the United States should increase its military presence in Singapore was shelved.

The ISG asserted that Singapore was situated in a strategic position in "the southern Asia and Pacific region from which the U.S. or USSR can project military, political, economic and psychological interests".[93] The ISG elaborated that

> [a]lthough the U.S. has no vital interests in Singapore, the free world and the U.S. do have an important concern that Singapore shall remain free of undue Soviet or PRC influence.... The consensus of this Interagency Study supports that summary. It is important that the U.S. maneuver in all areas (military, economic, political, and psychological) to maintain an advantageous position in Singapore relative to the Soviets, but this should not be done at the expense of other PACOM countries [countries under the protection of the US Pacific Command].[94]

---

[89] Ibid.

[90] Ibid.

[91] Ibid.

[92] Ibid.

[93] Ibid.

[94] The countries under the protection of US Pacific Command in 1972 were Australia, Japan, New Zealand, Republic of Korea and the Philippines. In 1979, Taiwan was included under the Taiwan Relations Act. After the Southeast Asian Treaty Organisation was disbanded, Thailand was included. Ibid.

Yet it was not "feasible or necessary … for the U.S. to occupy this [Singapore] base formally and conspicuously".[95] The ISG recommended that the US "must simply ensure that the facilities are operative and in friendly hands, and continuously receptive to the accommodation of U.S. vessels and aircraft".[96] In sum, Singapore was not sufficiently critical to free world interest to warrant a formal military deployment by the Americans. Singapore's significance lay in the possibility that America's enemies would have access to a potent asset against the 'free world' if Singapore allowed the Soviet Union or the PRC access to its naval dockyards.

The Singapore Study also evaluated the Singapore government's attitudes towards the United States vis-à-vis the Soviet Union. The ISG assessed that Lee Kuan Yew was "especially sensitive to China's intentions toward Singapore" and would continue with his "flirtation with the Soviet Union" in light of the reduction of forces by the US in Vietnam.[97] The study also highlighted that Lee had said publicly that the Soviet Union would be "one of the countervailing forces to China" in Southeast Asia, and he considered a Soviet naval presence "inevitable".[98] In fact, at the height of Lee Kuan Yew's anti-American press campaign in late 1965, he spoke of offering the Soviet Union a military base in Singapore if the Malaysian government invited American troops to replace the British presence.[99] At the same time, the ISG observed "definite indications that the USSR would like to use Singapore for ship repairs".[100] The study noted that

> Singapore's location is roughly halfway between the USSR's European and Asiatic ports along the optimum sea route. With a rapidly expanding merchant fleet and the possibility of a reopened Suez Canal, increased Soviet interest, activity and influence in Singapore is predictable.[101]

---

[95] Ibid.

[96] Ibid.

[97] Ibid.

[98] Ibid.

[99] King, "Singapore's Prime Minister Would Consider Offering Base to Russians if Malaysia Brings in G.I.'s", 16 September 1965.

[100] Interagency Singapore Study Group, "Singapore Study", August 1972.

[101] Ibid.

Although the United States had a head-start against the Soviet Union in the utilisation of Singapore's naval dockyards, it was "likely to have no more than a partial impact on Soviet influence with the GOS".[102] Since the US government feared the possibility of Singapore allowing access of its naval dockyards to the Soviet Pacific Fleet, they concluded that a proactive strategy was needed to ensure that the Singapore naval facilities were "adequately utilized by the UK, Australia, New Zealand, and the U.S.", so that "GOS [would] probably deny USSR access to those facilities".[103]

The Singapore Study, however, did not consider a high level of utilisation of the Singapore ship repair facilities to be sustainable after a reduction of US forces was announced by President Nixon in 1969.[104] The Interagency Study Group forecast that US withdrawal from Vietnam would reduce the number of ship repair contracts in Singapore and result in the following "disadvantages":

1. Loss of political clout with GOS
2. Might cause GOS to offer Sembawang facilities to Soviets
3. Might cause GOS to restrict US access to airfields for other than emergency needs.[105]

Hence, despite the gradual reduction of American forces in Southeast Asia, the ISG recommended an increase in the level of ship and aircraft contracts in Singapore for 1972 and 1973.[106] By creating anxieties within Washington through closer links with the Soviet Union, the Singapore government guaranteed a high and sustained level of revenue for its ship repair business.

The ISG predicted that a government in Singapore that was hostile to "Free World interests" would create "losses to U.S. investors [that] would be approximately several hundred million dollars".[107] Also, if the Singapore government made its strategic naval facilities "fully available to

---

[102] Ibid.
[103] Ibid.
[104] Bruns, "Memocon: PM Lee, McCain, Koren and Bruns", 6 August 1969.
[105] Interagency Singapore Study Group, "Singapore Study", August 1972.
[106] Ibid.
[107] Ibid.

the Soviets", it would give the USSR "a significantly improved strategic and psychological position in both the Pacific and Indian oceans".[108] Singapore, if aligned with the Soviet Union and "hostile to the free world ... would certainly ... [pose] a serious threat to free world commerce and [America's] ability to defend or exert influence in the southern Asia area".[109] The ISG concluded that: "For the above reasons, the U.S. has a clear stake in maintaining friendly and cooperative relations with Singapore."[110] But the policy of friendliness towards Singapore became increasingly unsustainable in Washington when the Singapore government appeared erratic in its attitude towards the US—most notably during Lee Kuan Yew's anti-American press campaign in late 1965 and Singapore's increased engagement with the Soviet Union after 1968.

PLAYING THE SOVIET CARD

American government officials and diplomats wanted to assess the attitude of the Singapore government regarding closer ties with the Soviet Union. In a conversation between Lee Kuan Yew and William Bruns of the American Embassy in Singapore, the American diplomat asked Lee about his views on the US, as well as the Soviet-Singapore relationship. After Johnson, Lee was certain that irrespective of who the next American president would be, the US would withdraw from Vietnam "as soon as possible".[111] Lee told Bruns that he was concerned that the next US president would "withdraw from Vietnam too soon".[112] It seemed clear that the Singapore government sought better ties with the Soviet Union in order to counter the PRC influence and to keep Washington engaged in Southeast Asia. It was a consolation to the American government that there seemed to be no hint of admiration by the Singapore government for the USSR or communist ideology. A State Department official, Robert Barnett, observed in another memorandum that Lee Kuan Yew did not hold the

---

[108] Ibid.
[109] Ibid.
[110] Ibid.
[111] Bruns, "Memcon: Lee and Bruns", 24 July 1969.
[112] Ibid.

Russians in high regard, especially with respect to the Soviet Union's engagement in Southeast Asia.[113] Barnett reported that Lee criticised the "Russians' inability to grasp the psychology of the peoples of Southeast Asia" and felt that they "lacked style or even any well-defined purpose" in their activities in Singapore, Malaysia and Indonesia.[114] Based on preliminary analysis by the US government in the late 1960s, Singapore's intention to close ranks with the USSR was aimed at keeping the US engaged in the region.[115] Although State Department officials understood Lee's views of the Soviet Union to be largely negative in 1969, they became worried when Lee began to speak favourably of the Russians after his visit to Moscow in September 1970.[116]

Formal Singapore-Soviet Union ties could be traced to the signing of their first trade agreement in April 1966.[117] Thereafter, both countries engaged in significant joint projects in shipping and aviation. In February 1967, a joint commercial shipping line—the Singapore-Soviet Shipping Agency (SinSov)—was established, running the route between Vladivostok and the Indian Ocean via Singapore.[118] With SinSov, Singapore became the first country in the region to form a joint venture with the Soviets at that time.[119] More than 500 Soviet ships called at Singapore ports in 1967,[120] followed by 520 in 1970, and the number steadily increased

---

[113] Barnett, "Views of PM Lee", 12 May 1969.

[114] Ibid.

[115] Buszynski argues that Thailand and Singapore began diplomatic engagements with the Soviet Union with the intention of preserving American interest in the region. See Buszynski, *Soviet Foreign Policy in Southeast Asia*, p. 71.

[116] Lucian W. Pye, "Letter to Ambassador Charles T. Cross, American Embassy, Singapore", 28 October 1970, in POL 7–1 Lee Kuan Yew Visit 1970 (Memoranda of Conversation, etc.), Box 8, Subject Files of the Office of Indonesia, Malaysia and Singapore Affairs, 1965–74, RG 59, NACP.

[117] Singh, *The Soviet Union in Singapore's Foreign Policy*, p. 14.

[118] Ibid. The Singapore-Soviet Shipping Agency was sometimes called Sosiak Line. See Brian Pockney, "Soviet Trade with the Third World", in *The Soviet Union and the Third World*, ed. Feuchtwanger and Nailor (New York: St. Martin's Press, 1981), p. 49.

[119] Singh, *The Soviet Union in Singapore's Foreign Policy*, p. 20.

[120] The first Soviet vessel recorded in Bilveer Singh's study was the *Frunze*, which arrived in Singapore in July 1962. See Singh, *The Soviet Union in Singapore's Foreign Policy*, p. 20. Nevertheless, Soviet ship visits significantly increased only after the signing of the Soviet-Singapore trade agreement.

each year.[121] In March 1975, a second joint Soviet-Singapore maritime company, Marissco, was formed.[122] Increased Soviet maritime trade in Asia was driven by a sharp growth in Soviet-Asian trade, which doubled from 600 million roubles in 1970 to 1.2 billion roubles in 1975, and exceeded 2 billion roubles in 1978.[123] The USSR bought 97 per cent of its rubber from Southeast Asia and was also destination to 12 per cent of Malaysia's exports.[124] Singapore further became a ship repair centre for Soviet Union,[125] which, by 1976, possessed the world's sixth-largest merchant fleet and ninth-largest tanker fleet.[126]

When Soviet ships stopped at Singapore's commercial ports, the western powers did not raise alarms. But when the Singapore government allowed Soviet use of Singapore's ship repair facilities, the ANZUK nations quickly objected. The Singapore government, however, ignored their protests. On 7 July 1971, a Soviet merchant ship arrived in Singapore for repairs; and a week later, a Soviet destroyer stopped at Singapore for repairs.[127] In fact, the appearance of the Soviet warship in Singapore was foreshadowed by Lee Kuan Yew in March 1971 when he had highlighted the usefulness of a Soviet fleet as a "counterweight" against both China and Japan, and accepted that the Soviets could make use of former British bases in Singapore for ship repairs during peacetime.[128] The US and ANZUK nations exerted diplomatic pressure on the Singapore government to minimise Soviet ship repairs at the island but had limited leverage on the issue. The western powers were mainly worried about Soviet ships visiting Sembawang shipyard located in the northern region of Singapore, where USN and ANZUK Navy vessels were berthed for repairs. The presence

---

[121] The US government recorded 346 Soviet merchant ship visits to Singapore in 1969 and approximately 480 in 1970. See Interagency Singapore Study Group, "Singapore Study", August 1972. From figures extracted from *Soviet News* (Singapore), Singh records over 500 Soviet ship visits in 1967, 521 in 1970, and 636 in 1974. See Singh, *The Soviet Union in Singapore's Foreign Policy*, p. 15.

[122] Singh, *The Soviet Union in Singapore's Foreign Policy*, p. 26. Marissco was sometimes called Merrisko. See Pockney, "Soviet Trade with the Third World", p. 49.

[123] Pockney, "Soviet Trade with the Third World", p. 35.

[124] Ibid.

[125] Singh, *The Soviet Union in Singapore's Foreign Policy*, p. 20.

[126] Pockney, "Soviet Trade with the Third World", p. 69.

[127] Interagency Singapore Study Group, "Singapore Study", August 1972.

[128] Singh, *The Soviet Union in Singapore's Foreign Policy*, pp. 23–4.

of Soviet warships in the same facility exposed the US Navy's classified technology and military intelligence to the Soviet Union.[129] Hence, the US government was determined to stop Soviet ships from entering the Sembawang facility. But the United Kingdom found it "difficult to take too hard a line" because the British government had allowed the Soviet Navy to use ports in the UK as well.[130] The Singapore government became "somewhat irritated" by ANZUK efforts to dictate the use of the naval facilities, which the British themselves had recently decided to abandon and the Australians too were reluctant to take over.[131] Recounting the Singapore-Soviet relationship, Eddie Teo from the Defence Ministry of Singapore puts it this way:

> From time to time, we felt the need to take a stand. We don't consider ourselves allies of the United States. We shouldn't be too unfriendly to the Soviets as well.[132]

The uncompromising stance taken by the Singapore government led the US government towards planning for the worst-case scenario where they would lose access to Singapore.

In August 1971, there were signs that Washington was moving Singapore to a less central position in US-Southeast Asian strategy. The shift was an outcome of the disagreement between the Singapore and the United States governments over the purpose of the naval dockyards in the northern part of Singapore. Washington had requested the Singapore government to keep Singapore's northern naval dockyards exclusively for ANZUK and US Navy use, but this was rejected by the Singapore government. As discussion between members of the Five Power Defence Arrangements neared its conclusion in mid-1971, the ANZUK nations informed the US State Department that two of the seven Stores Basins in Singapore's Sembawang naval base would be converted to service commercial ships by the Singapore government.[133] The US Navy had been using the Sembawang facilities for the repair of USN ships since

---

[129] Interagency Singapore Study Group, "Singapore Study", August 1972.
[130] Ibid.
[131] Ibid.
[132] Interview with Eddie Teo, 6 January 2015.
[133] Cross, "Memcon: US Repair Program", 24 July 1971.

1966 when the facilities were under ANZUK control. They had hoped to maintain the status quo after the Singapore government took over. Hence, in July 1971, American Ambassador to Singapore, Charles Cross, met Lee Kuan Yew to request for Sembawang to be preserved as a non-commercial naval facility in exchange for more US Navy repair contracts in Singapore.[134] Ambassador Cross argued that the US Navy did not wish to see parts of the Sembawang base turned into commercial berths because sensitive equipment onboard the USN ships would be less secure if the base would turn commercial. Cross also expressed concern that USN ships would be turned away if lucrative contracts from merchant ships competed with contracts from USN vessels.[135] Lee assured Cross that there would be "plenty of room" for US ships because Britain and Australia were going to reduce ship visits to the Stores Basins after 1971.[136] Lee also disagreed with Cross's assertion that USN ships would be less secure if a part of Sembawang was commercialised, telling Cross that the US Navy could "simply [lock] up its secret equipment" as Lee had seen being done in Malta.[137]

The issue of Soviet ships using Singapore's naval facilities became the most sensitive subject in US-Singapore diplomacy throughout 1972.[138] Washington feared that the Singapore government was "considering increased Soviet use of Singapore naval facilities".[139] Yet the US government could not impose its thinking on the Singapore government, especially when the latter strongly guarded its non-aligned image. Washington had to rely on the ANZUK nations to influence the views of the Singapore government regarding the matter of Soviet ships using the Singapore dockyards. But even the ANZUK powers had differing positions on the increase of Soviet ships in Singapore. Like the Americans, the Australians were "standing firm against any increase" of Soviet ships in the Singapore dockyards.[140] The British were uncertain if the Singapore

---

[134] Ibid.
[135] Ibid.
[136] Ibid.
[137] Ibid.
[138] Heavner, "Green's Asian Trip", 23 February 1972.
[139] Ibid.
[140] Heavner, "US and Soviet Use of Singapore", 15 February 1972.

government could be persuaded and they predicted that the US and the ANZUK nations might "in the end have to settle for keeping the Soviets out of the ANZUK naval base area of Sembawang".[141] London proposed that the Singapore government could be advised to take an "even-handed" approach and "bar both US and Soviet naval vessels" from using Singapore's naval facilities.[142] London's suggestion "incensed" the Australians, not only because it failed to share their view that the increased Soviet presence in Singapore was a security threat to its allies, but also that it revealed the remoteness of London's thinking vis-à-vis Canberra.[143] The British government promptly "dropped" the suggestion.[144]

Eventually, after consultation with the US government, the ANZUK powers formally submitted their protest to the Singapore government. ANZUK opposed any type of communist vessel berthing at any time in or near Sembawang, where USN and ANZUK Navy vessels were located.[145] They also opposed "communist intelligence-gathering vessels" visiting any part of Singapore. Finally, they objected to "communist warship repairs anywhere in Singapore", including "any communist warship calls except for brief, formal visits".[146] After ANZUK "reiterated to the GOS, both orally and in written form, their four major points", the issue of Soviet vessels using Singapore's naval facilities seemed to have "quieted down".[147] To ensure that the Singapore government was able to respond to ANZUK's protest, Washington planned to provide intelligence on the movement of Soviet ships in or near Singapore waters so that the Singapore government could turn away intelligence-gathering Soviet ships in advance.[148] The US State Department noted that "the Singaporeans seemingly accepted the points made by the ANZUK powers and probably the matter is now best left unmentioned by US officials".[149]

---

[141] Ibid.
[142] Heavner, "Talks with British and French", 17 May 1972.
[143] Ibid.
[144] Ibid.
[145] Heavner, "Green's Asian Trip", 23 February 1972.
[146] Ibid.
[147] Heavner, "Talks with British and French", 17 May 1972.
[148] Ibid.
[149] "Singapore: Bilateral Issues Paper", June 1972.

To keep the Singapore government more accountable, Washington would pass the information to the Singapore government through ANZUK, who would monitor the actions of the Singapore government. The US State Department opined that sharing key intelligence with Singapore would bind the Singapore government to be "more cooperative in general on this issue".[150] Country Director for Indonesia, Malaysia and Singapore at the US State Department, Theodore Heavner, also wanted to ensure that ANZUK would not pass on the information to the Malaysian government, a member of the FPDA. Heavner posited that "since the GOM has not asked for it, the potential for a security leak would be increased, and we see no direct benefit to the USG".[151] Furthermore, the State Department was concerned that the Malaysian government had recently "made a deal to let the USSR build a 400 million Singapore dollar dam in Pahang which will result in Soviets running all over the place".[152] In fact, among the five founding countries of ASEAN, Malaysia was the top trading partner with the Soviet Union from 1970 to 1975.[153] Soviet-Singapore trade was 8.4 million roubles in 1970, while Soviet-Malaysian trade hit 112.6 million roubles that year.[154] It was nonetheless crucial for the ANZUK powers to treat Malaysia and Singapore with parity. The passing of intelligence to Singapore without dispatching a copy to Kuala Lumpur could potentially damage the cohesion of the FPDA if the Malaysian government were to find out.[155] After months of negotiation between Washington, London, Canberra and Wellington, it was finally decided that US intelligence on Soviet movement near Singapore would be quietly passed to the Singapore government through the ANZUK nations. If the Malaysian government

---

[150] Heavner, "Talks with British and French", 17 May 1972.

[151] Ibid.

[152] State Department official, Robert Chin, in a memorandum to the Chargé d'Affaires in Singapore, was quoting officials from the Singapore government on the USSR dam-building project. Chin later added that: "Actually the dam, exclusively an irrigation scheme, will cost about only eighty million [Singapore] dollars." See Chin, "GOS Perceptions of Malaysia", 12 June 1972.

[153] ASEAN-Soviet trade as tabulated by Bilveer Singh indicated that Malaysia maintained the highest volume of trade with the Soviet Union from 1970 to 1988, with the exception of 1981, where Malaysia was outranked by Thailand. See Singh, *The Soviet Union in Singapore's Foreign Policy*, p. 17.

[154] Pockney, "Soviet Trade with the Third World", p. 41.

[155] Heavner, "Talks with British and French", 17 May 1972.

came to know about it, "the ANZUK response would be to the effect that [they] had regarded the matter as a Singapore problem and were therefore trying to deal with it in Singapore".[156]

The desire to use close ties with the Soviet Union to gain leverage against the United States did not reduce Lee Kuan Yew's frequent visits to the US. During his visits, American officials plumbed Lee's views on the Russians. In September 1970, Lee visited Moscow for eight days. He praised Soviet leaders for "displaying a profound understanding of the problems which Southeast Asian countries were facing".[157] Lee's Moscow visit was closely followed by a visit to the United States in October 1970. During Lee's visit to Boston, Lucian W. Pye from the Massachusetts Institute of Technology hosted Lee at the university. Over dinner conversations, Lee told his American hosts that "things have improved in the Soviet Union…, [but] gone down in this country".[158] President Nixon's National Security Advisor Henry Kissinger, "like everyone else in Washington", also pressed Lee to discuss "the Soviet ship business".[159] Lee's visit to the US signified that he would maintain personal relations with American officials and academicians despite disagreement between the two governments over the Soviet ship issue.

The issue of Soviet ships using Singapore's repair facilities was temporarily resolved in early 1973. Lee declared in an interview that "there was no reason for the Russians to develop a habit of using Singapore ship repair facilities since such facilities would not be available to them 'when they were really required'" by ANZUK and US ships.[160] Lee stated that "the ANZUK presence…preempt[ed] the use of the naval base against

---

[156] Theodore J.C. Heavner, "Memorandum of Telephone Conversation between Theodore J.C. Heavner, Director, and Michael J. Powles, First Secretary, Embassy of New Zealand", 22 June 1972, in DEF 13 Logistics Matters (Soviet Navy) 1972, Box 10, Subject Files of the Office of Indonesia, Malaysia and Singapore Affairs, 1965–74, RG 59, NACP.

[157] Singh, *The Soviet Union in Singapore's Foreign Policy*, p. 22.

[158] Pye, "Letter to Cross", 28 October 1970.

[159] Charles T. Cross, "Official-Informal Letter to Josiah W. Bennett, Country Director for Malaysia/Singapore Affairs", 8 December 1970, in POL 7–1 Lee Kuan Yew Visit 1970 (Memoranda of Conversation, etc.), Box 8, Subject Files of the Office of Indonesia, Malaysia and Singapore Affairs, 1965–74, RG 59, NACP.

[160] "US Naval Presence", 1 February 1973.

any possible <u>Russian</u> commercial uses".[161] Happily, the State Department concluded:

> [Lee] made it clear that we are welcome and the Russians are not. As a result of this apparent shift in the [Singapore] Government's public posture, we have felt confident that the GOS would tolerate, and, in fact, welcome a greater use of Singapore by the US Navy.[162]

The US State Department's optimism was short-lived. Disagreement over the issue of Soviet ships in Singapore was revived after the Australian government announced its withdrawal from Singapore in December 1973. Washington observed that there was "some erosion in the GOS position" on restricting Soviet ships visiting Singapore's naval dockyards.[163] State Department official, Theodore Heavner, reported in April 1974 that six Soviet merchant ships were docked at the Stores Basin in Sembawang, "at least three of which arrived without advance GOS notification to ANZUK".[164] The Singapore government attributed the lack of notification to a "bureaucratic mix up and promised to give notice in future".[165] Singapore made use of the occasion to assert that restrictions on Soviet vessels using Sembawang shipyard only applied to warships. Their interpretation was contrary to the ANZUK/US demand, which wanted the ban to apply to all types of Soviet vessels. Yet, with the FPDA weakened by the Australian decision and the complete British withdrawal that followed, the ANZUK powers surrendered their leverage over the matter.[166] It was then up to the United States government to increase USN usage of Sembawang to compensate for the declining ANZUK use with the announced withdrawals by the Edward Heath government in the UK and the Gough Whitlam government in Australia. It was now obvious to the US government that they needed to secure access to Singapore's northern dockyards, or at least keep the Soviet Pacific Fleet away from

---

[161] Ibid. Emphasis in original.
[162] Ibid.
[163] Theodore J.C. Heavner, "Soviet Use of Singapore Facilities", 10 April 1974, in DEF 15 Soviet Use 1974, Box 12, Subject Files of the Office of Indonesia, Malaysia and Singapore Affairs, 1965–74, RG 59, NACP.
[164] Ibid.
[165] Ibid.
[166] Ibid.

the area, and that the ANZUK nations could no longer be depended on to influence the Singapore government.

THE UNITED STATES AND SINGAPORE AT ARM'S LENGTH

The US government's attempt to establish a permanent naval presence in Singapore did not amount to much. In the July 1971 meeting between Ambassador Cross and Lee Kuan Yew, the American ambassador asked about the possibility of "maintaining some regular US Naval presence in Singapore over the long haul".[167] Lee's response, according to Cross, was "unclear".[168] Cross was testing the Prime Minister's initial reaction towards a proposal to homeport some USN ships after the US withdrew from Vietnam.[169] Lee rejected the homeporting arrangement because he was worried about "incidents" involving US servicemen on shore leave.[170] He told Cross that "any kind of 'punch up' would create grave political difficulties" for the Singapore government and could "cost him an election".[171] Ambassador Cross took offence in Lee's assertion that the British and Australians "had smooth ways of keeping their forces out of trouble with the [local] population" but the Americans were incapable of doing the same.[172] Lee's view on the sensitivity of American military presence could be attributed to attempts by the Barisan Sosialis to protest against the American R&R program in July 1966, and turn Vietnam into a domestic political issue against the PAP.[173] In fact, laws were passed by the PAP government in August 1966 to restrict press publications on the R&R program and US ship visits.[174] When opinions between the two men became too "obscure", the meeting ended with both parties agreeing that a permanent US naval presence in Singapore would only be considered if it benefitted both governments.[175] Throughout the meeting with Cross,

---

[167] Cross, "Memcon: US Repair Program", 24 July 1971.

[168] Ibid.

[169] Interagency Singapore Study Group, "Singapore Study", August 1972.

[170] Cross, "Memcon: US Repair Program", 24 July 1971.

[171] Ibid.

[172] Ibid.

[173] Ang, "Singapore and the Vietnam War", pp. 364–5.

[174] Ibid.

[175] Cross, "Memcon: US Repair Program", 24 July 1971.

Lee insisted that homeporting US Navy ships in Singapore and keeping Sembawang exclusive for USN ships was unnecessary and damaging to Singapore.

Commenting on the US request for homeporting USN vessels in Singapore, Bilahari Kausikan explained that Lee did not wish for Singapore to "get involved in this kind of thing" because he wanted to preserve his credibility.[176] Kausikan elaborates that Lee was "credible in the sense that he was not an American stooge or American ally who said that Vietnam War was worth fighting".[177] Furthermore, Lee was unwilling to allow the United States to establish a military base on the island because of Singapore's experience with the British bases that were leaving in December 1971. Lee's speech was quoted in the ISG study in August 1972:

> We do not want a U.S. base in Singapore. I have just gotten through all the problems of unemployment and dislocation of employees as a result of the British forces being drastically rundown.... We do not want to have our people working as servants, cooks, grocers and dry cleaners for American service families stationed in Singapore. But we shall be happy to do a technical job for them.[178]

Although Lee rejected the proposal for a permanent US military presence, he assured the American ambassador in July 1971 that Singapore would not turn away American ships that needed to use Singapore's repair facilities.[179]

The US State Department was looking for a stronger commitment from the Singapore government on American access to the Singapore naval dockyards after the British withdrawal. Since the US government could not establish an American naval base in Singapore, Washington had to consider the contingency that the USN might not be able to use the Singapore dockyards in the future. As a result, State Department planners reduced Singapore's role within US strategy in Southeast Asia. In 1971, Theodore Heavner stated that assessment of Singapore's

---

[176] Interview with Bilahari Kausikan, 8 January 2015.
[177] Ibid.
[178] Interagency Singapore Study Group, "Singapore Study", August 1972.
[179] Ibid.

significance should focus on "the strategic importance of the [Malacca] Straits or 'the water passageways between the Indian and Pacific oceans'".[180] The United States government did not regard Singapore to be a key element in its strategy for Southeast Asian security as it had in the late 1960s. Singapore was but one of several bases that could be used to secure a vital strategic area—the Strait of Malacca.[181] Heavner also stressed the need to ensure "the declining military significance of Singapore over the long haul".[182] According to Heavner's analysis, Singapore would only be "vital" in the case of naval conflict between the US and the Soviet Union in the Indian Ocean—a scenario considered to be "a remote contingency" in 1971.[183] Furthermore, easing tensions between Washington and Moscow in the early 1970s meant that Washington now aimed to "minimize" rather than "deny" Soviet influence.[184] Heavner further argued that technological development in weaponry and aircraft carriers meant that Singapore's geographical location had lost its "strategic value" in a "nuclear and missile age".[185] But as long as the US remained engaged in armed conflict in Vietnam, Heavner posited that

> the U.S. is interested in assuring continued pro-Western influence in Singapore and denying increases in Soviet influence. In terms of military facilities in Singapore, U.S. strategic interests are served to the extent that the GOS grants preferential access to the U.S. and other free world forces vis-à-vis the Soviets.[186]

---

[180] Heavner, "Heavner to Shaid", 17 August 1971.
[181] By 1974, the US Navy had already established a presence in the Indian Ocean from bases in Diego Garcia, which was situated in the centre of the Indian Ocean. See Theodore J.C. Heavner, "Official-Informal Letter to Edwin M. Cronk, American Ambassador, Singapore", 25 April 1974, in POL 2.3 PARA 1974, Box 12, Subject Files of the Office of Indonesia, Malaysia and Singapore Affairs, 1965–74, RG 59, NACP.
[182] Heavner, "Heavner to Shaid", 17 August 1971.
[183] Ibid.
[184] Ibid.
[185] Interagency Singapore Study Group, "Singapore Study", August 1972.
[186] Theodore J.C. Heavner, "DOD Changes in Singapore PARA", 22 March 1972, in Memoranda 1972, Box 10, Subject Files of the Office of Indonesia, Malaysia and Singapore Affairs, 1965–74, RG 59, NACP.

According to the US State Department, Singapore was not unimportant, but should gradually become less important strategically.

Theodore Heavner also pointed out in 1971 that Singapore did not possess "much political clout in the region".[187] All three of Singapore's nearest neighbours—Malaysia, Indonesia and the Philippines—were more important to the US in political and economic terms than Singapore.[188] Hence, to reflect the State Department's position on Singapore accurately, Heavner suggested that it was vital to consider the "political 'isolation' of Singapore" in the region, since Singapore's relations with regional countries were such that its political influence was "in many ways actually negative".[189] The US State Department concluded that the United States' relations with Malaysia and Indonesia outweighed those with Singapore in importance when measured by the higher degree of influence possessed by the two over Singapore in the Strait of Malacca. A Policy Analysis and Resource Allocation (PARA) Study conducted by the US State and Defense Departments in 1973 concluded that

> Malaysia's aspirations for sovereignty over and control of traffic in its claimed portion of the Malacca Straits poses the most immediate and serious threat to U.S. interests vis-à-vis Malaysia. A determined Malaysian prosecution of its position could cause a serious deterioration in our good relations with that country and jeopardize other U.S. interests in Malaysia. Indonesia's position on the issue will directly influence Malaysia, and other regional and developing nations' positions will also affect the GOM's negotiating stance.[190]

Within the context of American interests along the Malacca Strait, Singapore mattered far less than Malaysia and Indonesia.

On another level, personal relationships between US officials and the Singapore leadership began to lose the mutual admiration, as was evident from the State Department documents of the late 1960s. A background document drafted by the State Department in 1972 hinted at signs of tension between the Singapore and US government officials. The paper

---

[187] Heavner, "Heavner to Shaid", 17 August 1971.
[188] Ibid.
[189] Ibid.
[190] "PARA - Malaysia", 1973. Emphasis in original.

noted "a brief deterioration in 1971 when Lee again accused the U.S. of engaging in clandestine political action in Singapore".[191] In 1972, the US State Department drafted a briefing paper for American officials visiting Singapore that revealed a change of perception in Washington towards Singapore; words of praise and admiration for Singapore's leaders noticeable in the late 1960s were replaced by perfunctory, and somewhat cynical, notes on the Singapore government. Describing the Singapore leadership, the State Department remarked that

> [t]hey see themselves as the most successful, sophisticated, and cosmopolitan leaders in Southeast Asia, and they are accustomed to having high-level American and European statesmen listen courteously to them as "spokesmen for Asia".[192]

The State Department also outlined Singapore's non-aligned foreign policy and its influence on Singapore's perception of the United States:

> [T]he Singapore leadership ... seeks to "balance off" the great powers in order to maintain maximum independence for Singapore. They appear to be convinced that all the great powers, including the U.S., are unreliable in their relations with small countries and will quite readily sacrifice the interests of small partners.[193]

State Department's analysis reflected the thinking among Singapore leaders rather accurately. Former Ambassador to the US, Wong Lin Ken, who was appointed the Minister for Home Affairs delivered a speech to a Singaporean audience in August 1971, stressing that "no country is completely independent; not even the United States, in matters of security and economic growth. Today, all nations are inter-dependent, including ourselves. But within this inter-dependence, we should ensure that we have sufficient power on our own to take independent actions in our collective interests."[194] Sensing that Singapore did not acquiesce in giving unreserved support to Washington in every situation, the US government gradually became less sympathetic to Singapore's non-aligned policy.

---

[191] "Singapore: Bilateral Issues Paper", June 1972.
[192] Ibid.
[193] Ibid.
[194] "National interests must not suffer: Dr Wong", *The Straits Times*, 31 August 1971, p. 7.

The US State Department found itself in a weak negotiating position not only over the Soviet ship repairs, but also when the Singapore government requested to buy sophisticated military equipment from the US. The State Department attempted to prevent Singapore's 'poisoned shrimp' defence strategy from triggering a regional arms race. Nevertheless, US government officials hesitated to refuse the Singapore defence ministry's requests because "should Western sources deny purchase of a specific weapons systems or material which Singapore deems vital to its military posture, the possibility that it will turn to a communist source cannot be ruled out".[195] When the Singapore government showed persistent interest in the F-4 supersonic aircraft and modern artillery equipment, such as the M-109, US Embassy officials often resorted to delay tactics instead of rejecting Singapore's requests.[196]

For the sake of the interests of both the governments, however, political and strategic disagreements between Washington and Singapore from 1970–73 did not plunge US-Singapore relations into any crisis. In fact, a de-emphasis on Singapore's military role in the eastern Indian Ocean region did not exclude Singapore entirely from US strategic planning. US Defense Department policy in Southeast Asia now positioned Singapore as a provider of key "logistic support facilities for naval units conducting operations and port visits".[197] The approach of the US Defense and State Departments was to attenuate Singapore's military importance and accentuate its logistical and economic significance. Heavner argued that the US government should "continue our present policy of encouraging American investment and generally supporting economic development in Singapore".[198] During the early 1970s, Singapore did not seem to have experienced the much-forecast economic, political and strategic crises created by the British military withdrawal. The American Embassy in Singapore commented in March 1972 that: "The GOS considers that it has

---

[195] Interagency Singapore Study Group, "Singapore Study", August 1972.
[196] The US Embassy in Singapore and the US State Department tried to balance a dual policy of equipping Singapore's defence force and preventing a regional arms race. See Chapter 4.
[197] Laird, "US Utilization of Singapore Naval and Air Facilities", 3 August 1971.
[198] Heavner, "Heavner to Shaid", 17 August 1971.

no unemployment problem now."[199] In 1972, Singapore had accumulated reserves of up to US$2 billion, indicating the depth of its financial stability, and trade between Singapore and the United States amounted to US$650 million.[200] Soviet-Singapore trade, on the other hand, was fluctuating at approximately US$40–60 million per year between 1965 and 1973.[201]

The US government's approach towards Singapore in response to the Singapore government's strengthening ties with the Soviet Union was encapsulated in the Interagency Study Group's 1972 Singapore Study. The ISG recommended that the United States should maintain a policy of "current low key supportive role", with "certain modifications".[202] The US government would increase ship visits to Singapore to about 100 a year, maintain a volume of ship and watercraft repair contracts that would utilise Singapore's Sembawang naval base, maintain aircraft repair contracts in Singapore at a minimum level of US$2 million for 1973, and continue to promote American investments into Singapore.[203] The Singapore Study further recommended that the US government should continue to give low-key support to the FPDA in order to preserve the US Navy's continued use of the Singapore naval base. Most importantly, it recommended that the US government needed to expand the scope of military equipment that could be supplied to Singapore by modifying the National Disclosure Policy to give Singapore greater access to confidential information and munitions. By allowing Singapore more choices for purchasing US military equipment, the ISG argued that it would remove the constant irritant of Singapore having to wait for State Department's and Congress' clearance

---

[199] John J. O'Neill, Jr, "Official-Informal Letter to John P. Heimann, Country Officer for Indonesia, Malaysia and Singapore Affairs", 6 March 1972, in POL - Policy Study (Singapore) 1972, Box 10, Subject Files of the Office of Indonesia, Malaysia and Singapore Affairs, 1965–74, RG 59, NACP.

[200] "Singapore-U.S. Relationships", August 1973.

[201] Bilveer Singh extracts Soviet-Singapore trade figures from the *Yearbook of Statistics 1975/76* published by the Department of Statistics, Singapore. The figures are quoted in Singapore dollars by Singh, but converted to US dollars at the exchange rate of US$1 to S$3. Note that the Singapore currency was not introduced until 1967. Before that, the Malaysian Ringgit was used in Singapore. For figures compiled by Singh, see Singh, *The Soviet Union in Singapore's Foreign Policy*, p. 16.

[202] Interagency Singapore Study Group, "Singapore Study", August 1972.

[203] Ibid.

before purchasing equipment classified as 'Confidential'. Politically, giving Singapore more access to confidential US material and information would encourage Singapore to be more dependent on US military equipment and technical assistance. The move also demonstrated US support and trust towards the Singapore government.[204] A likely result of including Singapore into the National Disclosure Policy, however, would be a possible request by the Malaysian government to enjoy a similar status as that of Singapore—a consequence the ISG deemed as tolerable since both countries were governed by non-communist governments. A major concern was the risk that Malaysia and Singapore would start a regional arms race, but even with that, the ISG was confident the US government could manage.[205]

CONCLUSION

From 1968 to 1972, the United States-Singapore relationship became strained as result of the Singapore leadership's loss of confidence in the US government's commitment to Southeast Asian security. To ensure that the US would continue to maintain its strategic interest in Singapore, the Singapore government indicated its willingness to balance western influence by increasing Soviet-Singapore engagement. Closer diplomatic and commercial links with the Soviet Union led to a deterioration in US-Singapore relations, especially when the US State Department and Embassy in Singapore viewed Soviet ships in Singapore as a security threat. Still, in the interest of both Washington and Singapore, the US-Singapore nexus was kept sufficiently close through economic cooperation. By keeping diplomatic channels open, both governments were able to maintain a reasonably close relationship despite occasional disagreements arising from Singapore's non-alignment and signs of Washington's withdrawal from Southeast Asia. The final chapter examines the consolidation of United States-Singapore relations in the closing years of the Vietnam War until 1975.

---

[204] Ibid.
[205] Ibid.

CHAPTER 7

From Nixon to Ford

Cementing US-Singapore Relations

During the Nixon administration, the governments of Singapore and the United States enjoyed strong diplomatic relations, marred only by Singapore's increased engagement with the Soviet Union.[1] The benefits of maintaining close US-Singapore ties, albeit at arm's length, outweighed a shift towards the USSR. Singapore-US relations were more important than Singapore-Soviet ties because US economic and military support for Singapore was more significant than that given by the USSR. Hence, from 1969 to 1975, despite its non-aligned foreign policy, the Singapore government developed closer ties with Washington than it did with Moscow. After American involvement in the Vietnam War ended with a ceasefire in 1973, the Singapore government began to tilt even more towards the US to ensure that the superpower would not pull out completely from Southeast Asia. The Five Power Defence Arrangements suffered a major blow after Australian Prime Minister Gough Whitlam announced in 1973 that Australia was going to pull back its forces from Malaysia and Singapore by 1975. With the diminution of Commonwealth defence commitment in Malaysia and Singapore, the

---

[1] For an analysis of how Singapore-Soviet relations became a source of irritation for Singapore-US relations, see Chapter 6.

period between 1969 and 1975 turned crucial for the development of an enduring Singapore-American relationship.

A COMMUNIST THREAT IN SINGAPORE

The Singapore government depended on America to play the role of "the anti-communist anchorman" in Southeast Asia, a phrase used by Singapore Prime Minister Lee Kuan Yew to describe the United States.[2] The US government played the anti-communist role by containing the spread of communism far beyond its borders, including the Malaysia-Singapore subregion. Although the Malayan Communist Party (MCP) was defeated by 1960, the US State Department remained vigilant in monitoring MCP influence in Malaysia and Singapore in the 1960s. In March 1968, State Department reports revealed that the MCP had

> successfully infiltrated elements of the Labor Party of Malaysia (LPM) and the Partai Rakyat (PR or People['s] Party).... In addition, there is a group of armed insurgents, popularly referred to as the Communist Terrorist Organization (CTO), on the Thai side of the Thai-Malaysian border whose stated purpose is the "liberation of Malaya including Singapore".... Although there is no reliable evidence that the CTO is either directed or supported from Peking, the group slavishly follows the Peking line and could probably be counted upon by Peking as an implementing vehicle, should Peking decide to engage in a Malaysian adventure. The CTO is currently rather ineffective. However, should serious sustained communal friction occur in Malaysia, the CTO could be expected to become much more active and possibly much more effective.[3]

In addition to communist threats in West Malaysia, Kuala Lumpur had to manage the growing instability in East Malaysia. The Sarawak Communist Organization (SCO) was reported to have infiltrated the Sarawak United Peoples' Party (SUPP) and was perceived to be able to take over SUPP

---

[2] Lee, *From Third World to First*, p. 449.
[3] "Communist Threats to Malaysia and Singapore", 15 March 1968, in POL 23 Internal Security. Counter-insurgency 1968, Box 1, Subject Files of the Office of Indonesia, Malaysia and Singapore Affairs, 1965–74, RG 59, NACP.

with "little effort".[4] If the SCO were to come to power in Sarawak, the US State Department predicted that it would "attempt to bring about Sarawak's secession from Malaysia and establish an independent communist state".[5] The existence of an armed insurgent group across the Indo-Malaysian border further threatened the political stability and security of East Malaysia.[6]

The US government estimated that the risk of a communist threat in Singapore was lower as compared to Malaysia because leftist groups had been repressed effectively by the Singapore government. The US State Department posited that the Barisan Sosialis, an opposition political party in Singapore alleged to be sympathetic to the PRC, could not "pose any real threat to Singapore".[7] If there were "serious and sustained economic dislocation or communal friction in Singapore", however, the People's Action Party government in Singapore would be under threat.[8] Furthermore, if "Peking were to decide to engage in an adventure in Singapore, overt or covert, the BSP [Barisan Sosialis] would be the likely vehicle".[9] Hence, the US government's strategy of containment in Singapore was to reduce the risk of economic crisis in Singapore through proactive economic cooperation, a strategy that the Singapore government instinctively embraced. But beyond US economic assistance, the Singapore government also desired American military presence in the region.

The Singapore government held the view that the American determination to fight communism in Vietnam was critical to the security of Singapore. Any indication of the US giving up its anti-communist war campaign in Vietnam would jeopardise the security of Singapore, which was already imperilled by the planned British military withdrawal from 1968 to 1971. Lee feared that

---

[4] Ibid.
[5] Ibid.
[6] Ibid.
[7] Ibid.
[8] Ibid.
[9] Ibid.

> [i]f America disengaged, the tide would go against all non-communist
> countries. Thailand would change sides and Malaysia would be put
> through the mincing machine of guerrilla insurgency. After that, with
> fraternal communist parties in control, the communists would cut our
> throats in Singapore. The Chinese army would not have to march into
> Southeast Asia.[10]

By "holding the line" in Vietnam, the US forestalled a military and
political takeover of Southeast Asian states by the communists, and also
"bought time" for the rest of Southeast Asia to strengthen their resilience
against communist-inspired subversion or insurgencies.[11] At the same
time, the US government recognised that American military engagement
played a critical role in the region. A National Policy Paper prepared
by the US State Department in 1968 concluded that "the U.S. military
presence in eastern Asia and the Pacific … have tended to shield the
[Indonesia, Malaysia and Singapore] subregion from direct and severe
forms of external Communist pressure", thereby giving them "valuable
time to develop their own societies and plan for their own defense".[12]
After the Johnson administration left office, Lee visited President Richard
Nixon in 1969 to learn of the new administration's policy in Vietnam,
and more importantly, to present a strong case for the US troops to
remain in Vietnam.

COMING TO TERMS WITH THE NIXON DOCTRINE

In May 1969, after Lee's visit to President Nixon, the Singapore
government's overall impression of the new administration was that an
American withdrawal from Vietnam was imminent.[13] The American

---

[10] Lee, *From Third World to First*, p. 457. Lee's comments were written after the end of
the Vietnam War and after the collapse of the USSR. He expressed these views with
knowledge of hindsight and it is noteworthy that his predictions did not eventuate.
Nevertheless, these comments are significant because they reveal that Lee did not revise
his views on the vulnerability of the region to a communist takeover should the US
government disengage from Southeast Asia.

[11] Rogers, "President's Meeting with Lee", 2 May 1969; Ang, *Southeast Asia and the
Vietnam War*, p. 29.

[12] US Department of State, "NPP: Indonesia, Malaysia and Singapore", 6 February 1968.

[13] For details on Lee's May 1969 visit to the US, see Chapter 6.

Vice-President, Spiro Agnew, called on Lee during his January 1970 Asian tour to assess the reaction of the Singapore leader towards the Nixon Doctrine since its announcement in July 1969. According to a memorandum of conversation between Lee and Agnew, Lee's interpretation of the "Guam pronouncements" was that

> it was now quite clear that both the present and succeeding U.S. Governments will no longer acknowledge it as U.S. responsibility to prop up governments in the region, nor to spare U.S. manpower for the cause of others.[14]

For Southeast Asian countries not formally allied with the United States, Lee told Agnew that it was "crucial that the Thais, who had enjoyed U.S. support and protection for the last 20 years, did not lose the will to resist" communist attack from Vietnam, should Saigon fall to Hanoi after the Americans withdrew from South Vietnam.[15]

Expressing some confidence in the Nixon administration, Lee told Vice-President Agnew that Southeast Asian leaders had taken "a great deal of heart from the courage, resolution and political sagacity" in the way Nixon had taken over the conduct of the Vietnam War from Johnson.[16] Lee felt that most Southeast Asian governments would rate Nixon's policy as "most likely to get through both the House of Representatives and the Senate".[17] Emphasising the need to preserve "a climate of confidence" that the US could maintain a sense of security in Southeast Asia under changing circumstances,[18] Lee warned that "one should never name dates and targets" for military withdrawals.[19] He argued that "nothing would be more calculated to diminish the chances of a permanent non-Communist

---

[14] S.R. Nathan, "Notes of Conversation between P.M. and Vice-President Spiro Agnew of the United States of America which took place at 3.00 p.m. on Friday, 9th January, 1970", 9 January 1970, in POL 7 – Vice President's Visit (Singapore 1970), Box 8, Subject Files of the Office of Indonesia, Malaysia and Singapore Affairs, 1965–74, RG 59, NACP.

[15] Ibid. In 1970, South Vietnam, Thailand and the Philippines were the countries in Southeast Asia that had signed mutual defence treaties with the United States.

[16] Ibid.

[17] Ibid.

[18] Ibid.

[19] Ibid.

South Vietnam than by naming a date for total US withdrawal".[20] The US should, according to Lee, "leave the impression on the North Vietnamese, the Vietcong and the South Vietnamese that US non-combatant forces will be there indefinitely".[21] Agnew disagreed that the US government should create such an impression and reminded Lee of "the US domestic scene and the sad fact that there were Americans who were prepared to side with the enemy".[22] With the Nixon administration determined to withdraw from South Vietnam, both men came out of the meeting less assured that the US government could prolong the deployment of troops in Vietnam.

After the Lee-Agnew meeting, however, the US Embassy in Singapore observed that Lee had become more concerned over the "style and pace" of US withdrawal from Vietnam.[23] US Ambassador Cross observed that

> Lee's focus seems to be not so much on how much or what US actually does in this area, but rather on our style of carrying it out, particularly by showing consistency and coolness.... Our task, as Lee sees it, is to provide the confidence which is absolutely essential if governments in this area are to deal effectively with communist insurgencies.[24]

Lee was optimistic that the South Vietnamese would have the confidence and will to "carry on alone" if some US presence remained until November 1972.[25] Lee's comments hinted that the Singapore government was preparing for an American withdrawal just before the November 1972 presidential elections.

In August 1971, Singapore's Minister for Foreign Affairs, S. Rajaratnam, gave a speech that indicated some erosion of Singapore's confidence in

---

[20] Ibid.

[21] Ibid.

[22] Ibid.

[23] Charles T. Cross, "Lee Kuan Yew on Regional Security", January 1970, in POL 15–1 Ambassador's Corres. 1970, Box 8, Subject Files of the Office of Indonesia, Malaysia and Singapore Affairs, 1965–74, RG 59, NACP.

[24] Ibid.

[25] Ibid. In retrospect, Lee was overly optimistic because Saigon fell under the military offensive of the North Vietnamese in April 1975, soon after the US withdrew its troops in March 1973. See Michael Leifer, *Dictionary of the Modern Politics of South-East Asia*, 3rd ed. (London: Routledge, 2001), pp. 41–3 and 211–2.

America's commitment in Southeast Asia. Rajaratnam announced that the Singapore government was ready to adjust its policies to fit "new realities":[26]

> [T]his Government [of Singapore] believes that the people should be informed at the earliest possible moment when facts have become fiction. Not only tell them the facts but reshape policies in the light of new realities.... I would like to tell you of one big fact which is today fiction. It is no longer a fact that the Americans are going to save South East Asia—and that includes Singapore—from Communism and from Peking. We in the Government never believed this but for 20 years a great many people accepted this as a fact and built policies and attitudes on the basis of this fact.[27]

In his speech, Rajaratnam ostensibly denied that the Singapore government had ever held the belief that the United States was going to save Singapore from communism. Yet his speech also implied that the Singapore government wanted to inform the people that the ability of the US to hold back the spread of communism was now in question. Surely the Singapore government too had to grapple with this "one big fact which is today fiction".[28] In fact, Rajaratnam continued his speech by addressing the anxieties of Singaporeans who might feel that the Americans had betrayed Asians.[29] He said

> [s]o if today the Americans are pulling out militarily from Vietnam and Taiwan they are doing so not because they want to betray friends but because the rules of the Power Game leave them no choice.... And I for one will not judge the big powers harshly. If small nations think national interests come first who are we to deny this privilege to big powers? Instead of wailing that we have been betrayed by our big friends, far better if small nations were to spend this time thinking out

[26] S. Rajaratnam, "Text of Speech by the Minister for Foreign Affairs and Labour, Mr. S. Rajaratnam, at the Sixth National Day Celebrations of the Pasir Panjang Community Centre on Sunday, Aug. 22, at 7.30 p.m.", 22 August 1971, in POL 1 General Policy and Background 1972, Box 10, Subject Files of the Office of Indonesia, Malaysia and Singapore Affairs, 1965–74, RG 59, NACP.
[27] Ibid.
[28] Ibid.
[29] Ibid.

ways and means of not putting themselves in situations where they can be let down or if let down to emerge with the least possible damage.[30]

Lee and Rajaratnam had expressed the Singapore government's position towards major powers. Depending on big powers for survival could not sufficiently ensure Singapore's security and, hence, the Singapore government should think of ways and means to avoid being let down by big powers again. By the early 1970s, the Singapore leaders were beginning to articulate a balance of power strategy to safeguard its autonomy.[31]

In the early months of 1970, Ambassador Cross reported that Lee had "come around to think" that the US would not be "totally inept" in their handling of Vietnam.[32] Cross observed that Lee appeared to be "an admirer of Nixon's political style" and exchange of letters between Lee and Nixon showed "the former's being extremely warm".[33] Nevertheless, Cross noted that sentiments within the Singapore government were highly subject to changes in regional circumstances. The US ambassador, therefore, recommended that the American diplomatic mission "should be constantly taking temperature of Singapore opinion".[34] Cross also concluded that "nobody has reversed anything".[35] In fact, not only did the Nixon Doctrine effect minimal changes in the approach of the Singapore government, but even the US Embassy did not alter its approach towards Singapore. The US State Department and US Embassy's policy of keeping a low profile and promoting American investments in Singapore remained fully relevant under the Nixon Doctrine.[36] In a discussion with the American Chargé d'Affaires ad interim, John J. O'Neill, Jr, Rajaratnam opined that "the strength of the United States was its economic magnitude which far outstripped anything that either

---

[30] Ibid.

[31] Because of the Singapore government's balance of power strategy towards the US and the USSR, the Singapore government engaged in diplomatic, economic and cultural exchanges with the Soviet government. For an analysis of Singapore's balance of power strategy, see Chapter 6.

[32] Cross, "Embassy Conference 1970", 9 April 1970.

[33] Ibid.

[34] Ibid.

[35] Ibid.

[36] Ibid.

the PRC or USSR [could] offer".[37] He also applauded US economic contributions to regional projects that promoted cooperation among Southeast Asian countries. A 1973 Policy Analysis and Resource Allocation (PARA) study conducted by the US government summed up American perception of Singapore thus:

> Singapore is a good Nixon Doctrine country: self-reliant, developing with great success and rapidity, and cooperating in regional economic and security arrangements, Singapore requires little US attention and no US assistance, yet contributes significantly to US interests and objectives in the area.[38]

Washington would "seek no closer political and defense relationship with Singapore and take an essentially 'hands off' attitude toward it while maintaining correct and friendly relations".[39]

After President Nixon's summit in Beijing in 1972, the Singapore government was pushed to respond to the visit's implications on Singapore and the region. The US State Department reported:

> Prime Minister Lee Kuan Yew doubts that the PRC will stop its past program of support for local insurgencies, and he also doubts that China is seriously concerned with a revival of Japanese militarism. Fundamentally, China only fear[s] the USSR, and its foreign policy is designed primarily to counter the Russians. It is for this reason, Lee believes, that the PRC welcomed President Nixon's initiative for a summit in Peking. The summit, according to Lee, "bought time" for Southeast Asia in [which] to develop and strengthen its defense against China—ultimately the menace to all other powers in Asia.[40]

According to an Interagency Study Group report in August 1972, Lee still viewed the People's Republic of China "as the principal threat to Singapore's long-term viability,... and has consistently avoided close contact with [the] PRC".[41] The report added that

---

[37] O'Neill, "US Policy in East Asia", 20 June 1972.
[38] "Singapore PARA–FY 1974", 15 December 1972.
[39] Ibid.
[40] "Singapore: Bilateral Issues Paper", June 1972.
[41] Interagency Singapore Study Group, "Singapore Study", August 1972.

[d]iplomatic relations [between Singapore and the PRC] are avoided and trade relations are closely controlled. No PRC officials are allowed to reside in Singapore.... [Lee] resents Malaysian overtures toward the PRC because they may generate pressures in Singapore, particularly among the "Chinese Chinese" [Chinese-Singaporeans from China].[42]

Lee was carrying out a "nation-building program" that would involve "bring[ing] the development of a Singapore national consciousness to the point that it would be safe to end the present insulation from contact with Communist China".[43] Lee said in August 1971 that he needed ten more years to reach his goals but Malaysia's improving relations with the PRC could force the Singapore government to end the distancing of Singapore's people from PRC influence.[44]

But the US Embassy in Singapore observed that the Singapore government's policy towards the PRC was moving in a positive direction despite Lee's concerns about Beijing's influence on Chinese Singaporeans. Commenting on earlier drafts of the ISG report, O'Neill pointed out that Singapore was already responding to improving Malaysia-PRC relations despite expressing grave concerns to US Embassy officials. In March 1972, he highlighted that Singapore had sent a table tennis team and some reporters to the PRC.[45] The Singapore Chinese Chamber of Commerce also sent a trade mission, which was followed by a special mission dealing with shipping.[46] Despite Lee's anxieties towards Beijing, the Singapore leadership had to adapt to Sino-US rapprochement, which was a vital political development in Asia. In fact, Sino-American détente contributed to improving America's image among the Chinese population in Singapore.

The US Department of State observed positive changes in news reports on American policy in Singapore a year after President Nixon's visit to Beijing. In a country report on Singapore drafted in 1973, State Department officials noted that

---

[42] Ibid.
[43] Ibid.
[44] Ibid.
[45] O'Neill, "Letter to Heimann", 6 March 1972.
[46] Ibid.

[t]he treatment accorded United States policy in Asia by the Singapore press, both in general newsplay and editorials, has undergone demonstrable change over the past year. This has been particularly true of the Chinese language press which, as Prime Minister has clearly pointed out, is the most influential in Singapore.[47]

Commenting specifically on the changes in the two Chinese newspapers in Singapore, *Nanyang Siang Pau* and *Sin Chew Jit Poh*, the report highlighted that

Sin Chew also began to use in its columns almost everything offered by USIS, especially economic material.... Since the President's China trip,... Nanyang has also showed considerable sympathy for US foreign policy, including at times support for the US efforts in Viet-Nam.[48]

Although the report carried positive trends in Singapore's press reporting of the United States foreign affairs, the study also noted that "news coverage of US home affairs emphasize the negative and [Americans] are generally pictured as an example of a once great society rapidly coming apart at the seams".[49] Based on these reports, there seemed to be a gradual acceptance of US involvement in Southeast Asia, though manifested by anxieties of America's impending retreat from the region.

THE END OF AMERICAN-VIETNAM WAR

The United States signed a ceasefire agreement with the North Vietnamese government in Hanoi in January 1973. The Singapore government initially responded with cautious optimism. With a pragmatic tone, Rajaratnam foreshadowed Singapore's endorsement of the impending ceasefire in late 1972: "Whatever our views on the rights and wrongs of the Viet-Nam war, it gave non-Communist countries in the region time to prepare to

---

[47] "Press Treatment of the US", 2 February 1973, in Background (Singapore 1973), Box 11, Subject Files of the Office of Indonesia, Malaysia and Singapore Affairs, 1965–74, RG 59, NACP.

[48] Ibid. Since Nixon's visit to Beijing in 1972, *Nanyang Siang Pau* and *Sin Chew Jit Poh* had been publishing articles about closer Sino-American cooperation, vis-à-vis Sino-Soviet relations. See headlines on *Nanyang Siang Pau* and *Sin Chew Jit Poh* from February 1972 to December 1973. Emphasis in original.

[49] "Press Treatment of the US", 2 February 1973.

meet the new stresses and strains that the ending of this terrible war must bring."[50] His speech indicated that Singapore was ready to handle the dynamics of a post-Vietnam War Southeast Asia. After the ceasefire agreement was signed, Rajaratnam commented that: "[I]t is a necessary and important step towards restoring peace in the region.... But it is only one step, although a major one."[51]

After the ceasefire agreement was signed between Washington and Hanoi in January 1973, Lee visited Thailand. When asked in Bangkok about choosing a strategic partner for Singapore's security, Lee answered: "I think it should be a partner who will not let you down."[52] Since Lee had actively urged Washington to remain in South Vietnam until November 1972,[53] he would have found consolation that the Nixon administration had held on in South Vietnam until early 1973. In 1972, the US State Department reported Lee's changing stance towards an American withdrawal from Vietnam:

> Lee would have preferred that we [the US] keep large ground forces in Indo-China until the Communists were defeated, but he has adjusted to the reduction in our forces by arguing that Vietnamization is all right even if South Viet-Nam should eventually fall, so long as that fall is seen to be a result of the inadequacies of the GVN [Government of Vietnam] leadership who were given what they needed to survive if they had used it properly. It would have a disastrous effect on other governments, on the other hand, if it seemed to them that South Viet-Nam was lost because the United States pulled out prematurely and abandoned its responsibilities as a result of its own internal problems.[54]

---

[50] S. Rajaratnam, "Excerpt from Recent Speech by Foreign Minister Rajaratnam taken from 'The Mirror'", 11 December 1972, in Background (Singapore 1973), Box 11, Subject Files of the Office of Indonesia, Malaysia and Singapore Affairs, 1965–74, RG 59, NACP.

[51] "Ceasefire Agreement", 2 February 1973, in Background (Singapore 1973), Box 11, Subject Files of the Office of Indonesia, Malaysia and Singapore Affairs, 1965–74, RG 59, NACP.

[52] "Excerpts from Interview with Prime Minister Lee During Recent Visit to Thailand taken from 'The Mirror'", 29 January 1973, in Background (Singapore 1973), Box 11, Subject Files of the Office of Indonesia, Malaysia and Singapore Affairs, 1965–74, RG 59, NACP.

[53] Cross, "Lee on Regional Security", January 1970.

[54] "Chiefs of Mission Briefing Paper: Indo-China", 19 June 1972, in Background (Singapore 1973), Box 11, Subject Files of the Office of Indonesia, Malaysia and Singapore Affairs, 1965–74, RG 59, NACP.

The Singapore government's key concern had been to ensure that US withdrawal from Vietnam did not diminish America's prestige and its ability to stabilise the region.

In this regard, Lee Kuan Yew was proactive in shaping the Southeast Asian security environment after the American withdrawal from Vietnam. Lee had earlier indicated his view that a strong American presence in Thailand was critical to Southeast Asia's security if the US were to pull out of Vietnam.[55] Shortly after the ceasefire agreement, Lee described the American withdrawal as "inevitable" and emphasised that the United States needed to assure Thailand that the Nixon Doctrine would be implemented in Thailand—that the Nixon administration would "supply them with economic and military assistance to help them defend their independence".[56] "If Thailand is able to maintain her independence on the basis of the Nixon Doctrine," Lee claimed, "then the survival of the other countries in Southeast Asia will not be in jeopardy."[57] When asked by journalist Edwin Newman if he considered that the US had "achieved peace with honor in Vietnam", Lee rejoined:

> "You are asking me a very leading question, Mr. Newman. I cannot answer that question. I am a guest in this country. I think I can say this: that you disengaged from Vietnam in an honorable way. Whether there is peace in Vietnam is another matter."[58]

Despite expressing optimism about the future of peace in Vietnam after US withdrawal, the Singapore government remained sceptical of Saigon's ability to resist Hanoi's "indoctrination efforts and subversive activities".[59] Rajaratnam's view, as reported by State Department officials, was that the ceasefire meant that the US, China and Russia had decided "not to continue to confront one another in Indo-China".[60] In fact, the removal

---

[55] Green, "Letter to Cross", 13 January 1970. See also Ang Cheng Guan, *Lee Kuan Yew's Strategic Thought*, pp. 34–5; and "Lee wants US presence in South-east Asia", *The Straits Times*, 15 December 1972, p. 6.

[56] "PM Lee Interview in Thailand", 29 January 1973.

[57] Ibid.

[58] "Lee on why South-east Asia won't go communist", *The Straits Times*, 16 April 1967, p. 27.

[59] "Ceasefire Agreement", 2 February 1973.

[60] Ibid.

of the superpowers from the struggle without changing the underlying hostility of the contesting parties in the Vietnam conflict would intensify North Vietnam's subversive activities in South Vietnam, engagement in political assassination and other "standard Communist tactics".[61] Rajaratnam questioned South Vietnam's capability to counter these "Communist tactics".[62] In December 1973, the Governor of California, Ronald Reagan, visited Singapore and met Rajaratnam. During the meeting, Rajaratnam told Reagan that the Thieu government in South Vietnam would be able to put up a "fairly strong" fight if "the North launched an all-out attack".[63] But if the North followed "a policy of promoting the gradual disintegration of South Vietnam through political means", the Singapore foreign minister would be "pessimistic about the outcome".[64]

The Singapore government had understood the implication of US détente with the PRC and the USSR, as well as the American military withdrawal from Vietnam. According to Ang's analysis, the Lee government anticipated that small states, such as Singapore, no longer needed to avoid being drawn into the major power blocs. Instead, small states needed to ensure that their interests were taken into consideration when the major powers reached their compromises.[65] Since the United States presented no threat to Singapore, the Singapore government now moved overtly to establish closer ties with Washington. The US State Department reported a change in attitude of the Singapore government towards American military presence in Singapore as early as 1973. Theodore Heavner reported that

> [w]hile nothing dramatic has surfaced, the former GOS policy, i.e. holding us at arm's length and even flirting with the possibility of increased Soviet presence, now seems to be undergoing gradual change. In short, I think I discern a tilt toward the US—a tilt which raises questions about our own posture.[66]

---

[61] Ibid.

[62] Ibid.

[63] William B. Grant, "Memorandum of Conversation between S. Rajaratnam and Ronald Reagan", 4 December 1973, in POL 7 Visits and Meetings 1973, Box 11, Subject Files of the Office of Indonesia, Malaysia and Singapore Affairs, 1965–74, RG 59, NACP.

[64] Ibid.

[65] Ang, *Lee Kuan Yew's Strategic Thought*, p. 36.

[66] Heavner, "US Military Involvement with Singapore", 20 February 1973.

Heavner observed that the Singapore government had, over the recent months, made several requests through Ambassador Edwin Cronk to increase the number of US military personnel assigned to Singapore to perform missions directly involved with the Singapore Armed Forces.[67] The Singapore government asked for military training teams from the US to assist the Singapore defence ministry in logistics, flight training and classified projects, such as aerial photo interpretation.[68] The US Embassy in Singapore also asked for more US military personnel to staff the Lockheed facility and the US Navy office in Singapore due to increased workload.[69] The clearest signal that the Singapore government preferred US military presence to a Soviet military dominance in the region was Lee's request on 11 May 1973 for a joint naval task force comprising the US, Western Europe, Japan, Australia and New Zealand "to counter Soviet influence in the region".[70]

Only two years earlier, in 1971, the US government's proposal to homeport USN ships had been rejected by Lee.[71] The Singapore government's shift towards more direct military cooperation with the US was interpreted by the State Department as Singapore's departure from its "traditionally more or less even handed approach to the major powers".[72] Lee had been stressing the importance of a continued US military presence in Southeast Asia; he now began to cultivate a closer relationship with Taiwan at a time when other Southeast Asian countries were developing closer relations with the PRC.[73] Washington welcomed Singapore's apparent shedding of non-alignment but the Singapore government's overtures towards Washington were met with a degree of caution by the US government.

---

[67] Ibid.
[68] Ibid.
[69] Ibid.
[70] Buszynski, *Soviet Foreign Policy in Southeast Asia*, pp. 75–6.
[71] In 1971, at the height of US-Singapore disagreement over Soviet use of Singapore's naval dockyards, US Ambassador Charles Cross asked Lee Kuan Yew if the USN could homeport some warships in Singapore after the Vietnam War ended. Lee rejected the idea and the US government, hence, decided to drop the option and developed a base in Diego Garcia instead. For an analysis of the Cross-Lee meeting, see Chapter 6.
[72] Heavner, "US Military Involvement with Singapore", 20 February 1973.
[73] Ibid.

Heavner emphatically pointed out that America's basic policy was and should still be "to seek continued military access to Singapore's facilities with the least possible US involvement".[74] To safeguard against unwitting shifts away from the policy, Heavner reiterated the following guidelines for responding to future requests from the Singapore government:

1. Is it really important to continued US military access or to US/ GOS relations that we meet the request? If not, we should try to avoid it.

2. Could one of the ANZUK powers meet the request? If the answer is yes, we should try to put the burden on them.

3. What would the reaction be in Jakarta and Kuala Lumpur if we were known to be involved in the project? Our relations with both are more important than our relations with the GOS.[75]

It is striking that Heavner's recommendations reflected a return to the position held in the late 1960s—that Singapore was to remain a Commonwealth responsibility. Consistent with the Nixon administration's position on Singapore since 1969, State Department officials viewed America's relations with Indonesia and Malaysia as more important than US-Singapore relations.[76] Washington's emphasis over the stability of the subregion greatly influenced the supply of US military equipment to Singapore.

The United States was a major supplier of military equipment, not only to Singapore, but also to other countries in Southeast Asia. The US contributed to the stability of the region by ensuring that the supply of US military equipment did not trigger an arms race among Singapore and its neighbours. In 1971, the Singapore government had expressed interest in purchasing F-4 supersonic jets from McDonnell Douglas Corporation.[77] Heavner was concerned that Singapore's acquisition of F-4 jets would jeopardise future plans for Five Power Integrated Air Defence System, since the rest of the FPDA members did not possess

---

[74] Ibid.
[75] Ibid.
[76] Ibid.
[77] Heavner, "Singapore F-4", 18 August 1972.

F-4s.[78] More importantly, Heavner feared that selling F-4s to Singapore would create interest in other Southeast Asian countries to acquire these sophisticated aircraft and set off a "mini arms race".[79] The State Department warned that

> [i]f Singapore were to buy the F-4, it would be the first country in Southeast Asia to have anything approaching such an advanced weapons system. Such a quantum jump in weaponry would undoubtedly send shock waves throughout the region, and the probable result would be increased regional tensions, a Southeast Asian arms race, and quite possibly a deterioration in our relations with a number of important countries.[80]

The State Department assessed that Singapore's acquisition of the F-4 aircraft would "put heavy pressure" on Malaysia and Indonesia to acquire similar aircraft.[81] Indonesia and the Philippines might request similar aircraft from the US government under the Military Assistance Program. The US government could not afford to supply these expensive aircraft under the MAP and a refusal would put its relations with the two countries under strain if it were to supply the jets to Singapore.[82] The situation would be much worse for Malaysia as the US had recently sold the less advanced F-5 aircraft to the Malaysian government. Writing to Director of the Office of Munitions Control John Sipes, Heavner warned that "the Malaysians would feel they had been misled by the U.S. and their heavy investment in part nullified. Their envy and resentment of Singapore

---

[78] Theodore J.C. Heavner, "Official-Informal Letter to Edwin M. Cronk, American Ambassador, Singapore", 30 August 1972, in DEF 19 Military Assistance – Air Force 1972, Box 10, Subject Files of the Office of Indonesia, Malaysia and Singapore Affairs, 1965–74, RG 59, NACP.

[79] Ibid.

[80] Arthur W. Hummel, Jr, "F-4Es for Singapore", 1 May 1973, in DEF 19 Air F-4 1973, Box 11, Subject Files of the Office of Indonesia, Malaysia and Singapore Affairs, 1965–74, RG 59, NACP.

[81] Heavner, "Memcon: Heavner and Sipes", 23 April 1973.

[82] One squadron of 18 F-4 aircraft cost just under US$100 million and was also expensive to operate. The F-5, on the other hand, cost US$1 million each, and was also cheaper to maintain. See Christian Chapman, "Draft of Review of the USG's F-4 Sales Policy", 12 February 1973, in DEF 19 Air F-4 1973, Box 11, Subject Files of the Office of Indonesia, Malaysia and Singapore Affairs, 1965–74, RG 59, NACP.

would increase, and to some extent slop over on the U.S.".[83] Moreover, the US government had recently refused the sale of the F-4 aircraft to Taiwan. Selling the aircraft to Singapore would "probably outrage the ROC [Republic of China]".[84] John Sipes was willing to adhere to the State Department's recommendation to reject the F-4 sale to Singapore since McDonnell Douglas was also working at capacity and had more orders than it could handle for the next few years.[85]

The US Embassy in Singapore was relieved to find out in December 1972 that Singapore had shelved its plans to purchase the F-4s.[86] The Singapore government postponed the purchase of the F-4s because it had recently acquired forty A4B aircraft and was in the process of training pilots and maintenance technicians to support the new equipment.[87] Heavner remarked that

> [t]he GOS is fully occupied now in trying to digest the A4B purchase. They are very short of both pilots and maintenance technicians for that program.... At present the Singaporeans are overwhelmed by technical problems associated with the A4B purchase, and it will probably be some time before they will feel capable of taking on F-4s. In fact, the difficulties experienced with the A4 may lead them to postpone indefinitely the acquisition of such a sophisticated aircraft as the F-4.[88]

The Australian and New Zealand Air Force were equipped with the A4B aircraft as well. Hence, the Singapore government's decision

---

[83] Heavner, "Memcon: Heavner and Sipes", 23 April 1973.

[84] Ibid.

[85] Theodore J.C. Heavner, "Memorandum from Ted Heavner to Mr. Hummel: F4s for Singapore", 23 April 1973, in DEF 19 Air F-4 1973, Box 11, Subject Files of the Office of Indonesia, Malaysia and Singapore Affairs, 1965–74, RG 59, NACP.

[86] Edwin M. Cronk, "Official-Informal Letter to Theodore J.C. Heavner, Country Director for Indonesia, Malaysia and Singapore", 14 December 1972, in DEF 19 Military Assistance–Air Force 1972, Box 10, Subject Files of the Office of Indonesia, Malaysia and Singapore Affairs, 1965–74, RG 59, NACP.

[87] John W. Sipes, "Letter from John W. Sipes, Director, Office of Munitions Control, to R.W. Shick, Marketing Manager, McDonnell Douglas Corporation", 9 May 1973, in DEF 19 Air F-4 1973, Box 11, Subject Files of the Office of Indonesia, Malaysia and Singapore Affairs, 1965–74, RG 59, NACP.

[88] Heavner, "Memcon: Heavner and Sipes", 23 April 1973.

also contributed to the effectiveness of the Five Power Integrated Air Defence System.

After the United States withdrew from South Vietnam in 1973, a Surplus Property Disposal facility was set up in Singapore. In December 1973, the US Department of Defense proposed expanding the facility in Singapore from three personnel to thirty-three, by transferring US personnel from the Vietnam office to Singapore.[89] The US Ambassador to Singapore, Edwin Cronk, objected to the proposed increase on political grounds,[90] seemingly worried that a temporary increase in American military presence in Singapore would harm political relations between Singapore and the US in the long run.[91] The State Department concurred with the embassy's assessment and informed the Defense Supply Agency of the political implication of the DOD's proposal. "We were concerned that once the precedent of moving out of Vietnam and into Singapore had been established," Theodore Heavner told DSA, "others would try to follow suit as the deadline for cutting back in Vietnam draws near."[92] Even though an influx of US military personnel might make the Singapore government "relatively happy" at first, the eventual departure of the Surplus Property Disposal unit from Singapore "might be interpreted as a further sign of US disengagement from the area".[93] Consequently, DSA agreed to reduce the number of personnel to be transferred from Vietnam to Singapore.

---

[89] Philip C. Gill, "Expansion of Surplus Property Disposal Facilities in Singapore", 26 December 1973, in DEF 15 U.S. Use of Military Facilities 1974, Box 12, Subject Files of the Office of Indonesia, Malaysia and Singapore Affairs, 1965–74, RG 59, NACP.

[90] Ibid.

[91] It is not clear what Ambassador Cronk might mean by "political reasons". Philip Gill's memo referred to an earlier cable written by Ambassador Cronk titled "Singapore 4873". See previous footnote. The cable is not attached to Gill's memo and is missing from the folder. Nevertheless, subsequent correspondence between State Department officials points towards the fear of creating an impression in the Singapore government that the US government was planning to base American troops in Singapore after US withdrawal from Vietnam. See Theodore J.C. Heavner, "Official-Informal Letter to William B. Grant, Deputy Chief of Mission, American Embassy, Singapore", 8 January 1974, in DEF 15 U.S. Use of Military Facilities 1974, Box 12, Subject Files of the Office of Indonesia, Malaysia and Singapore Affairs, 1965–74, RG 59, NACP.

[92] Heavner, "Letter to Grant", 8 January 1974.

[93] Ibid.

Washington was similarly cautious about granting Singapore's request for military training teams (MTT) through the Defense Attaché Office at the American Embassy in Singapore. Consideration was given to how the rendering of assistance to Singapore would affect US relations with Malaysia and Indonesia. In 1974, the State Department spotted a statement in one of the proposals submitted through USDAO stating that one of the missions of the MTT was to "design and play a logistical exercise, as part of the training program, which assumes small unit deployment across water of approximately 3,000 men".[94] Heavner highlighted to Ambassador Cronk that:

> It seems to me we would want to avoid anything that might look like we are helping the GOS prepare for the invasion of one of its neighbors. We have told ISA [International Security Agency] that we have no objection to the MTT designing an appropriate exercise as part of their instruction, but they should steer away from the "across water" aspect.[95]

Heavner also advised Cronk that the MTT should keep a low profile by ensuring that the members "wear civilian clothes and the whole project be treated as classified".[96]

Apart from seeking close defence links with the US, the Singapore government also developed strong relations with countries in the region, especially states that were aligned with the US. The Singapore government began to form close, but discreet, defence links with Taiwan in the early 1970s. On the way to visiting Tokyo in June 1973, Lee Kuan Yew disembarked at Taipei and did not board the connecting flight to Tokyo with the rest of the Singaporean delegates. In a conversation with Taiwan's trade commissioner to Singapore, Peter Chang, the deputy Chief of Mission at the US Embassy in Singapore, John J. O'Neill, Jr, learnt that

---

[94] Theodore J.C. Heavner, "Official-Informal Letter to Honorable Edwin M. Cronk, American Ambassador, American Embassy, Singapore", 11 April 1974, in DEF 6 Armed Forces 1974, Box 12, Subject Files of the Office of Indonesia, Malaysia and Singapore Affairs, 1965–74, RG 59, NACP.

[95] Ibid.

[96] Ibid.

> Prime Minister Lee's visit … would have gone unnoticed were it not
> for the fact that some alert reporter in Tokyo noticed the passenger
> manifest did not include Prime Minister Lee after the plane left Taipei.[97]

Even the Singapore Foreign Ministry was not aware of Lee's visit to
Taipei beforehand.[98] According to Chang, Taiwan was providing Singapore
with pilots for Singapore's A4S programme and both countries were
cooperating in military training.[99] In fact, a group of Singapore military
personnel had been training in Taiwan and had recently returned to
Singapore.[100] The trade commissioner spoke about the continuity of the
programme and mentioned that high-ranking visitors from Singapore
had also visited Taiwan over the last year. Chang also noted that the
Singapore government had been pleased and impressed with the
ROC government's ability to "keep such visits from getting into the
press".[101] According to Mushahid Ali, Singapore's economic cooperation
with Japan and Taiwan was significant to the development of an
industrialised economy.[102]

While relations between the US and Singapore became warmer
after US military operations in Vietnam wound down, the reliability
of the FPDA became increasingly doubtful in late 1973. The nature of
Australia's military involvement in the FPDA was altered in December
1973 under the Labor government led by the Prime Minister Gough
Whitlam. As opposition leader, Whitlam had signalled that Australia
should withdraw ground troops from Singapore.[103] On 8 December

---

[97] John J. O'Neill, Jr, "Memorandum of Conversation between Peter B.T. Chang, Trade
Commissioner, Trade Mission Republic of China, and John J. O'Neill, Jr., Deputy
Chief of Mission, American Embassy Singapore: Prime Minister Lee's Visit to Taiwan",
11 June 1973, in POL Nationalist China 1973, Box 11, Subject Files of the Office of
Indonesia, Malaysia and Singapore Affairs, 1965–74, RG 59, NACP.

[98] Ibid.

[99] The A4B aircraft bought by the Singapore government were modified in Singapore and
subsequently renamed A4S.

[100] O'Neill, "Memcon: Chang and O'Neill, Jr.", 11 June 1973.

[101] Ibid.

[102] Interview with Mushahid Ali, 27 November 2014.

[103] Benvenuti and Dee, "The Five Power Defence Arrangements and the Reappraisal of the
British and Australian Policy Interests in Southeast Asia, 1970–75", p. 116; Huxley,
Defending the Lion City, pp. 37–8.

1973, the Australian Deputy Prime Minister and Minister for Defence, Lance Barnard, announced plans for the withdrawal of Australian ground combat troops stationed in Singapore.[104] Barnard also announced that Australia would retain 600 Australian personnel after 28 February 1974 and complete a full withdrawal by April 1975.[105] The fledging FPDA, established in November 1970 as a result of the planned British military withdrawal from Singapore and Malaysia, risked being unravelled by the Australian decision. The Australian withdrawal of ground combat troops led Britain to consider, once again, a complete retreat from the subregion after the Edward Heath government had partially reversed their predecessor's east of Suez policy.

When the United States Department of Defense conducted a study of the British force deployments in Singapore, it highlighted the impact that military withdrawal of both Australia and Britain would have on US strategic interests in the region. Having utilised the Singapore naval dockyards since 1968, the DOD did not foresee that American access to Singapore's ship repair facilities would be "greatly impaired".[106] The Country Director of Indonesia, Malaysia and Singapore, Edward Ingraham, was concerned, however, that

1. lack of a secure anchorage would increase the vulnerability of U.S. vessels to foreign intelligence collection; and
2. perhaps more important, present GOS restrictions on Soviet access to the base area and Sembawang shipyard would probably be lifted.[107]

In voicing concerns about increased vulnerability of USN vessels to foreign intelligence collection, Ingraham was echoing his predecessor, Theodore Heavner. In April 1974, Heavner reported that there appeared to be

---

[104] "Draft Press Release by the Government of Australia", 8 December 1973, in DEF 4 FPDA (Collective Defense) 1974, Box 12, Subject Files of the Office of Indonesia, Malaysia and Singapore Affairs, 1965–74, RG 59, NACP.

[105] Ibid.

[106] Edward C. Ingraham, "Defense Consultations with the British: Singapore", 6 November 1974, in DEF 4 FPDA (Collective Defense) 1974, Box 12, Subject Files of the Office of Indonesia, Malaysia and Singapore Affairs, 1965–74, RG 59, NACP.

[107] Ibid.

"some erosion on the GOS position" regarding the restriction of Soviet access to the Stores Basins located in Sembawang, the northern part of Singapore.[108] The Singapore government had allowed six Soviet merchant vessels to use the Stores Basins at Sembawang and insisted that its agreement with the ANZUK powers was only to restrict Soviet warships from using the Sembawang facilities. Objections from the ANZUK/US powers did not change Singapore's position. In the April 1974 report, Heavner highlighted that DOD officers were worried that personnel onboard the Soviet bloc vessels could photograph and collect intelligence on US warships.[109] The Soviet ship issue loomed larger for Washington when the British government announced in 1975 that it was planning to withdraw "virtually all" of its 2,200 military personnel from Singapore by March 1976.[110] Secretary of State Henry Kissinger proposed a National Security Study Memorandum to assess the impact of the British withdrawal and the increase of Soviet ship visits to Singapore, which was "apparently moving quickly in the wake of the British announcement".[111] Furthermore, by 1975, the resilience of the South Vietnamese government in the face of the communist North was in doubt.

In April 1975, North Vietnamese troops took over Saigon, reunifying Vietnam under a communist government. For the USSR, Vietnamese reunification under a communist regime represented the most favourable outcome for Soviet policy in Southeast Asia.[112] "In blood, in treasure, in the sullying of America's image in the world," writes Warren Cohen, "the war in Vietnam was enormously costly to the United States and a great boon to the Soviet Union."[113] The Soviet Union had outmanoeuvred the PRC diplomatically in Vietnam, enhancing Soviet influence in Southeast

---

[108] Heavner, "Soviet Use of Singapore Facilities", 10 April 1974.

[109] Ibid.

[110] Henry A. Kissinger, "Proposed NSSM on U.S. Military Access to Singapore", March 1975, in Singapore – NSSM 218, Box 10, National Security Adviser. NSC East Asian and Pacific Affairs Staff Files, GRFL.

[111] Ibid. NSSM 218 was promptly approved by President Gerald Ford. Nevertheless, details of the NSSM 218 remain classified under "National Security Restrictions".

[112] Buszynski, *Soviet Foreign Policy in Southeast Asia*, p. 31.

[113] Cohen, *America in the Age of Soviet Power, 1945–91*, p. 185.

Asia after supporting the North Vietnamese regime with military equipment during the Vietnam War.[114] Significantly, Moscow also wrote off Vietnam's debts incurred before August 1975 and promised continued economic aid for Hanoi's five-year plan.[115] Vietnam became a close ally of the USSR and allowed Soviet ships and aircraft to operate from Cam Ranh Bay and Danang.[116] Soviet military installations in Vietnam "put Soviet bombers within two hours of the Straits of Malacca" and enabled Soviet ships and planes to "easily monitor movements at the American naval bases" in the region.[117] The Soviet Pacific fleet was able to exert pressure in Southeast Asia as a result of its presence in Vietnam.[118] Feeling the threat of a growing Soviet military influence in the region, the Singapore government seemed to have ceased its flirtation with the Soviet Union and appeared to be less encumbered by its non-aligned image when engaging with the US.

LEE AND THE GERALD FORD YEARS

Lee Kuan Yew visited Washington in May 1975, this time to "get a first-hand appreciation" of US foreign policy after South Vietnam had been taken over by Hanoi.[119] Secretary Kissinger briefed President Gerald Ford that Lee was "wary of the PRC presence" and planned to be "among the last of Southeast Asian nations to recognize Peking".[120] Kissinger also commented that Lee recently declared that "the contest for influence" in

---

[114] Kelemen, "Soviet Strategy in Southeast Asia", pp. 340–2.

[115] Ibid.

[116] Ibid. Alagappa notes that Cam Ranh Bay and Danang were the largest forward deployment bases outside the Soviet Union in 1979. See Alagappa, "The Major Powers and Southeast Asia", p. 557.

[117] Kelemen, "Soviet Strategy in Southeast Asia", pp. 340–2.

[118] Ibid. Kelemen illustrates this point with two examples: one in March 1979, where the Soviet Pacific Fleet sent a 15-ship contingent to intercept Chinese battlefield communications; and another in November 1980, where the Soviet Pacific Fleet sent four warships and an aircraft carrier into the Gulf of Thailand to protest a "UN vote in favour of the ASEAN resolution on Kampuchea".

[119] Henry A. Kissinger, "Background Notes: Meeting with Singapore Prime Minister Lee Kuan Yew", May 1975, in 5/8/75 – Singapore – Prime Minister Lee (2), Box 8, National Security Adviser. Presidential Briefing Material for VIP Visits, GRFL.

[120] Ibid.

Southeast Asia would now be mainly between the PRC and the Soviet Union.[121] Finally, the briefing memo noted that Lee had worked with the US government in recent years when he

1. Facilitated U.S. naval and air access to Singapore, and cooperated with us [the US] to minimize that of the Soviets.
2. Urged the Thai not to press for a hasty withdrawal of remaining U.S. forces.[122]

In essence, the Secretary of State was preparing President Ford to welcome a friend and supporter of the United States in a region where American military influence was diminishing. Ford was advised to respond positively to Lee as much as possible, and at least be sympathetic if the President found Lee's requests hard to meet.[123]

In another briefing memorandum to Ford prior to Lee's May 1975 visit, US State Department official, Robert Ingersoll, highlighted that

---

[121] Ibid.

[122] Kissinger, "5/8/75 - PM Lee (2)", May 1975. Urging the Thai government not to force a precipitous US withdrawal from Thailand was critically important to US-Singapore interests. According to a background paper on US force levels in Thailand drafted by the State Department, the new Thai government, sworn into office on 19 March 1975, publicly called for "the complete withdrawal of all foreign forces in Thailand within one year". The report noted that American failure to "rescue the GKR and GVN, and particularly with the seeming impotence of US combat forces stationed in Thailand" had put the Thai government under pressure to force US troops out of Thailand. The US Embassy in Thailand was in negotiations with the Thai government to reduce US force levels from 27,000 to 19,000 by mid-1975. See US Department of State, "US Force Levels in Thailand", April 1975, in 5/8/75 – Singapore – Prime Minister Lee (3), Box 8, National Security Adviser. Presidential Briefing Material for VIP Visits, GRFL. It should be emphasised that the US government was keen to reduce US troops in Thailand and the Philippines as well, albeit not in a hasty fashion. See US Department of State, "U.S. Policy and Forces Deployment in Southeast Asia", April 1975, in 5/8/75 – Singapore – Prime Minister Lee (4), Box 8, National Security Adviser. Presidential Briefing Material for VIP Visits, GRFL.

[123] Kissinger, "5/8/75 - PM Lee (2)", May 1975. Kissinger expected that Lee would ask for more US Navy ships to use the Sembawang shipyard in Singapore for repairs. He urged President Ford to agree to discuss the matter further "urgently" at a "working level" but not to commit to Lee.

Lee has consistently followed a policy of holding all the major powers at arms' [*sic*] length, largely over concern that small but strategically-located Singapore might become the target of big power rivalry. In practice, however, Lee clearly does not regard the U.S. as posing a threat and has welcomed our [US] presence in Southeast Asia as a counter to China and the USSR. US-Singapore relations remain cordial and free from any serious points of contention.[124]

Ingersoll further pointed out that US-Singapore economic cooperation, "common values and a similar world outlook" constituted a firm basis for amicable relationship.[125] With regard to developments in Indochina, Ingersoll noted that Moscow's relationship with Hanoi would provide the Soviets with "a larger foothold in Southeast Asia".[126] It was in America's interest to encourage some growth in PRC influence in Southeast Asia, since a strong China might provide a useful check on the expansion of Soviet and North Vietnamese influence in Asia.[127]

Nevertheless, the Singapore government's position on the PRC had not changed significantly since Singapore's independence. In 1975, the US State Department still noted that

[a]s regards China, Singapore considers itself especially vulnerable to subversion because of Singapore's large Chinese population and their emotional ties with the mainland, and has therefore been apprehensive of closer contacts with the PRC.[128]

Ingersoll recommended that President Ford make clear to Lee that the US government would continue its policy of "normalization" of Sino-American relations,[129] but acknowledged that the question of PRC-Southeast Asian

---

[124] Robert S. Ingersoll, "Office Call May 8 by Prime Minister Lee Kuan Yew of Singapore", 2 May 1975, in 5/8/75 – Singapore – Prime Minister Lee (2), Box 8, National Security Adviser. Presidential Briefing Material for VIP Visits, GRFL.

[125] Ibid.

[126] Ibid.

[127] US Department of State, "China's Policy in Southeast Asia", April 1975, in 5/8/75 – Singapore – Prime Minister Lee (3), Box 8, National Security Adviser. Presidential Briefing Material for VIP Visits, GRFL.

[128] US Department of State, "Singapore's Foreign Policy", April 1975, in 5/8/75 – Singapore – Prime Minister Lee (4), Box 8, National Security Adviser. Presidential Briefing Material for VIP Visits, GRFL.

[129] Ingersoll, "Office Call by PM Lee", 2 May 1975.

diplomatic relations was "one for individual Southeast Asian governments to decide on its merits".[130]

On 8 May 1975, President Ford, Secretary Kissinger and Prime Minister Lee met in the Oval Office. The memorandum of conversation recorded during the one-hour meeting revealed a discussion resembling a monologue, with Ford and Kissinger asking for Lee's views on Asian affairs and Lee doing most of the talking.[131] When asking Lee to comment on the fall of Saigon, Ford said, "I would appreciate your unvarnished views of the situation and what to do. Don't worry about being frank."[132] In reply, Lee expounded on his views regarding the Thai, Indonesian and Philippine governments. He advised President Ford to keep Indonesia stable by restricting excessive military aid to Indonesia, for fear that President Suharto might be overthrown "from within".[133] He also urged the US government not to interfere with Thai overtures towards the PRC because according to Lee, China was Thailand's "insurance agent" against Vietnamese attack.[134] Lee ended his lengthy reply with this:

> If I may emphasize one point. There is a tendency in the U.S. Congress not to want to export jobs. But we [Southeast Asian countries] have to have the jobs if we are to stop Communism.... If we stop this process, it will do more harm than you can every [*sic*] repair with aid. Don't cut off imports from Southeast Asia.[135]

The meeting with Ford demonstrated the degree of respect that the American leadership had for Lee. Lee's statements reflected his proclivity for portraying other Southeast Asian leaders negatively and persuading

---

[130] Ibid.

[131] Brent Scowcroft, "Memorandum of Conversation: President Ford, Prime Minister Lee Kuan Yew of Singapore, Dr. Henry Kissinger, Secretary of State and Assistant to the President for National Security Affairs and Lt. General Brent Scowcroft, Deputy Assistant to the President for National Security Affairs", 8 May 1975, in President Ford Memcons (3), Box 16, National Security Adviser. NSC East Asian and Pacific Affairs Staff Files, GRFL.

[132] Ibid.

[133] Ibid. Lee's assessment could be attributed to the significant blow suffered by the Suharto administration after the 15 January 1974 Malari affair. For a brief account of the Malari affair, see Leifer, *Dictionary of the Modern Politics of South-East Asia*, p. 173.

[134] Scowcroft, "Memcon: Ford, Lee, Kissinger and Scowcroft", 8 May 1975.

[135] Ibid.

the US government to maintain American economic involvement in the region.

When Lee returned from Washington, he sent a "chatty and candid letter" to express admiration for President Ford's leadership.[136] In his letter to Ford, Lee wrote:

> America is still the anchorman of the free world in this three-cornered tug-of-war between the two communist centres of power and the free world. Hence, every major crisis, sooner or later, lands on the tray of the President of the United States.[137]

Lee assured the President that "most ordinary people in Southeast Asia, and certainly all the leaders in office, hold America in high esteem".[138] He concluded his letter with a statement that was as strong an encouragement as it was a warning: "Regardless of what some may have to say publicly, all would be dismayed if an American President were to meekly do what the liberals in the media advocate."[139]

A telegram from the American Embassy in Singapore to Washington in December 1975 revealed that Lee Kuan Yew was firmly committed to a close relationship between Singapore and the US. Ambassador John Holdridge reported in the telegram that

> [t]he very candor of our conversation suggests to me that we [the US government] retain a very high degree of rapport in our relationship with him [Lee]. I consider it implicit in our conversation that Lee realizes he has no one else to rely upon except the U.S. and will continue trying to work with us.[140]

---

[136] Henry A. Kissinger, "Reply to Letter from Singapore Prime Minister Lee Kuan Yew", 15 July 1975, in Singapore – Prime Minister Lee, Box 4, National Security Adviser. Presidential Correspondence with Foreign Leaders, GRFL.

[137] Lee Kuan Yew, "Letter from Lee Kuan Yew to Gerald Ford", 27 May 1975, in Singapore – Prime Minister Lee, Box 4, National Security Adviser. Presidential Correspondence with Foreign Leaders, GRFL.

[138] Ibid.

[139] Ibid.

[140] John H. Holdridge, "Habib Briefing of Lee Kuan Yew", December 1975, in Singapore – State Department Telegrams: To SECSTATE – NODIS, Box 16, National Security Adviser. Presidential Country Files for East Asia and the Pacific, 1974–77, GRFL.

American-Singapore military cooperation deepened after the fall of Saigon. In Lee's opinion, US assurance to the non-communist states in Southeast Asia was critical to the region's resilience against the spread of communist influence.[141] It was, therefore, critical for Singapore to engage closely with the US. In 1975, Singapore's Defence Ministry requested secondment of US Air Force officers.[142] The US State Department advised the American Embassy in Singapore to reject the proposal for secondment because "this request would have USG virtually running the RSAF [Republic of Singapore Air Force], in both command and staff capacities".[143] The Singapore government had asked for USAF personnel to hold nine RSAF positions which included the Director of the Air Staff, the Head of the Air Operations Department, the Head of Flying Operations Branch, and other staff and training officers.[144] The State Department assessed that secondment of USAF officers to the RSAF would introduce "a possibly discordant note into ASEAN" and the roles performed by these USAF officers would not be relevant to countering the communist threat in the region.[145] Hence, the move would not serve US interests. The US Embassy was instructed to offer other options to the RSAF, such as contracting a US firm to provide managerial skills, hiring qualified retired reserve US military officers, or requesting for US Mobile Training Teams.[146] Despite a cold US response, it is significant and noteworthy that the Singapore government maintained a high degree of openness towards American personnel in its defence force.

The end of American military involvement in Vietnam also marked the end of Lockheed Aircraft Service in Singapore. From 1969 to 1974, LASS had developed and trained 900 local staff in Singapore. By September 1975, LASS had reduced its work force to approximately

---

[141] Ang, *Southeast Asia and the Vietnam War*, pp. 107–9.

[142] US Department of State, "Singapore Request for Secondment of USAF Officers", 21 July 1975, in Singapore (1), Box 16, National Security Adviser. Presidential Country Files for East Asia and the Pacific, 1974–77, GRFL.

[143] Ibid.

[144] John A. Froebe, Jr, "Singapore Request for Secondment of U.S. Air Force Officers", 28 July 1975, in Singapore (1), Box 16, National Security Adviser. Presidential Country Files for East Asia and the Pacific, 1974–77, GRFL.

[145] Ibid.

[146] US Department of State, "Singapore Request USAF Officers", 21 July 1975.

300, and to less than 150 by the end of the year.[147] Lockheed was due to complete its last US contract by November 1975, and since the Singapore government had notified LASS that it was establishing a Singaporean organisation to take over the work for the RSAF, it was likely that Lockheed would terminate its operations in Singapore after its contract expired in April 1976. The State Department reported that Lockheed had met its obligations to Singapore by providing significant income from US military programmes and a US military presence through a commercial venture.[148] LASS was also instrumental in converting Singapore from an "all European equipped Air Force to a U.S. hardware oriented military service", making Singapore the only significant logistics and repair base with capabilities available to the US "from Guam in the East and across the Indian Ocean to the West".[149] The half a million dollars per year required to sustain Lockheed's operations in Singapore was nonetheless considered to be too high when weighed against US political and strategic interests in 1975.[150]

After 1975, the US Department of Defense and the Singapore Armed Forces continued to carry out military exercises. In May 1976, a US-Singapore military exercise was planned.[151] On 29 June 1976, five thousand personnel from the USN Commander Task Group and 204 personnel from the SAF took part in Exercise MERLION II. MERLION II was designed to be an anti-ship and anti-air training exercise involving four USN ships and four to six ships of the Republic of Singapore Navy. Through the exercise, the RSAF would demonstrate its capability to identify an aggressive surface force and its ability to coordinate its defence

---

[147] US Department of State, "Lockheed Aircraft Service Singapore Status Report", 15 September 1975, in Singapore (2), Box 16, National Security Adviser. Presidential Country Files for East Asia and the Pacific, 1974–77, GRFL.

[148] Ibid.

[149] Ibid.

[150] Ibid.

[151] M. Staser Holcomb, "Memorandum for Deputy Assistant to the President for National Security Affairs: Significant Military Exercise MERLION II", 25 May 1976, in Military Exercises (3), Box 15, National Security Adviser. NSC East Asian and Pacific Affairs Staff Files, 1974–77, GRFL.

with the RSN against an aggressor.[152] The political intention of conducting the military exercise was to "signal" to the North Koreans, the PRC and the USSR that the US and Singapore defence forces were able conduct a combined exercise and perform mutual support operations in the region.[153] After MERLION II, a similar exercise codenamed MERLION III was held on 25 January 1977, with intentions of leading foreign nations conducting ocean surveillance on Singapore to perceive this exercise as "a demonstration of US capability to conduct war-at-sea operations opposed by ships and land-based aircraft".[154] Through these joint military exercises, it was apparent that US-Singapore defence cooperation had developed a "strategic partnership",[155] albeit without signing a formal treaty. Eddie Teo highlights the significance of conducting joint military exercises with the US:

> Generally speaking, when we have joint exercise with a greater power like the US, our goal is to show them that we have what it takes to work with them, and that we have a credible force. We want to show that we can keep up with them, and almost be seen as equal. We want to convince them that it is worth their while to deal with us.[156]

In February 1976, the heads of government of ASEAN countries met in Bali, Indonesia, for the first time.[157] As a member of ASEAN, Singapore became party to the Treaty of Amity and Cooperation and the Declaration of the ASEAN Concord, signed during the Bali Summit. The Treaty of Amity and Cooperation provided a "machinery for regional dispute settlements and made provision for accession to it by non-members", which included communist Vietnam.[158] Michael Leifer interprets the treaty as a display of solidarity among the five ASEAN nations and notes that the

---

[152] R.E. Brubaker, "Commander in Chief Pacific: Brief of Significant Military Exercise MERLION II", 18 May 1976, in Military Exercises (3), Box 15, National Security Adviser. NSC East Asian and Pacific Affairs Staff Files, 1974–77, GRFL.

[153] Ibid.

[154] R.E. Brubaker, "Commander in Chief Pacific: Brief of Significant Military Exercise MERLION III", 24 November 1976, in Military Exercises (3), Box 15, National Security Adviser. NSC East Asian and Pacific Affairs Staff Files, 1974–77, GRFL.

[155] Interview with Bilahari Kausikan, 8 January 2015.

[156] Interview with Eddie Teo, 6 January 2015.

[157] Leifer, *Dictionary of the Modern Politics of South-East Asia*, pp. 67–8.

[158] Ibid.

machinery for dispute settlement has not been invoked since its inception.[159] Ly Tuong Van makes the claim that the Treaty of Amity and Cooperation was "the first binding treaty signed by the leaders of ASEAN that sought to promote regional peace, amity and effective cooperation".[160] Indeed the ASEAN governments were showing a united front against a Vietnamese threat through the signing of the treaty in 1976.[161] But beneath the confidence of unity among the non-communist governments in Southeast Asia lay the fear that American disengagement from the region was imminent. For the Singapore government, in particular, the loss of US presence in the region was considered to be highly detrimental to Singapore's security and economy.

In fact, so keen was Lee in trying to keep the Americans engaged in Southeast Asia that he tried to facilitate US-ASEAN dialogue. On the eve of Lee's visit to Manila in January 1977, he called Ambassador Holdridge at night after reading reports of Philippine President Ferdinand Marcos making strident remarks over the US government's statement on Philippine human rights and threatening to halt the progress of the US-ASEAN economic dialogue.[162] During the meeting, Lee expressed "dismay" that President Marcos, who served as coordinator for the economic summit, was stalling the progress of the US-ASEAN dialogue.[163] If President Marcos refused to proceed with organising the US-ASEAN economic dialogue, Lee felt that the progress could drag on for months.[164] Holdridge reported that

> [Lee] knew what Marcos' attitude would be—to hold out until he received $2 billion, or $3 billion, or whatever, from the U.S. The

---

[159] Ibid.

[160] Ly Tuong Van, "The Vietnamese Revolution in the Cold War and its Impact on Vietnam: ASEAN Relations during the 1960s and 1970s", in *Southeast Asia and the Cold War*, ed. Lau (Oxon: Routledge, 2012), p. 179.

[161] Ang, *Lee Kuan Yew's Strategic Thought*, p. 39.

[162] John H. Holdridge, "PM Lee Kuan Yew Expresses Concern over U.S.-ASEAN Economic Dialogue", January 1977, in Singapore – State Department Telegrams: To SECSTATE - NODIS, Box 16, National Security Adviser. Presidential Country Files for East Asia and the Pacific, 1974–77, GRFL.

[163] Ibid.

[164] Ibid.

PM was certain that Marcos would not move until he got what he wanted.[165]

Lee told the US ambassador that he "felt a statement of disinterest on Marcos' part would ... clear the way" for other ASEAN countries to start the talks.[166] Lee would meet Holdridge again after returning from Manila to discuss the results of his talk with President Marcos. Holdridge concluded his telegram, commenting that Lee's dismay over the likelihood of the Philippines dropping out of the US-ASEAN dialogue was indicative of "the great importance" he attached to these talks.[167] After a decade of trying to keep the United States at arm's length, the Singapore government recognised that Singapore's security and economic development hinged on continued US interest in the region.

Singapore and the United States enjoyed stable and cordial relations during President Gerald Ford's administration. In a letter to Ford after his defeat at the November 1976 Presidential Election, Lee Kuan Yew expressed his admiration for the former President. "Your integrity," Lee wrote, "had helped to restore confidence in the Presidency after the terrible trauma of Watergate."[168] Ford replied to Lee in January 1977, reciprocating the Prime Minister with kind words of his own:

> The steadfast support and friendship of Singapore during the past two and one half years enabled us to continue to play a constructive role in Southeast Asia and contribute to continued stability and peace. I trust that the friendship between our two peoples which has developed during my term in office will be continued and expanded in the future.[169]

---

[165] Ibid.

[166] Ibid.

[167] Ibid.

[168] Lee Kuan Yew, "Lee Kuan Yew's Letter to Gerald Ford", 10 November 1976, in CO 133 7/1/76–1/20/77, Box 0, White House Central Files. Subject File, 1974–77, GRFL.

[169] Gerald R. Ford, "Gerald R. Ford's Letter to Lee Kuan Yew", 18 January 1977, in CO 133 7/1/76–1/20/77, Box 0, White House Central Files. Subject File, 1974–77, GRFL.

The end of the Ford administration marked the close of a decade of US-Singapore relations through the tenure of three American presidents who oversaw the war in Vietnam.

CONCLUSION

Lyndon Johnson's presidency led to an escalation of US engagement in the Vietnam War. Richard Nixon's presidency created a thaw in US relations with the USSR and the PRC, paving the way for American withdrawal from Vietnam. Gerald Ford's presidency marked the beginning of US military disengagement from American allies in Southeast Asia. Indeed, the Vietnam War was a focal point of US-Singapore relations. By 1976, the Singapore government had weathered significant challenges such as the separation from the Federation of Malaysia and the removal of the Commonwealth security umbrella. At the same time, the PAP government also had to resolve Singapore's economic problems that arose from a failed merger with Malaysia and high unemployment caused by Britain's military withdrawal. Much of the reason for Singapore's successful development was the support from three consecutive American presidencies to a country that was small and thought to be insignificant, but still possessed strategic weight. US-Singapore's intimacy at a distance was an indispensable relationship that secured the Singapore government domestically, regionally and internationally.

Conclusion

Singapore gained independence in 1965, the same year that the United States deployed American troops to fight in the Vietnam War. As the Cold War raged in Southeast Asia during the 1960s and 1970s, newly decolonised Singapore found itself thrust into a bipolar global conflict. Singapore's non-communist government, led by Cambridge-trained lawyer Lee Kuan Yew, had clear preference for the West. Yet the need to gain popular support from Singapore's Chinese majority—who were sympathetic to the leftist opposition party—compelled the Lee government to project Singapore as a non-aligned country. Singapore had been under the security umbrella of the Commonwealth Strategic Reserve and was host to key British Royal Navy and Air Force bases in the region, making Singapore's claims of neutralism highly questionable. The United States adopted a containment strategy, which comprised political, military, economic and cultural instruments of statecraft, aimed at limiting the influence of communism in Asia. During the 1950s, major non-aligned countries such as India and Indonesia tilted more to the Sino-Soviet bloc than the United States, creating a perception that neutralism was not only anti-colonial but also anti-American. US containment strategy was, therefore, ostensibly incompatible with Singapore's public image of non-alignment.

In a span of ten years, diplomatic relations between the United States and Singapore oscillated time and again between periods of strong public discontent and a deep sense of solidarity. The Singapore government attempted to keep a distance from the US when Singapore sought the recognition of non-aligned countries in the United Nations. After gaining international acceptance for its independence, however, the Singapore government weighed the economic imperatives and began to increase economic cooperation with the United States. Singapore became a major fuelling station for US military vessels and a procurement centre for American military operations during the Vietnam War. American soldiers on combat leave in Singapore led to the growth of the island's tourism and hospitality industries. But beyond commercial benefits to Singapore, the US military presence provided a psychological boost for Singapore's security and economic stability. America's objective in Singapore was to maintain Singapore's non-communist status by tacitly endorsing Lee's pro-West government and supporting Singapore's economic growth.

In 1967, Singapore tilted to the US even more when Britain first announced plans to withdraw its troops from Singapore and Malaysia. Fearing the security and economic impact that could result from Britain's withdrawal, the Singapore government invited the US to take over the British bases. While there was a need for the US Navy to maintain access to Singapore's naval dockyards, the Johnson administration was unwilling to station American military forces in Singapore. Instead, the US Department of Defense assisted with the commercialisation of the British naval and air bases in Singapore and provided a stream of ship repair and maintenance contracts to keep the dockyards lucrative. The US government also supplied Singapore with military equipment to enhance its ability to build a credible defence force.

Although US-Singapore relations were close during this period, the Singapore government's overtures towards the Soviet Union between 1968 and 1972 created tensions between the United States and Singapore. The Singapore government lost confidence in Washington's commitment towards Southeast Asian security after President Lyndon Johnson announced that he would not run for a second presidential term, just as the Vietnam War had become increasingly unpopular in America. Johnson's successor, Richard Nixon, promised "peace with honour" during his presidential campaign, indicating that US military withdrawal from Vietnam was imminent. Hence, the Singapore government feared that America's withdrawal from Vietnam might lead to greater influence from the People's Republic of China in Singapore and the region. The Lee government increased diplomatic and economic engagement with the

Soviet Union in the hope of inducing Washington to remain committed in Southeast Asia. In 1971, the US Ambassador in Singapore, Charles Cross, voiced concerns that the Soviet ships berthed at Singapore's naval dockyards for repairs could compromise the security of USN vessels in the same facility. The US government, as well as Australia, New Zealand and the United Kingdom, formally protested against Soviet use of Singapore's naval dockyards. Lee eventually succumbed to the demands of the ANZUK nations and the US after initial resistance to give in. By 1973, the Soviet ship issue had been resolved.

After American troops withdrew from Vietnam in 1973, Vietnam was unified under the communist government in Hanoi two years later. With the fall of Saigon in 1975, the USSR was able to project its military presence in Southeast Asia through its alliance with Vietnam. Soviet strategic presence in the region became an impetus for closer US-Singapore relations. The Singapore government abandoned its public image of non-alignment and began to participate in joint military exercises with the United States.

This study on Singapore's close relationship with the United States from 1965 to 1975 sheds light on how global containment of communism intersected with Singapore's diplomacy after its decolonisation. It demonstrates how the leaders of Singapore navigated the bipolar dynamic of the Cold War in order to safeguard their country's independence and ensure the island's security and economic viability. While projecting a non-aligned foreign policy stance, the Singapore government invited US military presence on the island, took advantage of trade generated from the Vietnam War and encouraged the American government to prolong its military campaign in Vietnam. When the US government showed intentions to reduce America's commitment to Southeast Asia, the Singapore government played the Soviet card by increasing diplomatic and economic engagements with the Soviet Union.

The complicity of the non-communist regimes of Singapore, Thailand, Malaysia and the Philippines in prolonging the Vietnam War became apparent when they urged Washington to keep communism in check through a continued military intervention in Vietnam. Because the line was held in Vietnam, there was sufficient time to develop the resilience of Southeast Asia's non-communist regimes against communist influence. This book has highlighted the uncomfortable fact that the prosperity and stability of Singapore, as well as the wider region, had been built directly or indirectly on intense war efforts by the United States during the Vietnam War. As bystanders of the conflict, non-communist regimes in Southeast Asia contemplated the effects of the spread of communism into their borders and chose to endorse, tacitly or publicly, the devastation of Vietnam brought about by war. In this sense, the Vietnam War was a proxy conflict not just involving the US, the USSR and the PRC, but also their supporters cheering them on at the sidelines. Yet could a newly decolonised region, caught up in a prolonged and bloody war of national independence, have done better than to keep war out of its own borders? Indeed, regional efforts made to rebuild Vietnam after the war should not just be seen as serving the economic interests of rich Southeast Asian countries but also as a necessary tribute for a debt owed to a neighbour.

Many of Singapore's founding political elites, such as Lee Kuan Yew, Goh Keng Swee, Lim Kim San, S. Rajaratnam and S.R. Nathan, have published their memoirs or biographies, offering a history of Singapore's development as an independent state.[1] Their stories attempt to inform future generations of Singapore's key national interests and vulnerabilities, urging them to emulate the resolve and resourcefulness of the first generation of PAP leaders. Their rendition of Singapore's nation-building history has focussed on the contributions of the first generation of PAP leaders towards Singapore's political, economic and social progress. Singapore might not have become a politically and economically viable state had it not been for its enterprising and industrious leaders. This credible argument forms a foundational starting point for an understanding of Singapore's history since independence. At the same time, this research has argued that it was certainly also the meeting of these individuals with America's opportune entanglement in Southeast Asia that created the conditions for Singapore's survival. Without America's disposition to assist Singapore, albeit for US self-interest, the PAP leadership might not

---

[1] See Lee, *The Singapore Story*; Lee, *From Third World to First*; Ooi Kee Beng, *In Lieu of Ideology: An Intellectual Biography of Goh Keng Swee* (Singapore: Institute of Southeast Asian Studies, 2012); Asad-ul Iqbal Latif, *Lim Kim San: A Builder of Singapore* (Singapore: Institute of Southeast Asian Studies, 2009); Chan and Haq, eds., *S. Rajaratnam*; S.R. Nathan, *An Unexpected Journey*.

have succeeded in building a nation-state within such a short span of time. This research, therefore, has offered an important dimension to a dominant perspective of Singapore's nation-building history, which has not said enough about a major power on whom Singapore depended for its security and prosperity. Although the Singapore government wanted to keep Washington at arm's length during the Vietnam War, its actions displayed a keen desire to ensure that Singapore's relations with the United States remained intimate.

Sources and Bibliography

Primary Sources
Oral Interviews by the Author
- S.R. Nathan, former Singapore diplomat
- Mushahid Ali, former Singapore diplomat
- Eddie Teo, former Permanent Secretary, Ministry of Defence, Singapore
- Bilahari Kausikan, former Permanent Secretary, Ministry of Foreign Affairs, Singapore

National Archives and Records Administration II, College Park, USA (NACP)
- CIA Records Search Tool (CREST)
- State Department Central Files, Record Group 59
  - Bureau of European Affairs. Office of Northern European Affairs, Record Relating to the United Kingdom, 1962–74
  - Bureau of East Asian and Pacific Affairs. Office of the Country Director for Australia, New Zealand, and Pacific Islands, 1969–74
  - Bureau of Far Eastern Affairs. Office of the Country Director for Malaysia and Singapore. Records Relating to Malaysia and Singapore, compiled 1963–66
  - Bureau of Far Eastern Affairs. Office of Regional Affairs. Office of the Regional Planning Adviser. Subject Files, 1955–64
  - Executive Secretariat. Visit Files, 1966–70
  - Subject Files of the Office of Indonesia, Malaysia and Singapore Affairs, 1965–74

Lyndon B. Johnson Presidential Library, Austin, USA (LBJL)
- Files of McGeorge Bundy
- National Security File. Country File. Asia and the Pacific

Gerald R. Ford Presidential Library, Ann Arbor, USA (GRFL)
- Melvin R. Laird Papers
- National Security Adviser. NSC East Asian and Pacific Affairs Staff Files, 1974–77
- National Security Adviser. Presidential Briefing Material for VIP Visits
- National Security Adviser. Presidential Correspondence with Foreign Leaders
- National Security Adviser. Presidential Country Files for East Asia and the Pacific, 1974–77
- White House Central Files. Subject File, 1974–77

The National Archives, London, UK (TNA)
- Cabinet Files (CAB) 130/239
- CAB 133/374
- CAB 148/22
- CAB 148/29
- CAB 148/35
- CAB 148/116
- Foreign and Commonwealth Office Files (FCO) 7/875
- FCO 24/291
- FCO 24/292

National Archives of Australia, Canberra, Australia (NAA)
- Department of Foreign Affairs and Trade, Central Office, Files. Series A4359, 221/4/31/4 Part 1 and 2

Online Databases
- Harry S. Truman Library online database
- Lyndon B. Johnson Library online database
- Office of the Historian, US Department of State
- United Nations General Assembly Official Records
- United Nations Security Council Official Records

Official Documents in Edited Volumes
Boyce, Peter. 1968. *Malaysia and Singapore in International Diplomacy: Documents and Commentaries.* Sydney: Sydney University Press.

Newspapers
- *Petir: Organ of the People's Action Party*
- *The New York Times*
- *The Straits Times*

- *Sin Chew Jit Poh* 星州日报
- *Nanyang Siang Pau* 南洋商报

Memoirs

Lee Kuan Yew. 1998. *The Singapore Story: Memoirs of Lee Kuan Yew*. Singapore: Times Edition.

———. 2000. *From Third World to First: The Singapore Story, 1965–2000*. New York: HarperCollins.

Nathan, S.R. 2005. "My Foreign Ministry Years". In *The Little Red Dot: Reflections by Singapore's Diplomats*, ed. Tommy Koh and Chang Li Lin. Singapore: World Scientific.

———. 2011. *An Unexpected Journey: Path to the Presidency*. Singapore: Editions Didier Millet.

Speeches

Lee Kuan Yew. 2009. "The Fundamentals of Singapore's Foreign Policy: Then & Now". Presented at the S. Rajaratnam Lecture 2009, Shangri-La Hotel, Singapore.

———. 2012. *The Papers of Lee Kuan Yew: Speeches, Interviews and Dialogues, Vol. 3: 1965–1966*. Singapore: Gale Asia.

Nixon, Richard, "Informal Remarks in Guam with Newsmen", 25 July 1969, The American Presidency Project, Online by Gerhard Peters and John T. Woolley. http://www.presidency.ucsb.edu/ws/?pid=2140 [accessed 24 May 2013].

Truman, Harry S., "President Harry S. Truman's Address Before a Joint Session of Congress, March 12, 1947 ['Truman Doctrine']", 12 March 1947, The Avalon Project: Documents in Law, History and Diplomacy, Lillian Goldman Law Library, Yale Law School. http://avalon.law.yale.edu/20th_century/trudoc.asp [accessed 22 Dec. 2012].

Secondary Sources

Acharya, Amitav. 2008. *Singapore's Foreign Policy: The Search for Regional Order*. Singapore: World Scientific.

Alagappa, Muthiah. 1989. "The Major Powers and Southeast Asia". *International Journal* 44, no. 3: 541–97.

Ang Cheng Guan. 2009. "Singapore and the Vietnam War". *Journal of Southeast Asian Studies* 40, no. 2 (June): 353–84.

———. 2010. *Southeast Asia and the Vietnam War*. Oxon: Routledge.

———. 2011. "Malaysia, Singapore, and the Road to the Five Power Defence Arrangements (FPDA), July 1970–November 1971". *War & Society* 30, no. 3 (Oct.): 207–25.

————. 2011. "The Global and the Regional in Lee Kuan Yew's Strategic Thought: The Early Cold War Years". In *Singapore in Global History*, ed. Derek Heng and Syed Muhd Khairudin Aljunied. Amsterdam: Amsterdam University Press. pp. 235–67.

————. 2013. *Lee Kuan Yew's Strategic Thought*. Oxon: Routledge.

Armstrong, Hamilton Fish. 1963. "The Troubled Birth of Malaysia". *Foreign Affairs* 41, no. 4: 673–93.

Babaa, Khalid I. 1965. "The "Third Force" and the United Nations". *Annals of the American Academy of Political and Social Science* 362 (Nov.): 81–91.

Baker, Jim. 2005. *The Eagle in the Lion City: America, Americans and Singapore*. Singapore: Landmark Books.

Benvenuti, Andrea. 2008. *Anglo-Australian Relations and the 'Turn to Europe', 1961–1972*. Rochester, New York: Royal Historical Society.

Benvenuti, Andrea and Moreen Dee. 2010. "The Five Power Defence Arrangements and the Reappraisal of the British and Australian Policy Interests in Southeast Asia, 1970–75". *Journal of Southeast Asian Studies* 41, no. 1: 101–23.

Bresnan, John. 1994. *From Dominoes to Dynamos: The Transformation of Southeast Asia*. New York: Council on Foreign Relations.

Buszynski, Leszek. 1986. *Soviet Foreign Policy in Southeast Asia*. Kent: Croom Helm.

Chan Chin Bock et al. 2002. *Heart Work*. Singapore: Singapore Economic Development Board.

Chan Heng Chee. 1969. "Singapore's Foreign Policy, 1965–1968". *Journal of Southeast Asian History* 10, no. 1: 177–91.

————. 1971. *Singapore: The Politics of Survival, 1965–1967*. Singapore: Oxford University Press.

Chan Heng Chee and Obaid ul Haq, eds. 2007. *S. Rajaratnam: The Prophetic and the Political*. Singapore: Institute of Southeast Asian Studies.

Chang, David W. 1968. "Nation-Building in Singapore". *Asian Survey* 8, no. 9: 761–73.

Chen Jian. 2009. "Bridging Revolution and Decolonization: The 'Bandung Discourse' in China's Early Cold War Experience". In *Connecting Histories: Decolonization and the Cold War in Southeast Asia, 1945–1962*, ed. Christopher E. Goscha and Christian F. Ostermann. Washington, D.C.: Woodrow Wilson Center Press.

Chew, Melanie. 1996. *Leaders of Singapore*. Singapore: Resource Press.

Chiang Tao-Chang. 1969. *The Jurong Industrial Estate: Present Pattern and Future Prospects*. Singapore: Institute of Southeast Asia, Nanyang University.

Chin, C.C. and Karl Hack. 2004. *Dialogues with Chin Peng: New Light on the Malayan Communist Party*. Singapore: Singapore University Press.

Chin Kin Wah. 1983. *The Defence of Malaysia and Singapore: The Transformation of a Security System 1957–1971*. Cambridge: Cambridge University Press.

Christie, Clive. 2001. *Ideology and Revolution in Southeast Asia, 1900–1980: Political Ideas of the Anti-Colonial Era*. Surrey: Curzon Press.

Chua Beng Huat. 1995. *Communitarian Ideology and Democracy in Singapore*. London: Routledge.

Clutterbuck, Richard L. 1985. *Conflict and Violence in Singapore and Malaysia, 1945–1983*. Singapore: Graham Brash.

Cohen, Warren I. 1993. *The Cambridge History of American Foreign Relations Volume 4: America in the Age of Soviet Power, 1945–1991*. New York: Cambridge University Press.

Craig, Campbell and Fredrik Logevall. 2009. *America's Cold War: The Politics of Insecurity*. Cambridge, Massachusetts: The Belknap Press of Harvard University Press.

Elman, Colin and Miriam Fendius Elman. 2001. "Introduction: Negotiating International History and Politics". In *Bridges and Boundaries: Historians, Political Scientists, and the Study of International Relations*, ed. Colin Elman and Miriam Fendius Elman. Massachusetts: MIT Press.

Emmers, Ralf. 2012. "The Five Power Defence Arrangements and Defense Diplomacy in Southeast Asia". *Asian Security* 8, no. 3: 271–86.

Engerman, David C. 2010. "Ideology and the Origins of the Cold War, 1917–1962". In *The Cambridge History of the Cold War Volume 1: Origins*, ed. Melvyn P. Leffler and Odd Arne Westad. New York: Cambridge University Press.

Foster, Anne L., et al. 2010. "Ang Cheng Guan. Southeast Asia and the Vietnam War". *H-Diplo Roundtable Review* XI (46).

Gaddis, John Lewis. 2001. "In Defense of Particular Generalization: Rewriting Cold War History, Rethinking International Relations Theory". In *Bridges and Boundaries: Historians, Political Scientists, and the Study of International Relations*, ed. Colin Elman and Miriam Fendius Elman. Massachusetts: MIT Press.

———. 2005. *The Cold War: A New History*. New York: Penguin Books.

Gordenker, Leon. 1984. "The United Nations and Its Members: Changing Perceptions". *International Journal* 39, no. 2: 302–23.

Goscha, Christopher E. and Christian F. Ostermann, eds. 2009. *Connecting Histories: Decolonization and the Cold War in Southeast Asia, 1945–1962, Cold War International History Project series*. Washington, D.C.: Woodrow Wilson Center Press.

Grant, Bruce. 1969. "Toward a New Balance in Asia: An Australian View". *Foreign Affairs* 47, no. 4: 711–20.

Hogan, Michael J. 1995. "State of the Art: An Introduction". In *America in the World: The Historiography of American Foreign Relations since 1941*, ed. Michael J. Hogan. New York: Cambridge University Press.

Hong Lysa. 2011. "Politics of the Chinese-speaking Communities in Singapore in the 1950s: The Shaping of Mass Politics". In *The May 13 Generation: The Chinese Middle Schools Student Movement and Singapore Politics in the 1950s*, ed. Tan Jing Quee, Tan Kok Chiang and Hong Lysa. Petaling Jaya: Strategic Information and Research Development Centre.

Huff, W.G. 1994. *The Economic Growth of Singapore: Trade and Development in the Twentieth Century*. Cambridge: Cambridge University Press.

Huxley, Tim. 2000. *Defending the Lion City: The Armed Forces of Singapore*. New South Wales: Allen & Unwin.

Jackson, Richard L. 1983. *The Non-aligned, the UN, and the Superpowers*. New York: Praeger.

Jervis, Robert. 2001. "International History and International Politics: Why are They Studied Differently?" In *Bridges and Boundaries: Historians, Political Scientists, and the Study of International Relations*, ed. Colin Elman and Miriam Fendius Elman. Massachusetts: MIT Press.

Kelemen, Paul. 1984. "Soviet Strategy in Southeast Asia". *Asian Survey* 24, no. 3: 335–48.

Kennan, George. 1947. "The Sources of Soviet Conduct". *Foreign Affairs* 25: 566–82.

Krause, Lawrence B., Koh Ai Tee, and Lee (Tsao) Yuan. 1987. *The Singapore Economy Reconsidered*. Singapore: Institute of Southeast Asian Studies.

Kroef, Justus M. van der. 1969. "The Gorton Manner: Australia, Southeast Asia, and the U.S.". *Pacific Affairs* 42, no. 3: 311–33.

Larson, Deborah Welch. 2001. "Sources and Methods in Cold War History: The Need for a New Theory-Based Archival Approach". In *Bridges and Boundaries: Historians, Political Scientists, and the Study of International Relations*, ed. Colin Elman and Miriam Fendius Elman. Massachusetts: MIT Press.

Latif, Asad-ul Iqbal. 2009. *Lim Kim San: A Builder of Singapore*. Singapore: Institute of Southeast Asian Studies.

Lau, Albert. 2012. "Decolonization and the Cold War in Singapore, 1955–9". In *Southeast Asia and the Cold War*, ed. Albert Lau. Oxon: Routledge.

Lee Ting Hui. 1996. *The Open United Front: The Communist Struggle in Singapore 1954–1966*. Singapore: South Seas Society.

Leffler, Melvyn P. 1995. "New Approaches, Old Interpretations, and Prospective Reconfigurations". In *America in the World: The Historiography of American Foreign Relations since 1941*, ed. Michael J. Hogan. New York: Cambridge University Press.

Leifer, Michael. 1981. "The Soviet Union in South-East Asia". In *The Soviet Union and the Third World*, ed. E.J. Feuchtwanger and Peter Nailor. New York: St. Martin's Press.

———. 2000. *Singapore's Foreign Policy: Coping with Vulnerability*. Oxon: Routledge.

———. 2001. *Dictionary of the Modern Politics of South-East Asia*. 3rd ed. London: Routledge.

Lim Chong Yah and Ow Chwee Huay. 1971. "The Economic Development of Singapore in the Sixties and Beyond". In *The Singapore Economy*, ed. You Poh Seng and Lim Chong Yah. Singapore: Eastern Universities Press.

———. 1971. "The Singapore Economy and the Vietnam War". In *The Singapore Economy*, ed. You Poh Seng and Lim Chong Yah. Singapore: Eastern Universities Press.

Liu Hong and Wong Sin-Kiong. 2004. *Singapore Chinese Society in Transition*. New York: Peter Lang.

Liu Hong and Michael Szonyi. 2010. "Introduction: New Approaches to the Study of the Cold War in Asia". In *The Cold War in Asia: The Battle for Hearts and Minds*, ed. Zhang Yangwen, Liu Hong and Michael Szonyi. Leiden: Brill.

Litwak, Robert S. 1984. *Détente and the Nixon Doctrine: American Foreign Policy and the Pursuit of Stability, 1969–1976*. New York: Cambridge University Press.

Logistics Group Western Pacific Public Affairs Office. 20 August 2013. "Command History". 20 August 2013. http://www.clwp.navy.mil/history.htm [accessed 4 November 2013].

Loh Kah Seng. 2011. "The British Military Withdrawal from Singapore and the Anatomy of a Catalyst". In *Singapore in Global History*, ed. Derek Heng and Syed Muhd Khairudin Aljunied. Amsterdam: Amsterdam University Press, pp. 195–213.

Long, S.R. Joey. 2011. *Safe for Decolonization: The Eisenhower Administration, Britain, and Singapore*. Ohio: Kent State University Press.

Low, Linda, Toh Mun Heng, Soon Teck Wong, Tan Kong Yam, and Helen Hughes. 1993. *Challenge and Response: Thirty Years of the Economic Development Board*. Singapore: Times Academic Press.

Ly Tuong Van. 2012. "The Vietnamese Revolution in the Cold War and its Impact on Vietnam: ASEAN Relations during the 1960s and 1970s". In *Southeast Asia and the Cold War*, ed. Albert Lau. Oxon: Routledge.

Lyon, Peter. 1960. "Neutrality and the Emergence of the Concept of Neutralism". *Review of Politics* 22, no. 2 (April): 255–68.

Maddox, William P. 1962. "Singapore: Problem Child". *Foreign Affairs* 40, no. 3: 479–88.

Mason, Richard. 2009. "Containment and the Challenge of Non-Alignment: The Cold War and U.S. Policy toward Indonesia, 1950–1952". In *Connecting Histories: Decolonization and the Cold War in Southeast Asia, 1945–1962*, ed. Christopher E. Goscha and Christian F. Ostermann. Washington, D.C.: Woodrow Wilson Center Press.

Mastny, Vojtech. 2008. "The 1963 Nuclear Test Ban Treaty: A Missed Opportunity for Détente?" *Journal of Cold War Studies* 10, no. 1 (Winter): 3–25.

McIntyre, W. David. 1969. "The Strategic Significance of Singapore, 1917–1942. The Naval Base and the Commonwealth". *Journal of Southeast Asian History* 10, no. 1: 69–94.

McMahon, Robert J. 1999. *The Limits of Empire: The United States and Southeast Asia since World War II*. New York: Columbia University Press.

Ministry of Finance, Republic of Singapore. 1978. *Economic Survey of Singapore 1978*. Singapore: Ministry of Finance.

Ministry of Trade and Industry, Republic of Singapore. 1988. *Economic Survey of Singapore 1988*. Singapore: Ministry of Trade and Industry.

Mirza, Hafiz. 1986. *Multinationals and the Growth of the Singapore Economy*. Sydney: Croom Helm.

Ooi Kee Beng. 2012. *In Lieu of Ideology: An Intellectual Biography of Goh Keng Swee*. Singapore: Institute of Southeast Asian Studies.

Oyen, Meredith. 2010. "Communism, Containment and the Chinese Overseas". In *The Cold War in Asia: The Battle for Hearts and Minds*, ed. Zhang Yangwen, Hong Liu and Michael Szonyi. Leiden: Brill.

Pham, P.L. 2010. *Ending 'East of Suez': The British Decision to Withdraw from Malaysia and Singapore, 1964–1968*. New York: Oxford University Press.

Pockney, Brian. 1981. "Soviet Trade with the Third World". In *The Soviet Union and the Third World*, ed. E.J. Feuchtwanger and Peter Nailor. New York: St. Martin's Press.

Quinn-Judge, Sophie. 2008. "Through a Glass Darkly, Reading the History of the Vietnamese Communist Party, 1945–1975". In *Making Sense of the Vietnam Wars: Local, National and Transnational Perspectives*, ed. Mark Philip Bradley and Marilyn B. Young. New York: Oxford University Press.

Singh, Bilveer. 1990. *The Soviet Union in Singapore's Foreign Policy: An Analysis*. Kuala Lumpur: Institute of Strategic and International Studies.

———. 1999. *The Vulnerability of Small States Revisited: A Study of Singapore's Post-Cold War Foreign Policy*. Yogyakarta: Gadjah Mada University Press.

Sodhy, Pamela. 1991. *The US-Malaysian Nexus: Themes in Superpower-Small State Relations*. Kuala Lumpur: Institute of Strategic and International Studies.

Spector, Stanley. 1956. "Students and Politics in Singapore". *Far Eastern Survey* 25, no. 5: 65–73.

Starner, Frances L. 1965. "Malaysia's First Year". *Asian Survey* 5, no. 2: 113–9.

Stockwell, A.J. 1998. "Conceptions of Community in Colonial Southeast Asia". *Transactions of the Royal Historical Society* 8: 337–55.

Subritzky, John. 2000. "Britain, Konfrontasi, and the end of empire in Southeast Asia, 1961–65". *The Journal of Imperial and Commonwealth History* 28, no. 3: 209–27.

Suryadinata, Leo. 2007. *Understanding the Ethnic Chinese in Southeast Asia*. Singapore: Institute of Southeast Asian Studies.

Tilman, Robert O. 1963. "Malaysia: The Problems of Federation". *The Western Political Quarterly* 16, no. 4: 897–911.

Turnbull, Constance Mary. 2009. *A History of Modern Singapore, 1819–2005*. Singapore: NUS Press.

Vu, Tuong. 2009. "Cold War Studies and the Cultural Cold War in Asia". In *Dynamics of the Cold War in Asia*, ed. Tuong Vu and Wasana Wongsurawat. New York: Palgrave Macmillan.

Wallerstein, Immanuel. 2010. "What Cold War in Asia? An Interpretative Essay". In *The Cold War in Asia: The Battle for Hearts and Minds*, ed. Zhang Yangwen, Hong Liu and Michael Szonyi. Leiden: Brill.

Wang Gungwu. 1991. *China and the Chinese Overseas*. Singapore: Times Academic Press.

Wilarat, Kawin. 1975. *Singapore's Foreign Policy: The First Decade*. Singapore: Institute of Southeast Asian Studies.

Wolf-Phillips, Leslie. 1987. "Why 'Third World'?: Origin, Definition and Usage". *Third World Quarterly* 9, no. 4: 1311–27.

Yeo, Andrew. 2011. *Activists, Alliances, and Anti-U.S. Base Protests*. New York: Cambridge University Press.

Index